Studies in
Prose Writing

Studies in
Prose Writing

JAMES R. KREUZER
LEE COGAN
QUEENS COLLEGE

Rinehart & Company, Inc.
New York

Preface

It has long been our conviction that the best class hours in English Composition are those in which a single worthwhile point about writing is made—made once and for all. This book has been designed to provide the instructor with the classroom tools for such hours. It is organized not in terms of the "types" or subject matter of the reading selections but in terms of the fundamental principles of good expository writing. The supporting text—analyses, questions, and assignments—has been designed to focus attention on that principle of writing illustrated by the individual selection (or, occasionally, group of selections). Thus the student is led from reading and analysis to application, with one rhetorical principle under consideration at a time.

The order of the major divisions of content—from whole theme to paragraph, sentence, and word—is a matter of our own preference. We are aware, however, that many instructors prefer some other ordering of parts, and hence we have kept the major divisions sufficiently autonomous to allow for reordering.

One criterion has guided us in our treatment of each selection, namely, how can we most efficiently use the selection to teach a particular rhetorical principle. As a result, some treatments are longer and more intensive than others; some begin with a brief discussion of the principle under consideration; others consist only of questions aimed at directing the student's thinking about the rhetorical principle. The writing assignments grow out of the treatment of selections. Rather than merely listing a number of possible topics for student themes, the assignments guide the student in his thinking preparatory to writing and present in some detail various possibilities for handling the themes.

For the instructor who may find them useful, alternate selections for the teaching of each principle are suggested. It is our belief that

v

the apparatus for a given selection can be readily adapted to the alternate selections.

We have included adequate representation of the formal types of writing—exposition, description, narration, and argumentation. For example, under exposition we may list such selections as those by Alistair Cooke, Thomas H. Huxley, Erich Fromm, John Ciardi, and William Faulkner; under description, such selections as those by Charles Dickens, Virginia Woolf, Albert Camus, James Agee, and Thor Heyerdahl; under narration, those by Clarence Day, Richard Bissell, and Jan Struther; under argumentation, those by Russell Lynes, Learned Hand, Demosthenes, and Morris R. Cohen. In addition, autobiographical or biographical writing appears in the pieces by Hans Zinsser, Carl Sandburg, Joseph Wood Krutch, and Margaret Leech; and the process theme appears in the pieces by Kenneth Andler and Robert E. Rose.

We take pleasure in thanking Professor Charles Child Walcutt of Queens College for his contributions to the book when it was in the formulative stage and Judith Anne Kreuzer and Marie Sabatelli for their expert preparation of the typescript. Professor Richard S. Beal of Boston University and Professor James Edward Tobin of Queens College devoted many hours to painstaking reading, analysis, and constructive criticism of the whole volume. To our friends and families and to the College Department of Rinehart & Company, by whom we were helped beyond measure, we make most grateful acknowledgment.

James R. Kreuzer
Lee Cogan

JANUARY, 1960

Contents

THE PARAGRAPH

Coherence

III
Adequacy
Variety
Paragraphs in Combination

THE SENTENCE

I
Types of Sentences
Variety of Structure
Length

II
Parallelism
Balance
Subordination

III
Rhythm

DICTION

I
Succinctness

Organization of
the Whole

Concept of

Organization

Mamie

HANS ZINSSER

[1] THE first girl I ever noticed in what, later, I recognized as a sentimental emotion was called Mamie. She was the daughter of a truck driver in my father's chemical factory. We used to play in the large factory yard, where hundreds of barrels of resin were stored on end, and it was great fun to jump from barrel top to barrel 5 top. Mamie had a brother who became a bosom friend, and games of tag on the barrels were organized in which Mamie—being several years younger—was patronizingly allowed to participate. She and her brother were sweet children, amiable and gentle, and I loved them both very dearly. Their lives were hard. At twelve and ten, re- 10 spectively, they were called upon for severe domestic service, and their poor mother—a stout, red-faced woman—kind enough when she was sober, was less so when drunk. Their happy moments were the ones they spent with me, playing on the barrels; but when I went back to my playroom to have my feet dried and to be fed my supper, 15 they went back to a little frame house where dirt, noise, unmerited abuse, and frugal tolerance were their lot.

[2] Mamie was blue-eyed and blonde, with a bright blondeness

that shone through the dirt on her face and the squalor of her clothes.
20 And how humbly grateful she was to be allowed to be "It," chasing
us over the barrels. There must have been a faint dawning of the
endocrines in me even then, baneful prophecy of a long life of struggle, for while I was sorry for Jimmy when I happened to think of
being so, there was always a protective tenderness in my heart for
25 Mamie.

[3] One day—it was drizzling—the wet drove us from our play-
ground into a little shed where carboys of sulphuric acid were stored.
I dug a nickel out of my pocket and Jimmy was dispatched to the
store on the corner to buy some barber-pole candy sticks. Mamie
30 and I sat close together, for we were damp and a little chilly. She
stuck up her wet face to be kissed, and I gazed down at her with
the warm intention of kissing her. But when I looked into her face, I
saw two little rivulets running from Mamie's nose to her pouted upper
lip. I had never noticed them before, although I had often observed
35 her sticking her tongue out and upward, whenever she sniffed. For
ours was a catarrhal climate. Now I looked and saw. But I have
always been proud in later days that, even at this early age, I mastered my repulsion and kissed Mamie on her salty lips. Dear Mamie!
What has become of you since? You were a lovely child, in spite
40 of the rivulets on your upper lip, and—no doubt—you deserved
more consideration than the world has given you. What happened
to me at that moment has never left me since and is perhaps the
only achievement that may eventually entitle me to some measure
of self-approbation—namely, the mastery of arrogance and disgust
45 by tenderness and pity.

[4] We played in the great court of my father's chemical factory
and the atmosphere was redolent with odors of resin, sulphuric acid,
and amyl acetate. I never pass a chemical factory or smell amyl
acetate without thinking of Mamie and our games on the barrels.
50 Yes, the sense of smell is the most nostalgic of our senses. I recall
a charming lady from the West who stayed with us in New York,
but left suddenly—long before she had intended to. She was in the
recently cleaned bathroom one morning and, smelling the household
ammonia, got so homesick for her twins that she couldn't stand it
55 and had to go home.

The concept of organization can perhaps most easily be grasped by
thinking of it in terms of shooting a motion-picture scene. The cameraman stands behind a camera and looks through the view finder at a

panoramic scene. He has to focus upon details which best represent the whole. He must, however reluctantly, turn his camera away from some lovely spot, because it has nothing to do with the action. He must determine the order in which he will present the characters and the setting. He must adjust the angle of the camera so that some figures appear larger than others, since this is "their" scene. But most important of all, every move his camera makes—and doesn't make—must be determined by the ultimate meaning and purpose of the scene.

So the writer must determine his guiding purpose and then be "guided" by it, limit his topic to the expression only of ideas which can be adequately handled in the space available to him, express a consistent point of view, order his ideas most meaningfully, decide what to emphasize and what to de-emphasize, work out a beginning and an ending which will reflect his purpose and tone, find methods of being specific and exact, rule out material which is not consistent with or relevant to his purpose. In short, he must organize.

In the selection by Hans Zinsser, the author has explicitly stated his meaning or purpose: to show "the mastery of arrogance and disgust by tenderness and pity."

1. Restate this guiding purpose in your own words.

2. Knowing Zinsser's guiding purpose, we can determine from his first sentence that he decided to limit his topic to a single example. He chose to focus upon Mamie. But this was still not specific enough. He focused upon a single scene. Of what does that scene consist? Why is it particularly well suited to his purpose?

3. State briefly what Zinsser tells us paragraph by paragraph.

4. Why does he say "there was always a protective tenderness in my heart for Mamie"? Why does he place this statement so early in the selection?

5. What does the third paragraph do that the first two could not have done?

6. Why must paragraphs 1 and 2 come before paragraph 3?

7. Why has he included the last paragraph? Think again of our cameraman; to what device of his is this last paragraph comparable?

8. Why do you think Zinsser placed the statement of his purpose where he did? Where else might he have placed it? What would he have gained or lost?

9. Zinsser was a great doctor, a scientist. If you know this, what further meaning does the selection have?

Alternate selections for the study of the Concept of Organization: Charles Dickens, "August"; Margaret Leech, "General Winfield Scott"; Eric Sevareid, "This Telegram Smells."

Theme Assignment: Recall some person whom you have known who, though not aware he was doing it, taught you something or helped you to grow in some way. Select an incident involving this person which illustrates the meaning he has for you. Perhaps, for example, while the dramatics coach was directing you in your big scene, something he did or said suddenly made you realize that you didn't want to be an actor after all. Or, as a child, you may have explored a "haunted" beach house, to find that it was really occupied by an oceanographer who gave you your first inkling that learning can be exciting. Or, through your association with a local storekeeper, you may have seen for the first time the pride a man takes in his work.

Write a theme making selective use of your recollections. Remember that, although you are writing of someone else, you are telling about yourself. The organization of your material should reflect your guiding purpose.

Guiding Purpose

Getting Education

CARL SANDBURG

[1] WE didn't know we were getting education while having fun, Mary and Mart and I, in that little crowded kitchen when we read *Hostetter's Almanac* to each other. Besides pictures, jokes and sayings, it was crammed with all sorts of facts new to us and interesting—the morning and evening stars for any month in the year, 5 the ocean tides, the velocity of the earth, eclipses, and so on. We were hungry to learn. We didn't write a letter to Hostetter's thanking them for letting us have a free almanac every year but we could have and maybe we should have. We left it to the fellows who said they could get drunk on one bottle of Hostetter's. 10

[2] I remember reading Fowler and Wells' big book on "phrenology." To begin with, as I recall, they explained about physiognomy with pictures of different kinds of noses, the Aquiline, the Straight, the Executive, the Retroussé. I would go along Main Street and pick out noses like those in the book. Farther along in the book they got into 15 heads and bumps on heads. This was phrenology. Look at a man's head and you could tell what kind of man he was. Thick between the ears he was Combative, good in a fight. If your head had the bump of

From *Always the Young Strangers*, by Carl Sandburg. Copyright 1952, 1953 by Carl Sandburg. Reprinted by permission of Harcourt, Brace and Company, Inc. Selection title by the Editors.

Amativeness it meant you were good at love, handy with the women.
20 If you liked children and raised a big family you had somewhere
the bump of Philoprogenitiveness. Why did those big words stick in
my mind? They were as useless to me as the curl in a pig's tail is
to a pig. Why should I lug around in a corner of my mind that word
Philoprogenitiveness? Yet I did. I have seen a man pushing a baby
25 carriage on a walk with his wife and six children tagging along and
I would say, "There it goes, that's philoprogenitiveness." Of course
phrenology wasn't all nonsense. Nor, on the other hand, was it the
science that lecturers and writers of books claimed. Audiences paid
good money to hear a lecture with charts showing heads and bumps.
30 It was a fad, caught on for a while and then faded.

[3] In those years as a boy in that prairie town I got education
in scraps and pieces of many kinds, not knowing that they were
part of my education. I met people in Galesburg who were puzzling
to me, and later when I read Shakespeare I found those same people
35 were puzzling him. I met little wonders of many kinds among animals and plants that never lost their wonder for me, and I found
later that these same wonders had a deep interest for Emerson,
Thoreau, and Walt Whitman. I met superstitions, folk tales, and
folklore while I was a young spalpeen, "a broth of a boy," long
40 before I read books about them. All had their part, small or large,
in the education I got outside of books and schools.

In any writing, organization is a major problem which must be
solved if the writing is to be successful. The first step in the solution
is to determine and to state precisely the purpose guiding the writer.

1. State in your own words the guiding purpose of "Getting Education." For whom do you think Sandburg was writing?

2. On what evidence did you base your statements?

3. The author chose two books to illustrate his guiding purpose,
Hostetter's Almanac and "Fowler and Wells' big book on 'phrenology.' "
Do you think that he made a good selection? What does (or does not)
make the books appropriate?

4. How does paragraph 3 differ from paragraphs 1 and 2? Do you
think that, in making it different, Sandburg has strayed from his guiding purpose? Justify your answer, indicating the reason for the order
of the three paragraphs. Had they been ordered differently, what might
the essay have gained or lost?

5. Throughout the selection, Sandburg uses words and phrases which
may seem surprisingly slangy to you—"lug around," "handy with the

women," "young spalpeen," " 'broth of a boy.' " Why do you think he chose to express himself this way?

6. Is Sandburg saying that he is against formal education? How do you know?

Most writing assignments—in college and out—come in the form of fairly vague topics which in themselves do not supply the writer with much guidance. You may be asked to write a paper on the United Nations or on your home town or on the uses of the atom; you may have to write a letter explaining your absence from a final examination or breaking a date. One of the difficulties in writing on any of these "topics" is that each lends itself to almost numberless treatments—even those that at first glance look most specific and most limited. For example, a theme on your home town might have the guiding purpose of proving that the local government is utterly corrupt; an entirely different theme would stem from a guiding purpose of showing that your home town is an ideal place in which to grow up because of its educational, health, and recreational facilities. Clearly, the details you would use to illustrate one of these points of view would be most inappropriate to demonstrate the other.

The guiding purpose is what the writer uses to determine the length of his piece, the tone, the content to be included and excluded, the order of materials, the richness or paucity of illustrative material, the diction—everything, then, that makes the piece of writing what it is.

7. Formulate at least five guiding purposes for the "topics" suggested above. Then, by listing various items that might be included under several guiding purposes for one "topic," see how a guiding purpose governs the inclusion and exclusion of content.

Alternate selections for the study of Guiding Purpose: Learned Hand, "A Plea for the Freedom of Dissent"; Nathaniel S. Shaler, "Agassiz Plays a Game"; Erich Fromm, "Myths and Dreams."

Theme Assignment: Many character or personality traits make you the individual you are. For example, you may be irritable more frequently than you are gay, or you may be driven by a single ambition, or you may be a warm, friendly person or a shy, retiring person; you may love music, hate ballet, feel strongly about political issues, and read voraciously; you may tend to choose friends who are considerably older than you, react spontaneously rather than deliberately to new acquaintances, painfully relive your more embarrassing experiences.

Choose one—and only one—of your major personality traits as the basis for your theme. Your guiding purpose is to show how various incidents and experiences in your past contributed to the development of the trait. Be sure to make the trait convincing to the reader, but devote the major portion of your theme to explaining just how the incidents and experiences you select contributed to the development of the trait.

Formulate your guiding purpose so specifically that it will guide you exactly in determining which incidents and experiences to include and in what order. In doing this, you will, of course, have to take into account your reading audience.

Limiting
a Topic

The Autobiography of
My Friend Mark Van Doren

JOSEPH WOOD KRUTCH

[1] MORE distinguished men and women have acknowledged their deep indebtedness to Mark Van Doren than to any other
teacher of the humanities I know. Now that he is about to retire
after nearly forty years at Columbia many of them will certainly
testify again to his mysterious gift for influencing strong minds in ₅
ways (and often in directions) he neither intended nor was aware
of. No one who was listened to with attention by men whose careers
have been as different as (to take two amusingly extreme examples)
Thomas Merton and Allen Ginsberg can very well be accused of
merely encouraging reflections of himself. Because we were enrolled ₁₀
together at Philosophy Hall in 1915 I studied "with" rather than
"under" him, but I am sure that none who were formally his pupils
owe him more.

[2] In his recent autobiography (*The Autobiography of Mark
Van Doren;* Harcourt, Brace: 1958) he has told, not when we first ₁₅
met (like me he perhaps does not remember that) but when, very

"The Autobiography of My Friend Mark Van Doren," by Joseph Wood
Krutch. Reprinted from the *Columbia University Forum* (Winter, 1959) by
permission of the publishers.

shortly thereafter, we first became aware of one another on the rear
platform of a subway car and under those trying conditions began
a conversation which has been continuous ever since. The anecdote
20 as he tells it is extremely flattering to me; but if I were to write my
own autobiography I should be compelled to describe exactly that
incident and to give it a position of still greater importance.

[3] To have always at hand someone from whom understanding
and sympathetic attention to anything one has to say can be taken
25 for granted is itself a priceless boon. To be sure that he will also
"come back" with something which is illuminating just because it
is not *merely* sympathetic and understanding but is also a new insight
possible only from some different point of view or perspective, is
to have the perfect companion. And I have no doubt that it was
30 because his students sensed something approaching this kind of
response that they also could be so greatly helped to develop their
own so varied personalities and to find their ways along such diver-
gent paths.

[4] Mark was decidedly not one of those campus figures, gen-
35 erally called "prof," who make it a point to be one of the boys. He
did not attend football rallies or take much interest in extra-curricular
activities unless they were intellectual. But he was always ready to
discuss with any student any ambition, project, or problem actually
within his province. He gave himself whenever he could be useful;
40 he did not waste himself where he could not. Though I cannot
imagine him bothering to intercede for the student accused of tether-
ing a goat in the dean's office, there were notable and remembered
incidents (some of them dating back to the time when, for a young
instructor, it took great courage) in the course of which he came
45 to the defense of those whose intellectual or artistic daring threatened
to bring the wrath of the authorities down upon them.

[5] I think I have never heard any discussion of Mark's character
which did not sooner or later introduce the word "sweetness" and,
indeed, no one who knew him could be unaware of the characteristic
50 to which it referred. But there was never a hint of the saccharine
in that sweetness and there never could be for two reasons. One of
them is philosophical and comes down to the fact that if he tried
to understand all it was not because that would or should lead to
the toleration of all but rather because to understand all is to know
55 what ought to be and what ought not to be tolerated.

[6] The other reason is simpler: he had what is commonly called
"a terrible temper." John Dryden was the subject of his dissertation

and one of his first great literary enthusiasms. Dryden might have had him in mind when he wrote, "Beware the fury of a patient man."

[7] Mark was patient, so patient for instance that though he certainly did not tolerate bores and fools *gladly* he bore them (up to a point) so patiently that they often thought they were pleasing him. But when the storm broke it broke astonishingly out of a clear sky. I remember for instance hearing a roar which shook my adjoining office when the lightning finally struck a crank who had paid repeated visits, sure that Mark was listening sympathetically to his plan for an Owls Club—to be composed of Mark himself, along with the eleven other wisest men in the world, who would decide all policies for the universe and would have them accepted just because those who made them were so obviously the wisest men: "Damn it I don't *want* to be an Owl and I *won't* be an Owl. Get out of here!" Nor is it likely that even some of his favorite pupils will forget the times when, having listened with what seemed sympathy to some excuse or evasion or folly, he reached the end of his patience and the storm broke without so much as a single premonitory rumble.

[8] Once and once only during our long and so intimate association was I the victim of his anger and if he does not mention the incident in the autobiography I am sure it is not because he has forgotten it any more than I have. The date was 1920 and we were together in Paris, each on a Cutting Fellowship. At the moment, I remember, we were returning late at night on foot to our Left Bank hotel from some foray into Montmartre not strictly part of our academic work. For some time we had been walking in silence, I (and this was the occasion of the outburst) a foot or two ahead. Suddenly, in the same voice later to be used in declining the invitation to be an Owl, I was informed vehemently and profanely that he would not be bullied into walking faster than he wanted to walk. Though guilty, I was so unaware of it and so astonished at what came out of the darkness behind me that I made no reply whatever. We reached the hotel in silence. We parted for the night without a word. Next morning all was serene again and to this day neither of us has ever mentioned the incident to the other. Mark's anger is as short lived as it is seemingly sudden, and I say "seemingly" because I have no doubt that it had long been building up like the electrical charge in a cloud.

[9] "Discourse," "dialogue" and "dialectic" are words much favored today in intellectual discussion and indeed they threaten to become cant. But when I think what it has meant to me intellectually

to have called Mark Van Doren my most intimate friend for forty-
100 three years I cannot avoid using those words for the inescapable
reason that they define precisely the essential character of the
relationship. People sometimes speak of the ideal friend as an *alter
ego*; but talking to an *alter ego* is too much like talking to oneself—
soothing, no doubt, but otherwise not very profitable. There should,
105 to be sure, be some fundamental compatibility as well as the sense
that one will be comprehended, and I flatter myself there is that
compatibility between Mark and me. I believe, that is to say, that
at bottom we believe the same things and value the same things.
But we have arrived at our convictions by different routes and he
110 at least has learned things along the way I would never have known
had he not led me to them.

[10] I have often wondered just how this fundamental difference,
not inconsistent with equally fundamental similarities, might be defined, but I am afraid that I will never be able to do better than
115 to say that it has something to do with the fact that Mark is a poet
through and through while I have never been able to achieve anything except prose. I hope and believe this does not mean that I
am incapable of understanding poetry or, for that matter, incapable
of poetic feelings on my own. But my approach even to such mildly
120 mystical inclinations as I am proud to confess is always the plodding
approach of prose—and also, too often alas, of the prosy.

[11] But Mark is a poet twenty-four hours of the day as well as
through and through, and to say that means much more than to
say simply that the writing of poetry has been, ever since I first
125 knew him, his greatest interest—indeed, as he would probably
say in his somewhat extravagant way, his only real interest. It is to
say also that his approach is always via the leap and flight of a
poet's perception, so that in our intercourse I have often found
myself compelled to follow ploddingly after him, sometimes not
130 really understanding what he had said until days—in a few cases
years—afterward.

[12] I think it significant that when I felt impelled to write some
quarter of a century apart two books of non-technical philosophy
in which I tried to state what I believed about man and the universe
135 I thought the appropriate motto for both to be a few lines from two
of Mark's poems, written, I believe, with about the same interval
of time between them. This, I think, does not mean that I borrowed
my ideas from him and I am quite sure that he did not borrow his
from me. But it does illustrate how we arrived at compatible con-

clusions by different routes, and it makes clear why our relationship 140
has always been to me so rewarding.

[13] One of the most interesting and enlightening parts of his
autobiography is those many pages in which he describes the occasion and, as it were, the prose background, of a large number of
his poems. That he is willing to do so—one might say, willing to 145
take the risk of doing so—illustrates an important fact about him
as a poet, namely that although he is a completely "modern" poet
in every good sense of that word he has never been a member of any
cult or school, never adopted any of the cult affectations or mystifi-
cations. If any of his poems are "difficult" it is not because he wanted 150
to make them so, and he is perfectly willing—as many modern
poets are not—to give any pertinent information which can serve
to make them clearer. Like Robert Frost, to take another example,
he does not try to be modern—he merely *is* inescapably so, and he
does not need to prove it.   155

[14] Because he has always been so committed to poetry he has
often in conversation brushed aside all the considerable bulk of
criticism he has written as being, to him, of relatively little importance or interest. To readers it has been, on the contrary, of very
great interest and would perhaps be of more interest to Mark himself 160
(perhaps I should say that he would be more willing to recognize
the interest which he actually does take in it) if he realized how
unmistakably it is a poet's criticism. For the most part it consists,
not of painful intellectual analysis and judgments pronounced on
the basis of theories either conventional or eccentric, but, to use 165
again a phrase used before of the poetry itself, of the leaps and
flights of a poet into the heart and mind of some other creator and
his creation.

[15] He does not set out to prove any writer or any piece of
writing good or bad. He tells you instead what it means to him and 170
the result is that, unlike many modern critics whose professed aim
is to operate in a realm of discourse as far removed as possible
from the realm of the creative imagination, he keeps the reader
very close to the work criticized, both intellectually and emotionally.
When he writes about *Don Quixote* what he writes is funny in 175
precisely Cervantes' way. When—to take the example of another
recent and major piece of criticism—he writes about Thomas Mann's
"Joseph" he does not discuss the place of myth in modern literature.
What he does is to make the reader more effectively aware of Mann's
individual way of recreating the atmosphere of the myth.   180

[16] No ideal for criticism is today more generally assumed to be so completely discredited as "the adventure of the soul among the masterpieces." No doubt many weak attempts to achieve it deserve the discredit into which they have fallen. No doubt the 185 determination of the most characteristic recent critics to strive for something as different from that as possible has been responsible for highly interesting and important work. But—to cite a dictum almost as discredited as that concerning the adventures of the soul— all genres are good except the tiresome. And much of Mark's best 190 criticism actually is the adventure of a unique and perceptive soul among some of the masterpieces which have furnished him with richly meaningful adventures. Even more obviously his novels and short stories are a poet's prose fiction.

[17] Whatever aspects of the truth there may be in T. S. Eliot's 195 so famous pronouncement concerning the necessary "impersonality" of true works of art, the fact remains that a great deal of Mark's personality has been revealed to his readers in both his poetry and his criticism, as indeed it is revealed in the work of any writer. More of that personality—some of it described directly, some merely 200 inferable as it is in his other writings—is revealed in the autobiography, which has many of the same qualities as his criticism. For me and for various of his other friends it will to some extent also serve in lieu of any autobiography we might have felt the need to write. We will relive through it some of the most important moments of 205 our own existence.

[18] Just after reading this autobiography I wrote Mark that it had convinced me that we had both led very interesting lives—in the sense that we ourselves had always been interested in them. Also, that we had been so aware of that fact that, reading about them, I was 210 not ready to echo Colette's remark after seeing, shortly before her death, a movie based upon her career: "What an interesting life I had; and how I wish I had realized it sooner!"

Student writers are usually acutely—even painfully—aware of the need for answering the question, "What shall I say about this topic?" It is just as important, however, to answer another question: "What shall I not say about this topic?" We have already pointed out that a well-formulated guiding purpose is the key to determining what should be included in, and excluded from, a piece of writing. It is also the key to limiting the topic, to focusing the topic so sharply that not only is extraneous material excluded but adequate, satisfying treatment is given to relevant material in the wordage available.

A 500-word theme on college life obviously cannot adequately and satisfyingly treat all facets of the topic. A good guiding purpose might limit the topic in time: to describe college life at lunch time, showing that serious intellectual conversation is more important than the quality of the food. Or it might limit the topic in place as well as time: to describe college life in a typical dormitory from 7:00 A.M. to 8:30 A.M., showing particularly the annoyances of institutional living. Or it might limit the topic by focusing sharply on a single idea growing out of it: to show that college life with all of its complexities presents serious emotional problems even to well-adjusted students. However the guiding purpose limits the topic, it is essential for the writer that his topic be limited in proportion to the wordage he has available.

Joseph Wood Krutch faced a major problem in limiting a topic when he came to write "The Autobiography of My Friend Mark Van Doren." It was clearly not his intention to write a full-length biography of Van Doren; yet he had more to say about Van Doren than Zinsser had about Mamie or Sandburg about himself.

1. To what characteristic of Van Doren are the first three paragraphs devoted? Why do you think Krutch chose to begin with this characteristic rather than any of the others discussed in the essay? Don't fail to take into account the title of the essay. What additional light does paragraph 4 shed on Van Doren?

2. How is paragraph 5 related to paragraphs 6, 7, and 8?

3. How is paragraph 9 related to paragraphs 10 through 13? What qualities of Van Doren the poet are emphasized in these paragraphs?

4. Which paragraphs are devoted to Van Doren the critic? What quality of Van Doren's criticism is particularly emphasized?

5. With what do the remaining paragraphs deal? Why are these appropriate as concluding paragraphs?

After a close friendship of more than forty years, it is obvious that Joseph Wood Krutch has come to know Mark Van Doren intimately— to know the various facets of his personality, his likes and dislikes, his relations with the members of his family, his daily living habits, his tastes in food as well as in entertainment, his patterns of thought as well as his habits of dress. To select just the qualities of Van Doren discussed in the essay and to exclude the many others that might have been discussed must have taken not only much self-discipline on Krutch's part but also a clearly and exactly realized guiding purpose.

6. Formulate the guiding purpose of the essay. Test the adequacy of your formulation by demonstrating the relevance of each of the sections of the essay to the guiding purpose.

7. Add to the list of things about Van Doren that Krutch might be expected to know after a friendship of forty-three years. Which items in the total list might have been included in the essay without violating the guiding purpose you have formulated? Why do you think Krutch

did not include these items? Is he, perhaps, not so imaginative as you are? Or is your guiding purpose not correctly formulated? Would the inclusion of additional items have improved the essay? Justify your answer. Which items does your guiding purpose exclude from possible treatment in the essay? What is lost or gained by the exclusion of these items?

Alternate selections for the study of Limiting a Topic: Carl Becker, "History"; William Faulkner, "The Spirit of Man"; Inez Robb, "Not a Game She Likes to Play."

Theme Assignment: Krutch makes clear early in the essay just why he thinks Van Doren is an ideal intellectual companion. Each of us has different kinds of friends and various criteria for evaluating them. With some friends we enjoy serious discussions about politics or art or religion; with others, we enjoy such lighter forms of entertainment as going to the movies and card playing and dancing; and with still others we may have in common only an interest in photography or string-ensemble playing or woodworking. Write a theme in which you make clear your conception of one type of ideal friend; you may use an actual person or an imaginary one to exemplify your conception. Frame your guiding purpose so specifically that your instructor will know that you have learned to use a guiding purpose to limit and focus the content of your theme.

Point
of View

Teen-Agers Mirror Their Parents

RUSSELL LYNES

[1] THE number of 13-year-olds is increasing at a rate twenty times faster than the rest of the population. "Between 1958 and 1960," a recent report of the David L. Babson Company of Boston says, "the number of children crossing the 13-year-old threshold will rise by nearly 40 per cent. By 1965 there will be a 35 per cent increase in the 14-17 age group." The total population grows by a comparatively sluggish 2 per cent a year. We are obviously reaping the whirlwind of post-World War II romance.

[2] One of the specters that haunt our time is the sprawling expansion of the population, and it is more and more difficult not to picture the future as though it were going to be life in a sardine can. If the figures on the teen-age population are correct (and they must be), it's going to be a boisterous, noisy, squirming can indeed.

[3] There are those who view this prospect with alarm for they fear that civilization, as we know it, will be swept away by juveniles —if not entirely delinquent, then at least objectionable. Others, who have a hand in the teen-ager's pocket, consider the explosion the best sort of news. It seems to me unlikely that civilization is doomed,

"Teen-Agers Mirror Their Parents," by Russell Lynes, from *The New York Times Magazine,* June 28, 1959. © The New York Times. Reprinted with the permission of the author and The New York Times.

at least not by teen-agers, and I would like to suggest that if we
20 want to know what the teen-agers will do to us, we should look at
ourselves.

[4] In all the brouhaha about teen-agers we are inclined to forget,
it seems to me, that they are primarily reflections of us, of our foibles
and fumblings and aspirations, our fears and frustrations, our hopes
25 and our beliefs. They are, in effect, a magnifying mirror of their elders
—like a shaving mirror in which our eyes seem to bulge, our pores to
be extinct volcanoes, and our eyebrows thickets of thistles.

[5] Consider their rebellious natures. Of a New York Times
Youth Forum last year it was reported: "A group of high school
30 students said . . . that teen-agers were increasingly rebellious toward
authority—especially parental authority. And the tension behind
teen-agers' attitudes comes from a lack of close understanding with
their parents." The students also blamed this rebelliousness on "the
terrible age we live in" and the "looseness of family ties."

35 [6] This is where we come in. These are not things the teen-agers
thought up for themselves; they are ideas that have been impressed
on them by the rest of us. We have drummed into their heads their
"need to be understood," and they would be less than human not to
use this ready-made excuse as an escape hatch for their natural high
40 spirits.

[7] A few years ago two revealing studies of teen-agers appeared,
one of them something of a shocker, the other reassuring. They both
throw some light on ourselves. The first was a book called "The
American Teen-ager," a summary for the general reader of the
45 findings of a fifteen-year investigation of teen-agers made at Purdue
University under the direction of Dr. H. H. Remmers. The second
was called "Adolescent Girls" and was a study made for the Girl
Scouts by the Survey Research Center at the University of Michigan.

[8] From "The American Teen-ager" one gets the superficial im-
50 pression that our youngsters are monsters. (One also gets this
impression from the newspapers, of course.) Teen-agers believe, the
book says, in wire-tapping, in search without warrant, in "censorship
of books, newspapers, magazines and other media as protection of
the public against improper ideas." Furthermore, they believe that
55 "most people aren't capable of deciding what's best for themselves,"
and they "see no harm in the third degree." Not all of them, to be
sure, but a good many more than half of them.

[9] I find this rather chilling, less because of what it says about
the teen-agers than what it says about their parents. But the Girl
60 Scouts' report takes a somewhat more optimistic view.

[10] Their study found that by and large the youngsters of this era are "conservative." Far from being rebellious, the study exposed them as idealistic and practical, more eager than their mothers had been for advanced education, but not, in general, wanting to be high-powered executives or movie stars. Fewer than a fifth of them had 65 a good thing to say for "going steady." In many respects they are more independent than their mothers were at the same age. They have weekly allowances that give them more freedom to choose their fun; they have part-time jobs, and they play a larger role in making family plans. The attitude of the family has come a long 70 way since the "children should be seen and not heard" era. No one would now say, as my wife's grandmother used to, that there was nothing to do with children but "put them in a barrel and feed them through the bunghole until they're 21."

[11] Somewhere along the line we stopped thinking of teen-agers 75 as just young people in transition between childhood and the state of being "grown up," and we began to regard them as a minority pressure group in our society. We now look on them not as just "kids," as we used to, but as a sub-culture with a powerful effect on the culture as a whole. 80

[12] You will look in vain (or at least I have looked in vain) for references to "teen-agers" in the literature of my parents' day. You will find "youngsters" and "schoolboys" and "schoolgirls," but you will not find teen-agers as a group treated as though they were some-thing between menaces and the hope of the world, a class by them- 85 selves, a threat to adult sanity.

[13] The change came during and after the second World War, the result of the dislocation of families both physically and spiritually. Children were asked to adjust to change rather than to continuity, to pulling up stakes rather than to putting down roots. They began 90 to look more than ever to their contemporaries for security, and they began to look for their own set of rules to live by. The practice of "going steady," for example, was an attempt to establish formal relationships that promised some sort of continuity and sense of belonging to some one person. 95

[14] The songs popular with youth, you may have noticed, belie the old Tin Pan Alley cliché that a hit can't be made on the theme of married love. As Arnold Shaw has pointed out, "Honeycomb" and "Kisses Sweeter than Wine," both songs of marriage, have been taken to the hearts of teen-agers whose popular hits are "a growing 100 literature of . . . protest." "Born Too Late," they sing, and "Why Won't They Understand?"

[15] At the same time [that] they want to be a self-sufficient and rebellious group, they reach out for a hand to guide them. Their accu-
105 sation that adults "fail to understand" them is a reflection of our "wanting to understand," and their "rebelliousness" is, in part at least, a reflection of our fairly new belief in "permissiveness" and in our encouraging them to make up their own minds. They seem to be in a terrible hurry to be grown-up, to have grown-up respect paid to
110 them, at the same time that they resent the group they most want to be part of—a not uncommon human condition.

[16] They have reason to resent us, and if the reflection of ourselves that we see in them is not a pretty one, we should not be surprised. Let's look a little deeper into the mirror of our society
115 and see theirs.

[17] There was a time not long ago when parents not only preached the virtues of work but practiced them. The work week was ten or fifteen hours longer than it is now for father, and his day off each week was a restorative to enable him to do a better
120 job on the other six days. Now leisure has become a kind of job in its own right, and it is going to become still more of a job. When the work week shrinks, as economists say it will, to twenty hours, it is going to be difficult indeed for father to preach to his children the old gospel that "the devil finds work for idle hands." There is
125 plenty of evidence around us now of what happens to young people deprived of the opportunity to work and without the resources, either cultural or social, to put their time to good use.

[18] But time on parental hands has still further effects. At its worst it is corrosive and it is stultifying. It passively accepts what
130 is put before it. It wallows in ways to make time pass—hours of sitting before the television or in aimless puttering. Or it can be dangerously aggressive against society, or against self, as in dope addiction or alcoholism.

[19] Less spectacular, but also corrosive, undirected leisure takes
135 itself out in consumption for consumption's sake, in buying gadgets that save time, when time is the thing that least needs saving for the already time-ladened. It shows itself in ostentation and in competition with one's neighbors. Everyone wants to be the biggest Jones in the block. These are the lessons that the young learn when
140 leisure is not constructive and does not enrich the spirit. It can, of course, be otherwise, but it is the parents who show the direction.

[20] There is another direction they show. A good deal of journalistic space is occupied these days by articles about the number

of young people who cheat on exams. Is this, after all, very different
from padding an expense account or, more important, shading the 145
truth on an income-tax return? If colleges and universities promote
gifts in such a way that it is sometimes possible for a donor to make
money by giving gifts to them, doesn't the line of academic honesty
become a little blurred?

[21] Or take another matter that is related to schools. It is not 150
uncommon today to find youngsters who, when they have graduated
from high school, wish they had been made to work harder. Why?
Suddenly adults have been spurred into believing that only education
will save us from lagging behind the Russians; suddenly bright students have a new status which a few years ago they sadly lacked— 155
often to the point of being ostracized by their contemporaries. The
"grind" and the "brightie" were looked down upon, a reflection of
intellectual distrust on the part of parents. Now the winds blow in
a different direction.

[22] Or take the shibboleth of "conformity" with which the critics 160
of our society plague us. (In my opinion this is a convenient tag that
has been greatly overused to describe one aspect of a highly industrialized nation.) How is the teen-age custom of "going steady" a
reflection of our own insecurity? To what extent is it, as I have
suggested, an attempt to inject a kind of formality into relationships 165
among young people that they miss in this age of informality?

[23] The Girl Scouts may say that they are against it, but it has
become a tribal custom of the young that they observe with almost
universal respect all the same.

[24] We are inclined to be indulgent about the hero-worship of 170
the teen-ager for the movie glamour boys, for the Presleys and the
James Deans and Eddie Fishers and Ricky Nelsons. We should be.
We are hero-worshipers ourselves. It is evident in our political
attitudes, in the numbers of us who don't even bother to vote, presumably because we are willing to "leave it to the boss." It is evident 175
in our reverence toward leaders of business and industry, toward
scientists, toward anybody who we think can lead us by the hand
through the maze of complications that beset us.

[25] To what extent is our fear of the Russians, for example,
responsible for the teen-ager's belief in censorship, in wire-tapping, 180
in search without warrant? If we are worried, as we should be, about
their attitudes toward personal liberties, hadn't we better look to our
own?

[26] It is easy to take this subculture, this minority group, the

185 teen-agers, and read our characters and future in them as though
they were tea leaves. We can see adumbrated in them our attitudes
toward religion, toward the arts and toward education more clearly
than we can by looking at ourselves. We are likely to be more indulgent in looking at ourselves than at them; we smooth over our own
190 exaggerations while we view theirs with alarm.

[27] But I can see no reason why the simple statistical fact that
there are going to be a great many more teen-agers in the next few
years should be cause for anything more than the usual alarm. Unquestionably they will cause problems, just as we caused problems
195 when we were teen-agers. But they will also give delight. There will
be more noisy households than we are accustomed to, more telephones endlessly tied up, more records strewn around the living-
room floor, more starry-eyed young lovers, more hard questions
to answer, more nonsensical fads to throw up the hands about.

200 [28] There will be something that will take the place of rock
'n' roll, bobby socks, and hot rods, something that will seem ludicrous
to those who will have recently grown out of their teens into adult-
hood, and alarming to the parents who have to put up with it.

[29] Possibly I am lucky. I have just lived through the teen-ages
205 of a son and a daughter. There were moments when I thought
murder was too good for them; there were moments when they
thought murder was much too good for me. Sometimes their anguish
was my anguish; sometimes their cussedness was my fury; occasionally
their pleasure was my despair. But I saw myself sometimes distorted,
210 sometimes all too clearly, in them as a mirror. I suspect I learned
from them as much as I taught them, and I wouldn't have missed
it for anything.

1. Lynes' essay could have been written from any one of several
different points of view. Where does Lynes indicate two points of view
other than his own? Write guiding purposes for essays that might have
been written from both of these points of view. What major units of
content in the Lynes essay would be excluded by each of your guiding
purposes? What major units would be included?

2. What is the first hint we get of Lynes' point of view? Where
does he first make his point of view explicit? Where does he restate his
point of view?

3. Is Lynes' description of teen-agers as "a magnifying mirror of
their elders" (paragraph 4) farfetched? overstated? appropriate and
effective? ineffective? Why?

4. Explain the relevance of paragraphs 5 and 6 to Lynes' point of view.

5. Why does Lynes deal with the book called *The American Teenager* before the report, *Adolescent Girls?* Compare the lengths of paragraphs 8 and 10; how can you justify the disproportion?

6. What contribution do paragraphs 11 and 12 make to Lynes' central thesis? How are these paragraphs relevant to his point of view?

7. What do you understand by "rebelliousness" and "permissiveness" as these terms are used in paragraph 15?

8. Many people think the increased leisure of our day a blessing, but from Lynes' point of view it is potentially a danger. What are the effects of increased leisure that Lynes sees? What evidence can you bring to support or refute Lynes' position on leisure? What prescriptions would you give parents if they are to avoid the dangers of "undirected leisure"?

9. According to Lynes, how are padded expense accounts, dishonest income tax returns, the new status of bright students, hero-worship, and fear of the Russians mirrored in the attitudes and behavior of teen-agers?

10. What is Lynes' attitude toward "going steady"? How do you know?

11. Though Lynes' point of view is basically sympathetic to teenagers and their problems, he has to indicate some rather unpleasant facts about teen-agers in the course of his article—facts which may be offensive to teen-age readers. And, since he puts responsibility for much obnoxious teen-age behavior squarely on parents, Lynes may offend his adult reading audience. By what means does he either avoid giving offense or at least soften the offense for both groups of readers? In which paragraphs do you find one or another of his means most effectively used?

Alternate selections for the study of Point of View: Nicholas Monsarrat, "Around-the-World Grouch"; Jacques Barzun, " 'Say, Bud!' . . . 'Hiya, Baby!' "; Hal Borland, "Subtle Voices."

Theme Assignment: You can write a theme on teen-agers—their problems, their attitudes, their behavior—from any one of a number of points of view. You can write as a teen-ager defending your own generation or criticizing it; you can write as an atypical teen-ager—one with a strongly rooted home and close family ties—or as a typical teen-ager in rebellion against your generation; you can write as an adult (or near adult) with an adult's point of view on "the younger generation"; or you can write as a potential parent, expressing what you hope to do for, with, against your own teen-age children. Formulate a guiding purpose that will clearly reflect the point of view you have chosen and then write the theme.

or

Adopt the point of view of today's parent as he is characterized by Lynes and write a theme defending today's parents against Lynes' accusations. Your guiding purpose should clearly reflect your point of view and indicate specifically the accusations with which you will deal.

Unity

It's a Democracy, Isn't It?

ALISTAIR COOKE

[1]   I WAS standing on the corner of Lexington Avenue on
a Sunday in May waiting for a bus. It was a gorgeous day, hot and
golden, and there were not many people around. Sunday is more
than a bearable day in New York because for one thing there are
about a million less cars than usual. No trucks. Suburbanites in for   5
the day pointing up and down and walking with their feet out. A
couple of cabs parked outside a lunch-room, the drivers gone in for
a beer. A family or two hand in hand, taking the children off to the
park. A well-dressed upper-crust couple coming across from Park
Avenue also hand in hand—a very common sight in New York,   10
for Americans are not much concerned in such matters with what
looks proper or what the neighbors will think. A good day—the
sort of day when, for all the panicky newspaper headlines, your faith
in people, and their needs and inclinations, is restored.

[2] Suddenly, I heard a ghost. It was a familiar ghost, an invisible   15
man somewhere in mid-air saying in a brisk monotone—"Strike. The
count is two and two. Runners on first and third." This lingo, or
the language of which this is a snatch, is something you would hear
in a hundred places—homes, cafés, saloons, cars—from then till
the end of the first week in October. It is a radio sports announcer   20

Reprinted from "It's a Democracy, Isn't It?" from *One Man's America,* by
Alistair Cooke, by permission of Alfred A. Knopf, Inc. Copyright 1951, ©
1956 by Alistair Cooke.

covering a ball game—a ball game being, as you probably know,
a baseball game.

[3] The voice was coming from nowhere. A young couple, arm
in arm, was ambling towards me. But the man's free arm carried a
25 little box. Of course, it was a portable radio. They went down the
subway steps, and as they pattered down into the darkness the voice
went on floating up, more excited now: "A base hit to left field.
Fuselli's in, Rodgers coming into third." Nobody else on the street
seemed to notice or to care. But if you had cared, and wanted for
30 one day to get away from radio, I don't know where you could have
gone. Out at Coney Island, thousands of bodies would be lying in
close proximity not only to thousands of other bodies but to hundreds of other little boxes, tuned high. And the air would be so full
of "He's out" and "The bases are loaded" and "Full count," that
35 you'd have had quite a time knowing what the wild waves were
saying.

[4] This little picture is meant to produce a shudder in you. If
it doesn't, then Britons are not what they used to be, and their
passion for privacy, and what's more for respecting the next man's
40 privacy, is dead and gone. Don't misunderstand me. I approve myself
very strongly of this feeling. I share it. But it makes me all the less
of an American. Only a week ago, I heard a plonking sound, allied
to music, quite faint, coming up through the living-room floor. It
was a neighbor in our apartment house who is either six years of
45 age and a promising pianist or forty years of age and a dope . . .
because she—why do I say "she," I wonder—has been stuck on
that same piece for a month or two now. I grumbled about the
sameness of her repertory, and my twelve-year-old daughter, idling
over a book, said, "Relax, Pop, you don't have to hear it if you don't
50 want to."

[5] By this simple remark my daughter didn't mean that I could
get up and go downstairs and start a riot, or that I could call the
police or take out an injunction. She simply meant I should shut
my mind to the sound. I made sure this is what she meant, because
55 when I played aloud with the idea of strangling our tinkling neighbor,
she said, "I don't think that's very nice. She paid *her* rent too, you
know."

[6] Now, I should like to say that I am proud of my daughter
and usually turn to her for a response that is commonsensical and
60 unshocked (by, so far as I can make out, anything in life). But I
wasn't aware she had acquired so young a fundamental mood or

attitude of what Americans call democracy. In Britain, one of the
minor duties of good citizenship is not to disturb the private life of
other citizens. In this country, it's the other way around—not to
disturb other citizens who are enjoying their private life in public. 65
That, as you see, is a heavily loaded interpretation of an attitude
that is universal among Americans. And there are limits. Just the
same, the decision of a Washington court of appeal not to let advertisers broadcast in public buses only shows how far you can go
in America without being stopped.   70

[7] Americans regard most of us born in Britain as dull, decent,
amiable people but given to being rather testy about our rights.
So "Relax, Pop," says my daughter and goes back to reading her
book with one third of her mind, listening to the pianist downstairs
with another lobe, and at the same time dreaming on all cylinders 75
about some absent male of the species. Quite aside from the principle involved, this attitude entails a considerable physical feat. It
is the ability not to hear what you don't want to hear, what the most
famous radio critic in America calls "selective deafness." He says
it is a faculty essential to an enjoyment of American radio, and it 80
is a faculty that most visiting Britons would rather not develop.
Because they soon learn, as Mr. Crosby—John, not Bing—remarks,
that the advertising people are aware of this conditioned reflex and
so from year to year, like drug addicts, they increase the dose of the
sales talk they cut into the programs. Still, nobody hearing his favorite 85
comedian or forum discussion or symphony concert bothers to turn
off the "plug." He lets it chatter on about some soap that "atomizes
dirt" or a toothpaste that is "kind to gums but murder on film." And
then the ecstatic announcer stops, and so back to Bob Hope or
"Whither Europe?" or the Second Symphony of Beethoven.   90

[8] To watch an American on a beach, or crowding into a subway,
or buying a theater ticket, or sitting at home with his radio on,
tells you something about one aspect of the American character:
the capacity to withstand a great deal of outside interference, so to
speak: a willing acceptance of frenzy which, though it's never self 95
conscious, amounts to a willingness to let other people have and
assert their own lively, and even offensive, character. They are a
tough race in this. You are expected—far beyond what other peoples
would say were the restraints of manners—to assume that one man's
opinion is as good as another's. The expert is an American idol, 100
but only in certain understood fields. He is safe from contradiction
if his expertness is in a science—in medicine, technology, industrial

research, or in making something with his hands (better, if he uses somebody else's hands, because that shows he has mastered a process
105 which can be left to drones): such things as an automobile, a waterproof watch, or a non-riding girdle. But when it come to ideas about life and love and religion and education and architecture and painting and music, indeed all forms of pleasure, there is a national conviction that an expert is a phony, or "wants to be different," and
110 that what matters is you should know what you like and—this is a democracy, isn't it?—speak up and say your piece. It may well be born from generations of living close to many races and many prejudices and temperaments and having to strike a livable compromise that may not be as smooth as some other societies; but at least it
115 is a society, a going concern, which had to be built not out of a theory but out of the urgent practical need to get along at all.

[9] At any rate, if you want to live here in any spiritual comfort you have to allow for a wide variety of temperament in your friends and neighbors and approve a sharp clash of tastes. An insistence on
120 privacy in such a society looks, as it would not look in Britain, like a form of conceit or neurosis, a refusal to admit the status quo by which you all live. So if the issue ever came up in argument, I think most Americans would say that it is merely elementary good manners and good citizenship to look on yourself as only one member of the
125 community, whether that community is a town, a party, or a family.

[10] It may be what makes Americans so easy-going about their children. I don't know if anyone has ever taken a statistical count, and there may be just as many nagging parents here as anywhere else, but my impression is that if you are what they used to call a
130 severe disciplinarian with children, you get known to the neighbors as a crank. There is a sort of cheerful, unstated assumption that children will grow up and be polite soon enough and that there's no sense for the first fifteen years or so in pretending they are anything but inhabitants of the jungle. (There is a certain family pride
135 in seeing your child become king or queen of the jungle.) The children themselves are of course not aware of being particularly bad or violent or ill-mannered. They have no other system to compare themselves with, and like all children don't even know that any other system exists. Remembering this, you can appreciate that if
140 a six- or a ten- or a fifteen-year-old passes you on the street, looks up and says, "Hi!" he is paying you far more the respect of genuine liking than if he said, "Good morning, sir"—which would be a very alien, not to say sarcastic, sound in these parts.

[11] The same sort of tolerance explains too, I think, such a seemingly irrelevant thing as the variety of men's clothes in a big city. There is not among Americans anything remotely resembling the uniform of the English city businessman. They dress for themselves, with their own tastes in ties, shirts, shoes; and this gives to an American street a color, often a garishness, and it makes it pretty impossible for a foreigner to guess at the occupation of the other men around. With women, it is even more difficult. A flock of girls comes into a restaurant and you can't tell the débutante from the shop girl. I remember a Swedish girl on a skiing party watching the swirl of people in the snow and saying, "Which are the nice people? Who are my kind? Give me a sign." There are signs. But they are small and subtle and would take her years to learn. And if she stayed here long, she would insensibly shed the signs she sought.

[12] I was taking an Englishman the other night up to my apartment, and as we approached the entrance of the apartment house, I saw a man who lives in the building polishing the radiator of his car. I hissed to call my friend's attention to him as we came close. "Tell me quick," I said, "what sort of an American is this—I mean is he a banker, a real-estate agent, a baseball player or what?—look him over." My friend leered politely at him sideways. He was a middle-aged dark man, with a black mustache and big eyes. He was hatless. He had on a blue sports coat, slacks of a different color, a button-down collar, and a bright tie. He was polishing away and coughing smoke all over the radiator. Then he bent down to start on the wheels. Standing genially over him was the janitor, saying the utterly meaningless sentence, as we came on it: "No, sir, not for my money . . . but some guys are that crazy, I reckon." When we got inside I looked at my friend.

[13] "Oh, I don't know," he said, "I should say an advertising man or perhaps the owner of a chain of drugstores."

[14] "That," I said, as we went into the elevator, "is a dethroned Archduke."

[15] He was dethroned by the bullet that shot his great-uncle and started the First World War.

When we say that a piece of writing is unified or that a writer has achieved unity in his work, we do not, of course, mean that the writing says only one thing over and over again. We do mean that all the elements that make up the writing work harmoniously toward the single end of achieving the writer's purpose. Each idea in a piece of writing, each example or illustration or detail, each description or exchange of dialogue must be integral to the whole and must make its contribution to the total meaning. Practically all the elements of writing treated in this book have a part, in one way or another, in achieving unity. If ideas are not placed in proper order, if point of view and tone are not consistent, if less important elements are not subordinated to more important elements, if relations among ideas are not made clear, if irrelevant materials are included, unity is bound to be adversely affected.

Unity in writing, as in all the arts, results, not in monotony, but in harmony. The painter does not achieve unity by using a single color or a single shape: his colors, his shapes, his lines, his masses all work together to produce a unity of effect which is a major source of the viewer's pleasure. Similarly, the composer does not achieve unity by using a single note or even necessarily by writing in a single key or tempo: the unity of his work, like that of painting and writing, comes from the integration of all the elements of which his music is comprised. The Alistair Cooke essay provides an opportunity for seeing how diverse elements can be welded into a unified whole.

1. Formulate the guiding purpose of Alistair Cooke's essay. In which paragraph is the purpose most explicitly achieved?

2. Did Alistair Cooke start his essay with the description of an idyllic summer day in New York just to show that he is a skillful enough writer to create a mood? If not, what is the function of the first paragraph in relation to the rest of the essay? What other paragraphs combined with paragraph 1 make up the first major unit of thought in the essay? State the thought in one sentence; what contribution does this unit make toward achieving the guiding purpose?

3. Where in paragraphs 2 and 3 do you find reflected the fact that Cooke is addressing himself to a British audience?

4. What is the justification for including the incident of the practicing pianist and Alistair Cooke's daughter's attitude toward her?

5. What fundamental British and American attitudes is Alistair Cooke contrasting? Is inclusion of material on the British attitude a violation of the guiding purpose? If you think not, justify your conclusion.

6. What is the logical relation between paragraph 7 and the preceding three paragraphs? between paragraphs 8 and 9?

7. What statement made earlier in the essay is illustrated by paragraphs 10 and 11?

8. What is the relevance of the incident about the dethroned archduke to the guiding purpose of the essay?

9. Your answers to the previous questions should have made you aware of how carefully Alistair Cooke must have planned his essay

before writing it. After all, he has brought together what, at first, might seem to be a lot of unrelated topics—a summer day in New York, the hazards of living in a New York apartment, British and American attitudes toward privacy, the nature of American democracy, bringing up children, American men's and women's clothes, a story about a dethroned archduke—but he has welded his materials into a logically organized, unified, and coherent essay. By listing the main divisions of the content, reconstruct the plan or outline that Alistair Cooke must have had in mind or on paper before he wrote the essay.

10. In the light of the outline you have reconstructed, justify inclusion of the material on radio commercials and American attitudes toward experts. How is this material relevant to the guiding purpose you formulated above?

11. Does the relation between Cooke and his daughter support Lynes' thesis in the previous selection? Explain.

Alternate selections for the study of Unity: Gilbert Highet, "The Study of Style"; Samuel Johnson, "The Happy Valley"; James Agee, "Knoxville: Summer 1915."

Theme Assignment: Many Americans are more concerned with the preservation of privacy than Alistair Cooke seems to realize. Many American families—financially able—supply each family member with a room of his own—largely in the interests of privacy. Better restaurants place tables far enough apart or use booths so that diners may have some measure of privacy. American trains have private compartments and roomettes. American summer vacations often enough are enjoyed in a rented cottage or "camp" on a secluded lake front where privacy is a main attraction. Inhabitants of a metropolitan apartment building—though living in close proximity for years—may never come to know one another socially because of an unwillingness to invade privacy.

Write a theme on privacy in American life. You must realize that this is merely a broad topic with innumerable possible focuses and guiding purposes. You may want to concentrate on your own family's methods for ensuring privacy or on evidence drawn from some area of American life to refute or support Alistair Cooke's contentions or on invasions of privacy you most resent or on the special problems of privacy created by camp living or dormitory living or on the attitudes toward privacy of some of your friends or of members of your family. Whatever focus you choose, formulate a specifically worded guiding purpose and plan your theme in the light of it, paragraph by paragraph, to achieve the unity illustrated in Cooke's essay.

Ordering
of Ideas

FROM
Henry Ford—A Complex Man

ALLAN NEVINS

[1] [FORD'S] technological genius was one aspect of a mind peculiar for its intuitive nature. [He] hit upon truths (and errors) by divination, not ratiocination. His aides credited him with what Dean Marquis called a "supernormal perceptive faculty" and W. J.
5 Cameron "some gadgets in his head that the rest of us didn't have." Marquis termed him "a dreamer," adding that he had a different view from other men of what was possible and impossible. "I suppose the reason is that men who dream walk by faith, and faith laughs at mountains." As Ford himself told Fred L. Black, he worked partly
10 by hunches. Even his understanding of his lieutenants was largely intuitive.

[2] Obviously, if intuition moved some mountains, it collided disastrously with certain more massive ranges. Reliance on intuition was one reason why Ford was so amazingly unpredictable; men
15 never knew which of a half-dozen Fords they were going to meet. It was also one reason for the crippling isolation of his mind, for

"Henry Ford—A Complex Man," by Allan Nevins, from *American Heritage, The Magazine of History*, VI, No. 1 (December, 1954), 56–58. Reprinted with the permission of American Heritage.

a brain that cannot be reasoned with is a brain that cannot be penetrated. Down to 1914 Ford was open to the counsel of men who had a right to insist on being heard: his partners Alex Malcomson and John S. Gray, his indispensable business manager James 20 Couzens, the brilliant designer Harold Wills, and others. Later, with the amazing expansion of the business, the rise of employees to six figures, his achievement of autocratic power by the ousting of all his partners, and increasing age, Henry Ford placed himself beyond advice. His mental isolation "is about as perfect as he can 25 make it," wrote Marquis as early as 1923. Charles E. Sorensen, who ought to know, believes that Ford had only two lifelong friends: Sorensen himself, and the strong head of his British company, Percival L. D. Perry.

[3] His complex, inconsistent, intuitive mind has naturally lent 30 itself to a Jekyll and Hyde concept of two (or more) Fords dwelling in the same body; but we may repeat that these efforts at pattern-making are delusive. One clue, however, does explain much in the Dearborn wizard. The dreamer, the man of intuitive mind, is usually an artist; and many puzzling vagaries, many contradictions, even 35 many repugnant acts in Ford become comprehensible if we view him as essentially a man of artistic temperament. His detachment, his arch, wry humor, his constant self-projection into the spotlight (though all his intimates call him essentially modest), his ability to lift himself above those business minutiae which absorbed most 40 industrialists, his readiness to do some terrible things with as little seeming consciousness of their quality as Byron or Swift showed in *their* misdeeds, all suggest an artistic bent. The Model T was homely awkwardness itself—but it had artistic elements. Highland Park was the most artistic factory, in architecture, shining cleanliness, 45 and harmonic arrangement, built in America in its day. The painter Charles Sheeler caught the beauty of the River Rouge plant. And what of the aesthetic element in the old dances, old folksongs, old buildings, and old machines Ford loved so well?

[4] Above all, he had the artist's desire to remake the world 50 after his own pattern. His gospel of abundant work, high wages, and low prices; his plans for decentralizing industry to combine it with rural life and rural virtues; his enthusiastic forays into "better" agriculture, "better" education, "better" recreation; his warm promotion from 1914-20 of the welfare work of his "sociological depart- 55 ment"—what else were these but the artist's effort to impose his own vision on life? He would remold American society and the

American economy to fit his vision, himself the potter at the whirling wheel.

60   [5] If there was a Jekyll and Hyde element in the man, it lay in the complex enmity between Ford the artist and Ford the untutored countryman whose parents had been Michigan pioneers, and whose own formal education was limited to a few years in a very common school. This conflict twisted the whole skein of his character. An

65 artist needs a cultivated background: Henry Ford's background was that of Anglo-Irish tenant farmers, and of Springwells Township lately wrested from the forest. Though from his homely early environment he drew many advantages, its limitations always fettered him.

70   [6] He always remained a countryman in his plain way of living, for despite Keith Sward's statements, it *was* plain. When his fortune first grew, he said plaintively that the chief difference in his way of life was that "Mrs. Ford no longer does the cooking"—and he preferred her cookery. He refused a butler, for he wanted no man

75 behind his chair at dinner "while I am taking the potatoes' jackets off." His puritanic condemnation of smoking, drinking and marital irregularities conformed to the principles described in Thorstein Veblen's essay *The Country Town*. He rejected the eminent Delancey Nicoll as attorney in the Sapiro case because, when the New York

80 lawyer came to Dearborn, Ford saw him chain-smoking cigarettes. "I'm for Mr. Coolidge if he will enforce the Prohibition laws," he said in 1923. He was a countryman also in his devotion to work as a virtue in itself. His cure for nearly all ills was more work.

   [7] True to the frontiersman's instinct, he consistently preferred

85 trial and error to precise planning. Contemptuous of elaborate record-keeping, he once shocked Perry by making a bonfire of forms used to keep track of spare parts. Hostile to meticulous organization, he ran even the huge Highland Park plant without formal titles or administrative grades. He long derided careful cost accounting. In

90 this, thinks one surviving executive, H. L. Moekle, he was right. Success in the automotive industry at first depended not on computation of costs to the third decimal point in Rockefeller's fashion, but on courageous innovations in design and engineering and on the acceptability of models and prices to the public. Ford stayed

95 in the field of bold experiment—cost accounting might have hampered him. He of course stuck to Model T too long; but meanwhile he was experimenting with tractors, a tri-motored airplane, a weekly journal, a railroad, and a dozen other matters.

   [8] He had also the frontiersman's intense hatred of monopoly

and special privilege. To be sure, he long enjoyed a practical monop- 100
oly of the low-priced car, but he could say that he achieved it
without favor and without warring on any competitor. His dislike
of patents, his earnest counsel to George Holley to take out no
patent on his carburetor, his course in throwing open to public view
and general use Ford machines and methods, his determined battle 105
against George Selden, all harmonized with the frontier attitude.
He extended the principle beyond automotive patents. His early
broadcasting station WWI carried on research, worked out (so associates say) the first directional airplane controls, and gained a patent
—which he shared with all. Once his purchaser, Fred Diehl, was 110
offered spark plugs free for River Rouge production if the supplier
were allowed to sell all replacements to dealers. "Mr. Ford himself
turned that down," reports a lieutenant. "He said he didn't want
anything from anybody for nothing." A true countryman's speech;
for a scheme that would have meant monopoly supply was abhorrent 115
to Henry Ford.

These paragraphs make up one section of a longer essay about
Henry Ford, but they may be considered here as a self-contained unit
or short essay.

Nevins discusses the personality of Ford in terms of three facets—
his intuitive mind, his artist's temperament, and his countryman's (or
frontiersman's) point of view.

1. Formulate the guiding purpose of the essay, including all three
facets.

2. What reasons do you suppose led Allan Nevins to choose the
order in which he presents the three facets? Would any other order
have been better? Why or why not?

3. What is the purpose of the first paragraph? How do the several
quotations in the paragraph help achieve its purpose?

4. What is the logical relation between paragraphs 1 and 2?

5. How is paragraph 3 related to paragraphs 2 and 4?

6. How is the transition made between paragraph 5 and the preceding paragraphs?

7. How are paragraphs 6, 7, and 8 related to paragraph 5? What
do you think determined the order of paragraphs 6, 7, and 8? Would
any other order have done as well? Why or why not?

8. Paragraph 6 supplies details in support of the contention that
Ford "always remained a countryman." What do you suppose determined the ordering of the details? Is the order effective? Why or why
not?

9. Much of the interest in the essay comes from the details Nevins

supplies to support and clarify his interpretation of Henry Ford's character and personality. To say that Ford had much of the artist in him is not particularly enlightening unless we know precisely what Nevins means by artist. Through what supporting details in paragraph 3 is Nevins' precise meaning made clear? Further details appear in paragraph 4. Why is a separate paragraph devoted to these? The clarity with which we grasp Nevins' meaning is largely a result of the organization of the materials first into the main divisions suggested by question 1 above and then into the details within the main divisions. It should be obvious that only careful planning can result in unified, coherent writing.

Alternate selections for the study of Ordering of Ideas: Demosthenes, from "On the Crown"; Richard Steele, from *The Tatler*, No. 25; Eric J. Dingwall, "Paradox of the American Woman."

Theme Assignment: Select a person whom you know well—a member of your family, a friend, an historical figure about whom you have read fairly widely; define for yourself three or four facets of his personality which help you to understand him as an individual; write a theme in which you reveal your understanding. Remember that you are not writing a full-length biography; you are making convincing and meaningful only certain qualities of your individual. Your guiding purpose should indicate the facets with which you will deal and their order; your plan or outline should contain the details (and their order) which will make the facets believable to the reader. In a brief statement following your theme, justify the order you have chosen for the details.

Coherence

Poetry for the
Perfectly Practical Man

JOHN UNTERECKER

[1] I AM out to sell poetry to people who don't read it, who don't like it, who don't want their children to read it, and who, especially, don't want their friends and business associates to think they read it. I want not only to persuade them to read poems but as well to transform them into a band of missionary spirits who, suspending poems on every shining television aerial, will convert the American landscape into a forest leafing out in literature.

[2] I have no illusions, of course, as to the possibilities of my succeeding in this project. It is a very idle dream. Most of us, by and large, give considerable lip service to poetry, and lip service seldom if ever brings poetry to the lip. We (properly) deplore the Russian treatment of Boris Pasternak, and we (improperly) congratulate ourselves that a Pasternak in America would never be subjected to such shabby treatment. We keep the anthology of poetry we always intend to read in some handy place—the guest room, usually. And we frequently regret, publicly, that we have just never had time to learn to appreciate poetry (thus assuring the world that we're on its side, that it has nothing to fear from us). Comforted by our virtuous attitudes, we're able to experience the joy of doing our cultural bit without struggling through the words on the page.

"Poetry for the Perfectly Practical Man," by John Unterecker. Reprinted from the *Columbia University Forum* (Winter, 1959) by permission of the publishers.

[3] And yet the words on the page have value. In escaping them we escape, perhaps, a kind of fullness we can experience in no other place.

[4] For the fact of the matter is that all the slogans we believe in and therefore ignore are right. Intellectual and artistic freedom *is* the great Western achievement we have claimed it to be. In making the uninhibited exploration of the word every man's right, we have, in fact, loosened the shackles of ignorance, prejudice, and fear. And in creating a society in which some leisure is available to that man we have made possible the great dream of the nineteenth century: a citizenry released by the machine to pursue those cultural objectives which make life not only bearable but valued. The arts, which in the past have opened the eyes of only those men lucky enough to be born to a leisured class (artists themselves, of course, are classless creatures), are now at last within reach of the man in the street.

[5] And yet we in America are not—as Robert Brustein pointed out in a recent *Forum* ["The Theatre Is Losing Its Mind"; Fall 1958] —conspicuous for our intelligent interest in the theatre. Nor is the theatre we attend conspicuous for its quality. Serious new music languishes in America. Try, for example, to assemble an audience for a program of contemporary chamber music. And poetry perishes.

[6] How did we get this way? How can we evolve toward a happier condition?

[7] Though how we got this way is a far more complicated story than the oversimplification I am about to offer, involved in it, at least, are the very machines that liberated us, the ones that created so much leisure. For as they created leisure they helped remove man from the sort of "organic" activities which had in earlier times given him the illusion that his little contribution helped establish the order of an essentially ordered world. The potter had made a whole thing, a shaped object from the blob of clay he wedged, whirled, and fired into form. The baker had measured out flour, milk and salt, stirred the mess himself, shaped loaves, baked and sold them. These men, though only in the broadest sense artists, experienced the artist's shaping function. Participants in ordering their world, they were able to watch an entire progression from disorder to order take place under their hands. And, adjusted to order, they were able to value those arts they *did* experience.

[8] The individual farmer, cabinetmaker, tinsmith, blacksmith of

the nineteenth century was a survivor of the earliest system of relatively personal production, and each of those survivors retained
some real measure of creative activity. Farmer, cabinetmaker,
tinsmith, blacksmith held out longest against the tide; but in our
time we have seen them, like most of us, go under to the powers   65
of corporate efficiency. And not in America only. In England,
France, Russia—in every successfully industrialized state—the person has lost contact with total processes. Almost always he fabricates
a part, seldom a whole.

[9] Even in education, departmentalized for efficiency, it is more   70
and more difficult for the whole man to shape the mind of the whole
man of the next generation. Rolled from impersonal class to impersonal class or polished by the glittering mechanical marvel of educational television, the modern student finds himself machined to
a well-rounded intellectual billiard ball.   75

[10] And these triumphs of the machine are, I think most of us
would agree, not only economically imperative (we have to be efficient in order to feed, clothe, and house the world's huge, growing,
gobbling population) but also inevitable.

[11] At the same time that organic work activity was being re-   80
placed by necessary industrial fragmentation (the cabinetmakers
replaced by sanders, gluers, and varnishers and each of these in turn
by button pushers), depersonalized states, and—at least in some
places—depersonalized religions began to emerge. Compartmental-
ized, isolated from order in his amusement, much of his education,   85
most of his work, frightened by the huge uncontrollable disorders
about him (and by the powers of total destruction which lie at last
in his hands), twentieth-century man seeks not happiness but dis-
tractions. It is no wonder that he buries his head in the Great American Comic Book.   90

[12] And yet, in spite of everything that has contributed to his
feeling that he is only a meaningless part of a meaningless world,
man is essentially the systematizer that he has always been. His
happiness is still the struggle for form, the construction of images
of order from the apparent chaos which surrounds him. Not often,   95
but occasionally, he has the craftsman's sense of design. Happiness
can come from the invention of a master form letter that will be
good for all nonsense inquiries. The scientist—though he may incidentally discover the most efficient device to finish us off—still
pursues principles of order. Architect, engineer, executive still strug-   100

gle to give shape to things and, keeping chaos from the door, find
moments of joy. Perhaps joy comes even to advertising copy writers
and those poets, gone over to nightmare, who compose singing commercials for otherwise reputable products, which—their brand name
105 hammered home—some of us have learned scrupulously to avoid.

[13] That many of us really do try to escape from the fragmentation in which we seem to be caught is attested not only by the
astonishing popularity of adult education courses but by the even
more astonishing sale of how-to-do-it books. We really do want to
110 understand philosophy, music, painting, and poetry. We attend thousands of lectures. We consume—or at least buy—hundreds of
thousands of books that tell us how to read philosophy, how to listen
to music, how to paint and how to look at paintings, how to read
poetry and how to choose poets to read.

115   [14] In this welter of educational opportunity, most of us, for
perfectly good reasons, never get to examine philosophies, never
attend concerts, never go to art galleries, never read poems. Timid,
knowing what we don't know, sure only of our ignorance and our
inability to understand the self-help books, we conclude either that
120 the arts are beyond us or that the opinions of the critics are safe
substitutes for paintings, quartets, or poems.

[15] If we successfully delude ourselves in either of these ways,
we are, of course, doomed. We are also, of course, wrong. For no
critic, present company included, is a safe substitute for anything, let
125 alone a work of art. The critic's only function is to lead the audience
to the work or to point up (to an audience that is in the presence of
the work) some of the elements that make it operate. He can hardly do
anything else of real value. And the man who—with or without critic
—subjects himself to the work of art, who stares long enough at it,
130 almost always experiences it exactly as it should be experienced.
(If he hears, say, a Yeats poem as often as he hears the average
singing commercial, he can scarcely avoid "getting" the poem. He
may also, perhaps, come to admire its order quite as much as he
may come to detest the commercial's disorder.)

135   [16] And now, at last, I have worked around to the selling point.
It is here that I mount the soapbox. It is here that I want to make
my pitch for poetry.

[17] For poetry, among the arts, has certain very real advantages.
Like the "book bar" I saw displayed this morning in the window of
140 the local liquor store ("Closed, it's a handsome volume you'll be

proud to display on your desk, bookshelf, or end table. Open, it's
a handy container for two full fifths of your favorite liquor!"), poetry
is portable, potent, and practical. Unlike most of the arts, it can be
dragged about easily from place to place. It can be consulted in
spare moments. It can be sampled privately. (It can, even, be a secret 145
vice.)

[18] For the reader who has always wanted to read poetry but
has never quite known how to go about it, I have a few very practical
suggestions.

[19] In the first place, he should begin with the poetry itself. 150
No self-help book is as good for the novice as a book of poems.
After one is fairly well acquainted with an author, one can very
profitably go on to sample critical opinion, explications, etc. Criticism can function, and function well, during the reader's second trip
through an author. But on the first round it is all too often deadly. 155
It is, after all, almost always intended to make difficult matter clear.
But if one reads it before the poetry, one inevitably gets the mistaken impression that nearly all of the poems are well-nigh impenetrable.

[20] For a beginner, one volume of poetry should do—prefera- 160
bly not an anthology. (The "book bar" analogy holds here too:
casually mixed poets—say, Allen Ginsberg, Wordsworth, Dylan
Thomas, and Pope—are no more palatable than a cocktail compounded from absinth, beer, champagne, and sherry.) Ideally the
first book should be a Collected Works. There is a real advantage 165
in being able to see a writer's full development from start to finish.
Not only is each poem clearer in the context of the neighbors it
started out with, but a second wholeness, the sort of unity a life
necessarily imposes on a lifetime's work, begins to appear to the
diligent reader, the one who does not pick and choose but who reads 170
carefully through a volume in the way the author intended him to
read through it. If my notion is correct that the source of much
modern anguish is a sense of disorder, this sort of chronological
approach to a writer should give many readers pleasure. For they
will be able to apprehend not only the little ordered worlds that the 175
individual poems are but also the larger ordered world that the body
of work becomes and, beyond that, the organic thing, the organizer,
the poet himself.

[21] My second recommendation is that the reader give the poems
a chance to work on him. No poem, as I've already suggested, gives 180

up everything on a first reading; some give up very little. If he plans to spend about as much time reading *back* as he does reading forward, the reader will have a much better chance of liking both the poems he is looking at and poetry in general. Getting used to a poem
185 in the way one gets used to a popular song—by casual repetition half a dozen times, say, in a month—is a very satisfactory system. Here, a little strategy is helpful. The housewife interested in finding out what T. S. Eliot is doing might very well want to secrete his *Collected Poems* among her cookbooks, or, if she eats breakfast
190 after the rest of the family is out of the way or before they arrive, put it perhaps among the cold cereals. (With what delight, in that setting, she would come upon Eliot's "A Cooking Egg"!) Or the busy executive could take the two bottles *out* of the portable "book bar," substitute in their place Yeats' *Collected Poems,* and, without
195 arising, be able inconspicuously to go to Innisfree. My point is, of course, that the book of poems has to come out of the guest room. It has to be readily available. I know one man who, immersed in a bathtub, has made his way through all of John Donne and most of Blake.

200   [22] My third recommendation is that one go to poetry for what it can give and not for what it cannot. Poems may incidentally inspire readers to all sorts of deeds, but, by and large, poems—unlike essays of this sort—are not primarily propagandistic. The poet may be trying to inspire, and inspiration may come of his efforts; but his
205 primary purpose almost always is to assemble the organized thing that a poem is. The "message" is part of poetry, but it is only a part. Like rhymes, rhythms, metaphors, images, symbols, repeated words—all the other materials of poetry—themes help hold the whole business together. They are not, however, the normal poem's
210 reason for being. If we visualize the poem as a kind of an architectural unit, a framework compounded from various kinds of tensions (rhyme and rhythm, for instance, lacing together a structure of sound; definable themes and a paraphrasable prose sense shaping the outward thrust of metaphor and symbol) we may better be able
215 to see it for what it is.

    [23] More simply yet, all I am really saying is that the poem ought to be approached as a work of art, a structured thing, a shape. That does not mean that we do not have to worry about what the poem is saying. Of course, we have to. But it does mean that we
220 must not for a moment assume that what the poem is saying *is* the

poem. (The dog says "Arf" but "Arf" is not the dog.) The thing that ultimately satisfies us in a work of art is not its subject matter but the way that subject matter is decked out: the balances that make any painting, building, poem, trio an organic whole.

[24] If we can apprehend the work of art as a totality—by looking at it long enough, often enough, carefully enough—it will give us the satisfaction that only whole things can give us. It will remind us of order. It will remind us that man, for all the chaos he creates, shapes too. It will—in offering design—provide the sort of image that can bring to our eyes, focused so long on fragmented things, essential constructions to set against the rubble landscape of our world.

225

230

1. Unterecker divides his essay into six sections of various lengths. Though some of the sections have as many as five or six paragraphs, each section is so closely knit together, so coherent, that it can be adequately summarized in a single sentence. Using a carefully worded sentence for each section, summarize the content of the essay. Test the adequacy of your sentences: does the main idea of each paragraph in a section appear in your summarizing sentence either by implication or directly?

If your sentences are adequate, you will notice that, Unterecker's purpose being what it is, the sentences follow one another with the inevitability of logical sequence. The first section announces the writer's purpose and ends with questions which are answered in the second section. The third section points out that, in spite of what was said about man in the second section, man still has desires which poetry can help to satisfy. The final three sections supply some of the characteristics of poetry and the author's specific recommendations to potential readers of poetry. Clearly, the sections are so closely interrelated that the whole has unmistakable unity, and so coherent that the reader moves smoothly from section to section.

Good writing has the quality of "hanging together"—of coherence—from sentence to sentence, from paragraph to paragraph, from section to section. Coherence is basically a matter of having the parts of a piece of writing in the right order (logical, chronological, climactic, etc.) with the relations among the parts made clear to the reader. Often enough these relations are obvious, but just as often they must be pointed up for the reader. One way of doing this is to raise a question (as Unterecker does in paragraph 6) at the end of one section and answer it in the following section or sections. Another way of achieving coherence is to indicate at the end of a section the over-all direction the thinking will take in subsequent sections. Some-

times a paragraph is used—a paragraph of one or several sentences—
to show the relation of what has been said to what is about to be
said. Ideas may even be labeled "first," "second," "third" to keep
the reader aware of their progression. Constantly valuable for increasing coherence are such transitional words or expressions as *however,
nevertheless, in addition, consequently, but, indeed, finally, as a result,
in contrast to, in spite of, again, most of all, least of all.* Coherence
may also be achieved through judicious repetition of key words and
expressions (Unterecker, in paragraph 1, says that he is "out to sell
poetry" and in paragraph 16 that he has "worked around to the
selling point"; in both paragraphs 17 and 20 he makes use of the
" 'book bar' analogy") and through pronouns which, by referring back
to their antecedents, may link one section or paragraph or sentence
to another.

2. By what means does Unterecker effect a transition from section
2 to section 3? from section 3 to section 4? from 4 to 5? from 5 to 6?

3. What transitional expressions does Unterecker use at the beginnings of paragraphs 2, 3, 5, and 6? Supply a better transition for
paragraph 5 than the repeated "And yet."

4. Analyze the remaining sections of the essay to determine precisely how coherence from paragraph to paragraph is achieved. You
will need to take into account not only explicit transitions but also
relations among ideas.

5. The items below suggest a not too infrequent incident in any
large American city. Using all of the items, write a paragraph on the
incident in which you achieve coherence by reordering the items and
supplying adequate transitions.

> heavy traffic
> no casualties
> ambulance driver's first day
> rain
> bus accident
> sale of umbrellas
> jaywalker
> well-meaning bystander

Alternate selections for the study of Coherence: Lloyd Morris,
"A Coating of Cold Chocolate Sauce"; Thomas B. Macaulay, "The
Country Squire"; Virginia Woolf, "A Memorable Hand."

Theme Assignment: Unterecker's avowed purpose is to convert
people to doing something he thinks is important. In the course of
his essay he shows why people don't do what he wants them to do,

why it is important for them to do it, and how they should go about doing it.

Write a theme with essentially the same main sections; choose something you feel (or should feel) strongly about that you wish to convert people to. For example, you may want to convince your readers to listen to more and better music or to learn to play a musical instrument or to take a more active part in local politics or to spend more time and effort in extracurricular activities or to travel widely during summer vacations or to engage actively in your favorite hobby or to learn the fine art of exotic cooking or to become Red Cross First Aid experts.

Your sections need not be as long as Unterecker's, but you must achieve coherence between sections as well as between paragraphs. Call your instructor's attention to the transitional devices you are ingenious enough to use by underlining those between paragraphs with a single line and those between sections with a double line.

Logic

FROM *Areopagitica*

JOHN MILTON

[1] GOOD and evil we know in the field of this world grow up together almost inseparably; and the knowledge of good is so involved and interwoven with the knowledge of evil, and in so many cunning resemblances hardly to be discerned, that those confused 5 seeds which were imposed on Psyche as an incessant labour to cull out and sort asunder, were not more intermixed. It was from out the rind of one apple tasted that the knowledge of good and evil, as two twins cleaving together, leaped forth into the world. And perhaps this is that doom which Adam fell into of knowing good and evil, 10 that is to say, of knowing good by evil. As therefore the state of man now is, what wisdom can there be to choose, what continence to forbear, without the knowledge of evil? He that can apprehend and consider vice with all her baits and seeming pleasures, and yet abstain, and yet distinguish, and yet prefer that which is truly better, 15 he is the true warfaring Christian. I cannot praise a fugitive and cloistered virtue, unexercised and unbreathed, that never sallies out and seeks her adversary, but slinks out of the race where that immortal garland is to be run for, not without dust and heat. Assuredly we bring not innocence into the world, we bring impurity much 20 rather; that which purifies us is trial, and trial is by what is contrary. That virtue therefore which is but a youngling in the contemplation of evil, and knows not the utmost that vice promises to her followers, and rejects it, is but a blank virtue, not a pure; her whiteness is but an excremental whiteness, which was the reason why our sage and

48

serious poet Spenser, whom I dare be known to think a better teacher   25
than Scotus or Aquinas, describing true temperance under the person of Guyon, brings him in with his palmer through the cave of
Mammon and the bower of earthly bliss, that he might see and know,
and yet abstain. Since therefore the knowledge and survey of vice is
in this world so necessary to the constituting of human virtue, and   30
the scanning of error to the confirmation of truth, how can we more
safely, and with less danger, scout into the regions of sin and falsity
than by reading all manner of tractates and hearing all manner of
reason? And this is the benefit which may be had of books promis-   35
cuously read.

[For treatment of this selection, see below.]

"Smooth Cream" Advertisement

GOOD LOOKS

AND

GOOD TIMES

GO

TOGETHER

Get into the social whirl this summer!

Have you always said "No" to beach dates—afraid that
unsightly blemishes would mar your good times? Good looks can
be yours . . . and the good times that go with them.

SMOOTH CREAM works so fast that in twenty-four hours
you can be radiant.

These two selections have certain elements in common. Both begin
by making a statement. "Good looks and good times go together";
"Good and evil . . . in . . . this world grow up together. . . ." These
statements, notice, are like each other in form. Both selections then
go on to present other statements which are presumed to follow from
the first. Each selection follows an order which the writer intended
to be meaningful.

1. Follow this order in each piece by summarizing the points made
sentence by sentence.

2. Can you find any flaws in either of the arguments? Why are you either convinced or not convinced by each?

3. Note that an argument may be sound even though you may not agree with its conclusions, or unsound, though you may agree with its first assumption or premise. Give evidence from the two selections for this statement.

Much prose writing consists of the presentation of ideas. The order of this presentation is of great importance; the reader must be led along the path of reason to a valid conclusion. To be able to lead him successfully, the writer must be aware of the pitfalls and avoid them.

The most common of these pitfalls, or fallacies, are (1) the *non sequitur* or the conclusion which does not follow from the premise (She broke up with Tom; now she'll never get married); (2) the *argumentum ad hominem*: "argument to the man," an attack on a person's ideas based on an attack against the person (He's a beatnik; how could anything he says be right?); (3) the false analogy (Homework should be abolished; after all, factory workers aren't expected to work at home after hours); and (4) the favorite indoor sport of jumping to conclusions without sufficient evidence (Two students cheated on their examinations; you just can't trust students these days).

Once you have become aware of these fallacies, you will begin to see examples of them in print. They are used—sometimes innocently and sometimes not so innocently—most frequently in persuasive writing, writing which is attempting to convince the reader that some stand or point of view or action is correct.

4. Bring to class at least one example of each type of fallacy drawn from your reading of newspapers, magazines, or any other printed source. Be prepared to explain the logical fallacy in each of your selections.

Alternate selections for the study of Logic: Demosthenes, from "On the Crown"; "Hard Sell."

Theme Assignment: Assume that you have been hired by one or another political party to write campaign literature—throwaways to be distributed in your local precinct. This is a party with which you are in sympathy, and the men and women in charge of the campaign are sincere and well meaning. You may be asked to write copy about your candidate's position on a balanced budget; deductions from income taxes for tuition costs at institutions of higher learning; making sixteen the age throughout the country at which a driver's license may be obtained; federal loans to aid local communities to improve hospitals and nursing homes; legislation which would make it a crimi-

nal offense to threaten falsely that a bomb has been set in a public
place; extending the minimum wage law to cover a greater number
of men and women; reducing the voting age to eighteen.

Write a theme presenting your candidate's views (pro or con) on
any one of these issues. Remember that this leaflet will be read by
your neighbors—the voters—and that its ultimate objective is to convince them to vote for your candidate. Remember, too, that you are
to avoid fallacies in logic; your candidate is an honorable man!

Emphasis

A Plea for the Freedom of Dissent

LEARNED HAND

[1] WHAT do we mean by "principles of civil liberties and human rights"? We cannot go far in that inquiry until we have achieved some notion of what we mean by Liberty; and that has always proved a hard concept to define. The natural, though naïve, opinion is that it means no more than that each individual shall be allowed to pursue his own desires without let or hindrance; and that, although it is true that this is practically impossible, still it does remain the goal, approach to which measures our success. Why, then, is not a beehive or an anthill a perfect example of a free society? Surely you have been a curious and amused watcher beside one of these.

[2] In and out of their crowded pueblo the denizens pass in great number, each bent upon his own urgent mission, quite oblivious of all the rest except as he must bend his path to avoid them. It is a scene of strenuous, purposeful endeavor in which each appears to be, and no doubt in fact is, accomplishing his own purpose; and yet he is at the same time accomplishing the purpose of the group as a whole. As I have gazed at it, the sentence from the Collect of the Episcopal prayerbook has come to me: "Whose service is perfect freedom."

[3] Why is it, then, that we so positively rebel against the hive

"A Plea for the Freedom of Dissent," by Learned Hand, from *The New York Times Magazine*, February 6, 1955, pp. 11 ff. Reprinted with the permission of the author and The New York Times.

52

and the hill as a specimen of a free society? Why is it that such proto-
types of totalitarianisms arouse our deepest hostility? Unhappily it
is not because they cannot be realized, or at least because they cannot
be approached, for a substantial period. Who can be sure that such 25
appalling forecasts as Aldous Huxley's *Brave New World* or Orwell's
1984 are not prophetic? Indeed, there have often been near ap-
proaches to such an order.

[4] Germany at the end of 1940 was probably not far removed
from one, and who of us knows that there are not countless persons 30
today living within the boundaries of Russia and perhaps of China who
are not willing partners, accepting as their personal aspirations the
official definitions of the good, the true and the beautiful? Indeed,
there have been, and still are, in our own United States large and
powerful groups who, if we are to judge their purposes by their 35
conduct, see treason in all dissidence and would welcome an era in
which all of us should think, feel and live in consonance with duly
prescribed patterns.

[5] Human nature is malleable, especially if you can indoctrinate
the disciple with indefectible principles before anyone else reaches 40
him. (I fancy that the Janissaries were as fervent Mohammedans as
the authentic Turks.) Indeed, we hear from those who are entitled
to an opinion that at times the abject confessions made in Russia
by victims who know that they are already marked for slaughter are
not wrung from them by torture or threats against their families. 45
Rather, they come from partisans, so obsessed with the faith that
when they are told that the occasion calls for scapegoats and that
they have been selected, recognize and assent to the propriety of the
demand and cooperate in its satisfaction. It is as though, when the
right time comes, the drones agreed to their extinction in the interest 50
of the hive.

[6] Nor need we be surprised that men so often embrace almost
any doctrines, if they are proclaimed with a voice of absolute assurance. In a universe that we do not understand, but with which we
must in one way or another somehow manage to deal, and aware 55
of the conflicting desires that clamorously beset us, between which
we must choose and which we must therefore manage to weigh, we
turn in our bewilderment to those who tell us that they have found
a path out of the thickets and possess the scales by which to appraise
our needs. 60

[7] Over and over again such prophets succeed in converting us
to unquestioning acceptance; there is scarcely a monstrous belief

that has not had its day and its passionate adherents, so eager are
we for safe footholds in our dubious course. How certain is any one
65 of us that he, too, might not be content to follow any fantastic creed,
if he was satisfied that nothing would ever wake him from the dream?
And, indeed, if there were nothing to wake him, how should he
distinguish its articles from the authentic dictates of verity?

[8] Remember, too, that it is by no means clear that we are
70 happier in the faith we do profess than we should be under the spell
of an orthodoxy that was sage against all heresy. Cruel and savage
as orthodoxies have always proved to be, the faithful seem able to
convince themselves that the heretics, as they continue to crop up,
get nothing worse than their due, and to rest with an easy conscience.
75 [9] In any event, my thesis is that the best answer to such systems is not so much in their immoral quality—immoral though they
be—as in the fact that they are inherently unstable because they are
at war with our only trustworthy way of living in accord with the
facts. For I submit that it is only by trial and error, by insistent
80 scrutiny and by readiness to re-examine presently accredited conclusions that we have risen, so far as in fact we have risen, from our
brutish ancestors, and I believe that in our loyalty to these habits
lies our only chance, not merely of progress, but even of survival.

[10] They were not indeed a part of our aboriginal endowment:
85 Man, as he emerged, was not prodigally equipped to master the
infinite diversity of his environment. Obviously, enough of us did
manage to get through; but it has been a statistical survival, for the
individual's native powers of adjustment are by no means enough
for his personal safety any more than are those of other creatures.
90 The precipitate of our experience is far from absolute verity, and
our exasperated resentment at all dissent is a sure index of our
doubts. Take, for instance, our constant recourse to the word, "subversive," as a touchstone of impermissible deviation from accepted
canons.

95 [11] All discussion, all debate, all dissidence tends to question
and in consequence to upset existing convictions: that is precisely its
purpose and its justification. He is, indeed, a "subversive" who disputes those precepts that I most treasure and seeks to persuade me
to substitute his own. He may have no shadow of desire to resort to
100 anything but persuasion; he may be of those to whom any forcible
sanction of conformity is anathema; yet it remains true that he is
trying to bring about my apostasy, and I hate him just in proportion
as I fear his success.

[12] Contrast this protective resentment with the assumption that

lies at the base of our whole system that the best chance for truth 105
to emerge is a fair field for all ideas. Nothing, I submit, more completely betrays our latent disloyalty to this premise to all that we
pretend to believe than the increasingly common resort to this and
other question-begging words. Their imprecision comforts us by
enabling us to suppress arguments that disturb our complacency and 110
yet to continue to congratulate ourselves on keeping the faith as we
have received it from the Founding Fathers.

[13] Heretics have been hateful from the beginning of recorded
time; they have been ostracized, exiled, tortured, maimed and butch-
ered; but it has generally proved impossible to smother them, and 115
when it has not, the society that has succeeded has always declined.
Façades of authority, however imposing, do not survive after it has
appeared that they rest upon the sands of human conjecture and
compromise.

[14] And so, if I am to say what are "the principles of civil liber- 120
ties and human rights," I answer that they lie in habits, customs—
conventions, if you will—that tolerate dissent and can live without
irrefragable certainties; that are ready to overhaul existing assump-
tions; that recognize that we never see save through a glass, darkly,
and that at long last we shall succeed only so far as we continue to 125
undertake "the intolerable labor of thought"—that most distasteful
of all our activities.

[15] If such a habit and such a temper pervade a society, it will
not need institutions to protect its "civil liberties and human rights";
so far as they do not, I venture to doubt how far anything else can 130
protect them: whether it be Bills of Rights, or courts that must in
the name of interpretation read their meaning into them.

[16] This may seem to you a bleak and cheerless conclusion, too
alien to our nature to be practical. "We must live from day to day"
—you will say—"to live is to act, and to act is to choose and decide. 135
How can we carry on at all without some principles, some patterns
to meet the conflicts in which each day involves us?" Indeed, we
cannot, nor am I suggesting that we should try; but I *am* suggesting
that it makes a vital difference—*the* vital difference—whether we
deem our principles and our patterns to be eternal verities, rather 140
than the best postulates so far attainable.

[17] Was it not Holmes who said: "The highest courage is to
stake everything on a premise that you know tomorrow's evidence
may disprove"? "Ah"—you will reply—"there's the rub. That may
be the highest courage, but how many have it? You are hopelessly 145
wrong if you assume the general prevalence of such a virtue; ordinary

men must be given more than conjectures if they are to face grave dangers."

[18] But do you really believe that? Do you not see about you every day and everywhere the precise opposite? Not alone on the battlefield but in the forest, the desert and the plain; in the mountains, at sea, on the playing field, even in the laboratory and the factory—yes (do not laugh), at the card table and the racetrack— men are forever putting it "upon the touch to win or lose it all." Without some smack of uncertainty and danger, to most of us the world would be a tepid, pallid show.

· · · · ·

[19] By some happy fortuity man is a projector, a designer, a builder, a craftsman; it is among his most dependable joys to impose upon the flux that passes before him some mark of himself, aware though he always must be of the odds against him. His reward is not so much in the work as in its making; not so much in the prize as in the race. We may win when we lose, if we have done what we can; for by so doing we have made real at least some part of that finished product in whose fabrication we are most concerned—ourselves.

[20] And if at the end some friendly critic shall pass by and say, "My friend, how good a job do you really think you have made of it all?" We can answer, "I know as well as you that it is not of high quality, but I did put into it whatever I had, and that was the game I started out to play."

[21] It is still in the lap of the gods whether a society can succeed, based on "civil liberties and human rights," conceived as I have tried to describe them; but of one thing at least we may be sure: the alternatives that have so far appeared have been immeasurably worse, and so, whatever the outcome, I submit to you that we must press along. Borrowing from Epictetus, let us say to ourselves: "Since we are men we will play the part of a Man," and how can I better end than by recalling to you the concluding passage of "Prometheus Unbound"?

> To suffer woes which Hope thinks infinite;
> To forgive wrongs darker than death or night;
> To defy Power, which seems omnipotent;
> To love, and bear; to hope, till Hope creates
> From its own wreck the thing it contemplates;
> Neither to change, not falter, nor repent;
> This, like thy glory, Titan, is to be
> Good, great and joyous, beautiful and free;
> This is alone Life, Joy, Empire, and Victory.

Learned Hand's essay is a closely reasoned and eloquent argument on a subject of vital importance to every American. Part of its power comes from its organization and the emphasis given to certain ideas.

1. What is the answer to Hand's question (paragraph 1), "Why, then, is not a beehive or an anthill a perfect example of a free society?" Why need we not "be surprised that men so often embrace almost any doctrines, if they are proclaimed with a voice of absolute assurance" (paragraph 6)?

2. The first nine paragraphs constitute the first major division of Hand's thinking; indeed, he explicitly announces his thesis in paragraph 9. Formulate in a single sentence the basic idea developed through paragraphs 1 through 9.

3. Why is "our exasperated resentment at all dissent . . . a sure index of our doubts" (paragraph 10)? In what sense is anyone "who disputes those precepts that . . . [we] most treasure" a "subversive" (paragraph 11)?

4. Paragraphs 10 through 15 form the second major division of Hand's thinking. Formulate in a single sentence the basic idea developed through these paragraphs.

5. The remaining paragraphs form the third major division of Hand's thinking. Again, in a single sentence formulate the basic idea developed through these paragraphs.

6. What is the relevance of the quotation from "Prometheus Unbound" with which Hand ends the essay to the third main division of thought?

7. In the first paragraph Hand asks the question, "What do we mean by 'principles of civil liberties and human rights'?" and explicitly answers it in paragraph 14. Does the rest of the essay developing his third major unit of thought violate the unity of the whole? Why or why not?

8. Of the three main units of thought, which is most important, most basic to Hand's thinking? Justify your answer.

9. Hand could have ordered his main ideas differently; for example, he might have reversed the second and third units or he might even have begun with the third followed by the first and second. Show just why Hand's order is unquestionably the best.

10. Indicate all the ways in which Hand has given emphasis to the unit of thought that you have decided is most important.

Alternate selections for the study of Emphasis: John Unterecker, "Poetry for the Perfectly Practical Man"; John Ciardi, "An Ulcer, Gentlemen, Is an Unwritten Poem."

Theme Assignment: Learned Hand points out that the unquestioning adherence to an idea or set of ideas appeals to many persons because it seems to provide a sense of security in a world of inse-

curities, "safe footholds in our dubious course." Give several examples of such ideas or sets of ideas drawn from your knowledge of
world history. Most American families subscribe unthinkingly to ideas
in many areas of living: "financial success is a sure indication of
intelligence"; "a college education is good for everyone"; "anything
that appears in print must be true"; "a girl who stays out on a date
later than midnight is immoral"; "summer jobs give teen-agers a sense
of responsibility."

Write a theme on one such idea to which you or your family
subscribes. You may wish to examine the idea in order to refute or
confirm it, or you may be interested in tracing the origin of the
acceptance of the idea or in showing its effect on your daily life or
set of values. In a brief statement at the end of your theme, indicate
what you have done to give emphasis to your most important point.

Subordination

Chuan and the Wild Geese

GEORGES BLOND

[1] THE man was bracing himself against a wall of rock which rose vertically more than six hundred feet above him. His crushing load, whose weight was at least as great as his own, was jammed against the wall. He could just manage to maintain this position by the wide spread of his spindly legs, which were already 5 trembling in a pair of blue cotton trousers, and indeed were visibly on the point of giving way. He wore tattered, rope-soled, canvas shoes, which had held out only by a miracle this far, and his torn trousers flapped like a flag in the freezing wind that blew over the whole width of the mountain pass. It was only August, and the wind 10 came from the south, but for all that it was icy. The caravan, with its bearers and horses, was making its way slowly and painfully over the mountains, battling against the wind, and the man leaning his back against the wall of rock surveyed it with an impenetrable expression. 15

[2] He might have been thirty-five years old, or else sixty—how is one to guess at the age of a Chinaman? This human machine, worn down to the thread, had no age whatsoever. His skinny forearms emerged from the amputated sleeves of an American army jacket, which had incredibly bargained and bartered its way to the 20 heart of Asia. The caravan was traveling from Qulja to Aqsu, on

From *The Great Migrations*, by Georges Blond, trans. Frances Frenaye. Reprinted with the permission of The Macmillan Company. Selection title by the Editors.

the edge of the desert, three hundred miles as the crow flies, and the horses seemed as near the point of collapse as the men. From Qulja to the Muzart Pass, they had covered two hundred miles, most of
25 it through the mountains.

[3] The man leaning against the rock, whose knees were now slightly bent, so that he was even less erect than before, had covered the two hundred miles in the following manner: first he took fifty short, quick steps, with his back bent under his load at a 45-degree
30 angle; then he stopped, stuck his stick into the ground or ice, spread his two hands over the top and let his stomach rest upon them, while he breathed heavily, making a noise like that of a pair of defective bellows. Two to five seconds later, he began the cycle again with fifty more steps. For at least two hundred years, as every traveler's
35 account tells us, the technique has been exactly the same, and caravan bearers have carried as much as two hundred and fifty pounds of tea on their backs. Naturally, they do not live to a ripe old age; but then, in most of Asia, the care and feeding of a man is less expensive than that of a horse.
40 [4] The Muzart Pass is in the middle of the high central range of the Tien Shan Mountains: a vast agglomeration in Turkestan, whose area is greater than that of France. These mountains are never in the newspapers; they hold no interest for famous climbers, because their highest peak is only about twenty-four thousand feet above sea
45 level. Indeed, the topography of the central range is in many places uncertainly defined, for few geographers are tempted to haul their instruments to this far-away and chaotic region. And any pilot who flies over it watches his dials and listens to his motors with particular attention, knowing that a landing is impossible and a parachute jump
50 would unquestionably be the prelude to slow death from exposure. The Muzart Pass crosses this range at an altitude of twelve thousand feet, rimmed by glaciers which sweep down from the surrounding mountains, every one of them higher than the Mont Blanc. For three-quarters of the year, violent winds raise tempests of snow. The whole
55 length of the pass and some distance to either side are littered with bones, but snow conceals them most of the time from view.

[5] The man leaning against the rock watched as the caravan passed slowly before him. Every now and then a bearer, with his back bent at a 45-degree angle, stopped to rest on his stick. The
60 furious blast of the wind and the chatter of a mountain stream smothered the bearers' groaning sighs and the tread of the horses, which other men, bending their bodies to meet the wind's impact,

were leading by their bridles. The men moved like so many pale ghosts, and indeed their whole existence had something unreal and ghostlike about it. 65

[6] For convenience, let us give the man leaning against the rock a name. Let us call him Chuan. It is more than likely that neither this name nor any other which the reader may choose was ever entered in the birth records of a village or town. A peasant family from the borderland of Chinese Turkestan has little legal existence, 70 and for years no one had had occasion to call Chuan anything at all. A caravan bearer doesn't wait to be called; he is there, with fifty ghostly companions, and if he is not there no one is going to miss him. He may be dead, or he may be curled up in a corner, smoking remnants of opium; it doesn't really matter. 75

[7] Chuan felt himself slipping, and closed his eyes. His legs had crumpled, and finally he sat on his haunches, with his load resting partially on the ground although the straps still dug into his shoulders. From this sloping position he could no longer see the stooping men of the caravan pass before him. His head was turned 80 slightly to the right, and beyond the pass, to the southeast, between two snow-clad mountains, he saw a slope, slightly lower than the rest, covered with pines. The dark green trees, with a ray of sunlight upon them, stood in closed ranks, like the soldiers of a motionless army. Neither poverty nor wind had bent them over; they carried no 85 load and stood marvelously straight, just as they had grown, pointing toward the sky. The picture they made was one of dignity and freedom and power.

[8] Chuan relaxed his legs and stretched them out in front of him. Still feeling the straps cut into the area between his chest and 90 his shoulders, he threw back the upper part of his body and at once obtained relief. The pine forest was now lower in his line of vision, and without moving his head he could see a large part of the snowy mountain summits. Twenty times or more he had crossed the Tien Shan Mountains, and his eyes had been blinded by the dazzling 95 whiteness of the plateaus, but never for more than a fleeting second had he been able to lift them to see the jagged, white peaks stand out against the sky. For a bearer marches bent over at an angle of forty-five degrees.

[9] Chuan looked, then, upon the jagged, white peaks. The moun- 100 tains ceased to form the infernally hostile world to which a bearer must return over and over again in order to make his wretched living; they seemed now like the immobile waves of a majestic white

ocean, tinged here and there with rose and blue lights. Chuan no
105 longer saw the caravan pass by or wondered whether one of the
ghostly figures would come to a halt before him; the caravan and
its ghostly figures had gone out of his mind. The cold had dangerously invaded his thin, ill protected body, but he did not feel either
the cold or the bite of the wind on his parchmentlike skin. Only the
110 great snowy waves rolled over and penetrated him. By now he was
lying alongside his load, flat on the ground. For a long moment he
closed his eyes, and when he opened them he saw the sky filled with
birds.

[10] The infinite depth of the sky was pale blue and absolutely
115 cloudless, and the wild geese, flying at a single level, cut it horizon-
tally in two. There were dozens and dozens of groups of birds, all
of them in chevron or V formation, flying straight from north to
south. As far as Chuan could see, the birds filled the sky, flying in
the rarefied air high above the mountain pass. The air was so clear
120 that Chuan could make out every bird, every neck outstretched
parallel to the one next to it and every pair of wings making the
same regular, powerful rowing motion. Although the wind was blow-
ing from the south and the geese were flying against it, their pace
was faultlessly even. Each chevron was like a compass, with un-
125 equally long legs; the compasses were all open at exactly the same
angle, but without rigidity. They might be compared, also, to large,
lightweight, flexible kites, pulled by invisible strings in the same
direction.

[11] The rays of the setting sun lit up the ranks of wild geese
130 from below, and those on the western side seemed to be of a lighter
color than the rest, a pale gray very close to white. Chuan knew
their exact shading, for as a child he had watched them go by, once
in spring and once at the end of summer. At dawn he had seen them
fly low over the plains, and occasionally his father had got him out
135 of bed at night and led him into the dark and silent fields in order
that he might hear the strange whirring noise produced by the beat
of thousands of wings. Sometimes, he remembered, the noise had
continued for hours on end, and long after he had gone back to bed
the geese were still flying over.

140 [12] How many years had gone by since these dawn and midnight
vigils? How long had it been since the stopped caravan bearer had
looked up to see the great migration of the graylag geese, high in
the sky? All this time the birds had continued, at the same seasons,
to fly over. The bearer's body had become more and more bent,
145 and turned into a rag more miserable than the rags which covered

it; the insectlike steps he took under his killing load were increasingly
jerky, and his hoarse breathing was very painful to the ear. And yet
the movement of the birds was just what it had been before. Now
the intermediate period of time was contracted and wiped out, and
the birds' motion seemed to Chuan like a part of himself which had 150
been preserved from age and poverty and degradation. A great peace
came over him. Probably none of the bearers or the men who were
leading the horses through the wind-swept pass had noticed that the
flight of the geese had begun. Only Chuan, to all appearances a still,
parchment-skinned mummy, discolored by the icy cold, but delivered 155
forever of the crushing load it had been his lot to carry, was aware
of what was going on. As long as he liked, he would gaze upon this
unparalleled sight, yes, just as long as the child Chuan, for whom
the passage of time had no meaning.

[13] The graylag geese were flying over the Tien Shan Mountains; 160
soon they would cross the Desert of Takla Makan, the wild Altyn
Tagh, the stifling Tibetan plateau and finally, at an altitude of twenty-
six thousand feet, the Himalayas, which no other migrant birds are
known to pass. Just now their first line was passing over the Muzart
Pass, above the only human face turned in their direction, the face 165
of a miserable caravan bearer, whose stare was gradually congealing.
Chuan's eyes no longer moved, but he could still see the passage of
the great flexible kites overhead. The sky was beginning to darken,
but still the wild geese flew over. Their great flight across the high
heaven was the last movement registered by the retinas of the poor 170
bearer, who had for so long bent nearly double over the ground.

Though many elements of good writing could profitably be studied
in the Georges Blond selection, it is particularly useful for consideration of the problem of proportion and subordination.

1. Formulate Blond's guiding purpose. Account not only for Chuan
but the wild geese, the caravan, and the Muzart Pass as well. From
what point of view is Blond writing?

2. Why does Blond start with Chuan and the caravan rather than
with the setting, which is certainly exotic enough to catch a reader's
attention? What would have been gained or lost had paragraph 4
started the piece?

3. The migration of the wild geese is a most necessary ingredient
of the whole. Has Blond waited too long to introduce the birds? Why
or why not? Why did he not at least mention them toward the end
of paragraph 4?

4. Paragraph 10 is devoted almost entirely to the wild geese and

almost half of paragraph 13 to their itinerary. Do you consider this amount of space disproportionate to that given to Chuan in the last four paragraphs? in the rest of the piece? Why or why not?

5. How does Blond keep his piece from splitting into halves—one about Chuan, the other about the birds?

6. Why does Blond tell us three times—in paragraphs 3, 5, and 8—that a caravan bearer walks with his back bent at a 45-degree angle?

7. Blond says the very existence of a caravan bearer has "something unreal and ghostlike about it" (paragraph 5) and refers to bearers as "fifty ghostly companions" (paragraph 6) and as "ghostly figures" (paragraph 9). Just what does he mean by "ghostlike" and "ghostly"? How is the meaning particularly applicable to Chuan?

8. What is the relevance to the piece as a whole of the description of the "slope . . . covered with pines" in paragraph 7?

9. What statement about the life of man is implicit in the piece? Or, if you prefer, what is the theme of the piece?

Alternate selections for the study of Subordination: William James, "A Ferocious Metaphysical Dispute"; René Fülöp-Miller, from *Triumph Over Pain*; Ralph E. Lapp, from *Atoms and People*.

Theme Assignment: Through your analysis you have seen how a skillful writer handles a problem in proportion, how a subordinate element can be adequately treated, its significance and relationship to the main element made clear and yet its subordinate position maintained. This assignment tests your skill in handling a similar problem.

One of the marks of maturity is knowing that few opinions can be held without awareness of some validity in an opposing opinion. For example, a man may believe passionately that television is a major instrument of education; but he may, at the same time, be aware that much television broadcasting is an utter waste of time. Or a person who believes that travel is a major source of pleasure may nevertheless admit that travel can be an unmitigated bore. Partisans of athletics as an integral part of a liberal arts education may still realize that time spent in athletic endeavor is taken away from serious intellectual pursuits. People who feel strongly that advertising is a necessary public service may also be aware that advertising can be a public menace.

Write a theme in which you take a strong position in favor of one of the opinions indicated above, taking into account nevertheless the validity of the opposing position which should be kept subordinate but related to your main argument. You will not, of course, be guilty of using any fallacies in logic.

Beginning
and Ending

The Children's Hour

ROBERT BENCHLEY

[1] I DON'T want to be an alarmist, but I think that the Younger Generation is up to something. I think that there is a plot on foot.

[2] I base my apprehension on nothing more definite than the fact that they are always coming in and going out of the house, without any apparent reason. When they are indoors, they sit for a while without doing anything much. Then they suddenly decide to go out again for a while. Then they come in again. In and out—in and out.

[3] Of course, this applies only to Saturdays and vacation time. I don't know what they do at school but presumably they stay put. They can't just wander in and out of classrooms and school buildings as they do at home.

[4] This foot-loose tendency is most noticeable during spring and summer vacations. Let us say that two or three of them leave the house right after breakfast. In answer to the question: "Where are you going this morning?" they say: "Oh, just around."

[5] In half an hour they are back, with possibly three others. They

don't talk. They just come in. Sometimes they sit down in various
20 attitudes of abandon. Sometimes they walk slowly around the room.
Sometimes they just stand and lean against the wall. Then, after
perhaps five minutes of this, they start outdoors again in a body.

[6] This goes on all day. Each time they return, they have two
or three new ones with them, but there seems to be no reason why
25 fresh members have come. They don't act as if it made any difference to them *where* they were. They do not even appear to enjoy each
other's company very much. They are very quiet about it all, except
for slamming the screen door. It is ominous.

[7] All that I can figure out is that they are plotting a revolution.
30 When they go out, I think that they work secretly on laying cement
foundations for gun-bases, or even lay mines. Then they come indoors to look around and see if the old folks have begun to suspect
anything yet. Assuring themselves that all is well, someone gives the
signal and they are off again to their plotting.

35   [8] I don't think that anyone but mothers and fathers of adolescent families will know what I mean, but I have spoken to several
parents about it and they have all noticed the same thing. There is
a restlessness abroad among the Young Folk, but it is a quiet, sham-
bling sort of restlessness which presages a sudden bugle call some
40 day, at which they will all spring into action.

[9] All that I ask is that they let me in on their plans. It would
help if they were noisier about the thing and did a little yelling now
and then. It's this constant coming in and going out of the house like
slippered Moslems fomenting a revolt that gets me down.

45   [10] All I hope is that they start something—anything—before
I am too old to run.

A piece of writing is a unit. It has architecture—structure, order.
It has parts which must be developed separately but which must be
made to hold together. The relationships among these parts must be
clear, and the parts must be weighted appropriately. Also, this organized, ordered whole has strategic, sensitive spots. It is mere common
sense that the beginning and ending are strategic. Robert Benchley
was particularly adept at utilizing the potentialities of these strategic
spots.

1. How does the beginning of "The Children's Hour" get your
attention?

2. How does it arouse your curiosity about what is to follow?

3. Why does Benchley capitalize Younger Generation? Why does
he say "*on* foot"?

4. Is Benchley an alarmist? Who is? What is his attitude toward alarmists? How do you know? In the light of your answers to these questions, state in your own words Benchley's guiding purpose.

5. Beginnings and endings, of course, need not be held to one paragraph each. How long is the beginning of "The Children's Hour"? the end? How do you know?

6. An aphorist has been quoted as saying, about the structure of a piece of writing, "First I tells 'em what I'm gonna tell 'em, then I tells it to 'em, and then I tells 'em what I've told 'em." Does this piece fit that formula? How, or how not?

7. What purposes does the ending serve here? Why does Benchley say "—anything—" in the last paragraph?

8. If you have read the essay by Russell Lynes, state what he and Benchley have in common. How do Benchley's beginning and ending mirror these similarities?

9. Why and in what ways does this essay give the author the opportunity to make the most of his beginning and ending?

10. Select one other (nonhumorous) essay which you have already studied—the Lynes or the Cooke or the Hand, perhaps—and analyze the beginning and ending of that essay. How has the author caught your attention by his beginning? What tone does he set? What issue does he raise? Does the ending summarize his position or conclude his argument? Is the ending used for any other purpose? Explain.

Alternate selections for the study of Beginning and Ending: Joseph Wood Krutch, "The Autobiography of My Friend Mark Van Doren"; Russell Lynes, "Teen-Agers Mirror Their Parents."

Theme Assignment: Write a theme in which you say the opposite of what you mean. Thus you will be persuasive in an indirect way; you will employ humor; you will adopt—tongue in cheek—a point of view entirely different from your own. For example, if you believe that weight is a medical problem, and that everyone should keep his weight down (or up) to a certain figure, assume the attitude that weight is of no importance, and that everyone should eat whatever and whenever he likes. Or, if you believe that rock and roll is here to stay, adopt—exaggeratedly—the position that rock and roll music disgusts and bores you. If you think that going steady is not harmful to teen-age development, write as though you thought it most harmful. Keep your theme short, and make full use of the possibilities of the beginning and ending. Keep your tone light; this is not weighty disputation, but argument by indirection.

Concreteness

Agassiz Plays a Game

NATHANIEL SOUTHGATE SHALER

[1] AT the time of my secession from the humanities, Agassiz was in Europe; he did not return, I think, until the autumn of 1859. I had, however, picked up several acquaintances among his pupils, learned what they were about, and gained some
5 notion of his methods. After about a month he returned, and I had my first contact with the man who was to have the most influence on my life of any of the teachers to whom I am indebted. I shall never forget even the lesser incidents of this meeting, for this great master by his presence gave an importance to his surroundings, so
10 that the room where you met him and the furniture stayed with the memory of him.

[2] When I first met Louis Agassiz, he was still in the prime of his admirable manhood; though he was then fifty-two years old, and had passed his constructive period, he still had the look of a young
15 man. His face was the most genial and engaging that I had ever seen, and his manner captivated me altogether. But as I had been among men who had a free swing, and for a year among people who seemed to me to be cold and super-rational, hungry as I doubtless was for human sympathy, Agassiz's welcome went to my heart—I was at
20 once his captive. It has been my good chance to see many men of engaging presence and ways, but I have never known his equal. . . .

[3] The examination Agassiz gave me was directed first to find that I knew enough Latin and Greek to make use of those languages; that I could patter a little of them evidently pleased him. He didn't care for those detestable rules for scanning. Then came German and 25 French, which were also approved: I could read both, and spoke the former fairly well. He did not probe me in my weakest place, mathematics, for the good reason that, badly as I was off in that subject, he was in a worse plight. Then asking me concerning my reading, he found that I had read the *Essay on Classification,* and 30 had noted in it the influence of Schelling's views. Most of his questioning related to this field, and the more than fair beginning of our relations then made was due to the fact that I had some enlargement on that side. So, too, he was pleased to find that I had managed a lot of Latin, Greek, and German poetry, and had been trained with 35 the sword. He completed this inquiry by requiring that I bring my foils and masks for a bout. In this test he did not fare well, for, though not untrained, he evidently knew more of the *Schläger* than of the rapier. He was heavy-handed, and lacked finesse. This, with my previous experience, led me to the conclusion that I had struck 40 upon a kind of tutor in Cambridge not known in Kentucky.

• • • • •

[4] Agassiz's laboratory was then in a rather small two-storied building, looking much like a square dwelling-house, which stood where the College Gymnasium now stands. . . . Agassiz had recently moved into it from a shed on the marsh near Brighton bridge, the 45 original tenants, the engineers, having come to riches in the shape of the brick structure now known as the Lawrence Building. In this primitive establishment Agassiz's laboratory, as distinguished from the storerooms where the collections were crammed, occupied one room about thirty feet long and fifteen feet wide—what is now the 50 west room on the lower floor of the edifice. In this place, already packed, I had assigned to me a small pine table with a rusty tin pan upon it. . . .

[5] When I sat me down before my tin pan, Agassiz brought me a small fish, placing it before me with the rather stern requirement 55 that I should study it, but should on no account talk to any one concerning it, nor read anything relating to fishes, until I had his permission so to do. To my inquiry, "What shall I do?" he said in effect: "Find out what you can without damaging the specimen; when I think that you have done the work I will question you." In the 60 course of an hour I thought I had compassed that fish; it was rather an unsavory object, giving forth the stench of old alcohol, then

loathsome to me, though in time I came to like it. Many of the
scales were loosened so that they fell off. It appeared to me to be
65 a case for a summary report, which I was anxious to make and get
on to the next stage of the business. But Agassiz, though always
within call, concerned himself no further with me that day, nor the
next, nor for a week. At first, this neglect was distressing; but I saw
that it was a game, for he was, as I discerned rather than saw, cov-
70 ertly watching me. So I set my wits to work upon the thing, and in
the course of a hundred hours or so thought I had done much—a
hundred times as much as seemed possible at the start. I got interested in finding out how the scales went in series, their shape, the
form and placement of the teeth, etc. Finally, I felt full of the sub-
75 ject, and probably expressed it in my bearing; as for words about it
then, there were none from my master except his cheery "Good
morning." At length, on the seventh day, came the question, "Well?"
and my disgorge of learning to him as he sat on the edge of my
table puffing his cigar. At the end of the hour's telling, he swung
80 off and away, saying: "That is not right." Here I began to think that,
after all, perhaps the rules for scanning Latin verse were not the
worst infliction in the world. Moreover, it was clear that he was
playing a game with me to find if I were capable of doing hard,
continuous work without the support of a teacher, and this stimulated
85 me to labor. I went at the task anew, discarded my first notes, and
in another week of ten hours a day labor I had results which astonished myself and satisfied him. Still there was no trace of praise in
words or manner. He signified that it would do by placing before
me about a half a peck of bones, telling me to see what I could make
90 of them, with no further directions to guide me. I soon found that
they were the skeletons of half a dozen fishes of different species;
the jaws told me so much at a first inspection. The task evidently
was to fit the separate bones together in their proper order. Two
months or more went to this task with no other help than an occa-
95 sional looking over my grouping with the stereotyped remark: "That
is not right." Finally, the task was done, and I was again set upon
alcoholic specimens—this time a remarkable lot of specimens representing, perhaps, twenty species of the side-swimmers or Pleuro-
nectidae.
100   [6] I shall never forget the sense of power in dealing with things
which I felt in beginning the more extended work on a group of
animals. I had learned the art of comparing objects, which is the
basis of the naturalist's work. At this stage I was allowed to read,
and to discuss my work with others about me. I did both eagerly,

and acquired a considerable knowledge of the literature of ichthy- 105
ology, becoming especially interested in the system of classification,
then most imperfect. I tried to follow Agassiz's scheme of division
into the order of ctenoids and ganoids, with the result that I found
one of my species of side-swimmers had cycloid scales on one side
and ctenoid on the other. This not only shocked my sense of the value 110
of classification in a way that permitted of no full recovery of my
original respect for the process, but for a time shook my confidence
in my master's knowledge. At the same time I had a malicious pleasure in exhibiting my "find" to him, expecting to repay in part the
humiliation which he had evidently tried to inflict on my conceit. 115
To my question as to how the nondescript should be classified he
said: "My boy, there are now two of us who know that."

[7] This incident of the fish made an end of my novitiate. After
that, with a suddenness of transition which puzzled me, Agassiz
became very communicative; we passed indeed into the relation of 120
friends of like age and purpose, and he actually consulted me as to
what I should like to take up as a field of study. Finding that I wished
to devote myself to geology, he set me to work on the Brachiopoda
as the best group of fossils to serve as data in determining the
Palaeozoic horizons. So far as his rather limited knowledge of the 125
matter went, he guided me in the field about Cambridge, in my reading, and to acquaintances of his who were concerned with earth
structures. I came thus to know Charles T. Jackson, Jules Marcou,
and, later, the brothers Rogers, Henry and James. At the same time
I kept up the study of zoology, undertaking to make myself ac- 130
quainted with living organic forms as a basis for a knowledge of
fossils.

[For treatment of this selection, see p. 78.]

Thinking like a Scientist

THOMAS H. HUXLEY

[1] THE method of scientific investigation is nothing but
the expression of the necessary mode of working of the human mind.
It is simply the mode at which all phenomena are reasoned about,

From *Darwiniana*, by Thomas H. Huxley (New York: Appleton-Century-Crofts, Inc., 1896). Selection title by the Editors.

rendered precise and exact. There is no more difference, but there
⁵ is just the same kind of difference, between the mental operations
of a man of science and those of an ordinary person, as there is
between the operations and methods of a baker or of a butcher weigh-
ing out his goods in common scales, and the operations of a chemist
in performing a difficult and complex analysis by means of his
¹⁰ balance and finely-graduated weights. It is not that the action of
the scales in the one case, and the balance in the other, differ in the
principles of their construction or manner of working; but the beam
of one is set on an infinitely finer axis than the other, and of course
turns by the addition of a much smaller weight.

¹⁵   [2] You will understand this better, perhaps, if I give you some
familiar example. You have all heard it repeated, I dare say, that
men of science work by means of induction and deduction, and that
by the help of these operations, they, in a sort of sense, wring from
Nature certain other things, which are called natural laws, and
²⁰ causes, and that out of these, by some cunning skill of their own,
they build up hypotheses and theories. And it is imagined by many,
that the operations of the common mind can be by no means compared with these processes, and that they have to be acquired by a
sort of special apprenticeship to the craft. To hear all these large
²⁵ words, you would think that the mind of a man of science must be
constituted differently from that of his fellow men; but if you will
not be frightened by terms, you will discover that you are quite
wrong, and that all these terrible apparatus are being used by yourselves every day and every hour of your lives.

³⁰   [3] There is a well-known incident in one of Molière's plays,
where the author makes the hero express unbounded delight on being
told that he had been talking prose during the whole of his life. In
the same way, I trust, that you will take comfort, and be delighted
with yourselves, on the discovery that you have been acting on the
³⁵ principles of inductive and deductive philosophy during the same
period. Probably there is not one here who has not in the course
of the day had occasion to set in motion a complex train of reasoning,
of the very same kind, though differing of course in degree, as that
which a scientific man goes through in tracing the causes of natural
⁴⁰ phenomena.

     [4] A very trivial circumstance will serve to exemplify this. Sup-
pose you go into a fruiterer's shop, wanting an apple—you take up
one, and, on biting it, you find it is sour; you look at it, and see that
it is hard and green. You take up another one, and that too is hard,

green, and sour. The shopman offers you a third; but, before biting 45
it, you examine it, and find that it is hard and green, and you immediately say that you will not have it, as it must be sour, like those
that you have already tried.

[5] Nothing can be more simple than that, you think; but if you
will take the trouble to analyse and trace out into its logical elements 50
what has been done by the mind, you will be greatly surprised. In
the first place, you have performed the operation of induction. You
found that, in two experiences, hardness and greenness in apples
went together with sourness. It was so in the first case, and it was
confirmed by the second. True, it is a very small basis, but still it 55
is enough to make an induction from; you generalise the facts, and
you expect to find sourness in apples where you get hardness and
greenness. You found upon that a general law, that all hard and
green apples are sour; and that, so far as it goes, is a perfect induction. Well, having got your natural law in this way, when you are 60
offered another apple which you find is hard and green, you say,
"All hard and green apples are sour; this apple is hard and green,
therefore this apple is sour." That train of reasoning is what logicians
call a syllogism, and has all its various parts and terms—its major
premiss, its minor premiss, and its conclusion. And, by the help of 65
further reasoning, which, if drawn out, would have to be exhibited
in two or three other syllogisms, you arrive at your final determination, "I will not have that apple." So that, you see, you have, in the
first place, established a law by induction, and upon that you have
founded a deduction, and reasoned out the special conclusion of 70
the particular case. Well now, suppose, having got your law, that
at some time afterwards, you are discussing the qualities of apples
with a friend: you will say to him, "It is a very curious thing—but
I find that all hard and green apples are sour!" Your friend says to
you, "But how do you know that?" You at once reply, "Oh, because 75
I have tried them over and over again, and have always found
them to be so." Well, if we were talking science instead of common
sense, we should call that an experimental verification. And, if still op-
posed, you go further, and say, "I have heard from the people in
Somersetshire and Devonshire, where a large number of apples are 80
grown, that they have observed the same thing. It is also found to be
the case in Normandy, and in North America. In short, I find it to be
the universal experience of mankind wherever attention has been
directed to the subject." Whereupon, your friend, unless he is a
very unreasonable man, agrees with you, and is convinced that you 85

are quite right in the conclusion you have drawn. He believes, although perhaps he does not know he believes it, that the more
extensive verifications are—that the more frequently experiments
have been made, and results of the same kind arrived at—that the
90 more varied the conditions under which the same results are attained,
the more certain is the ultimate conclusion, and he disputes the
question no further. He sees that the experiment has been tried
under all sorts of conditions, as to time, place, and people, with
the same result; and he says with you, therefore, that the law you
95 have laid down must be a good one, and he must believe it.

[6] In science we do the same thing; the philosopher exercises
precisely the same faculties, though in a much more delicate manner.
In scientific inquiry it becomes a matter of duty to expose a supposed law to every possible kind of verification, and to take care,
100 moreover, that this is done intentionally, and not left to a mere
accident, as in the case of the apples. And in science, as in common
life, our confidence in a law is in exact proportion to the absence
of variation in the result of our experimental verifications. For
instance, if you let go your grasp of an article you may have in your
105 hand, it will immediately fall to the ground. That is a very common
verification of one of the best established laws of nature—that of
gravitation. The method by which men of science establish the existence of that law is exactly the same as that by which we have
established the trivial proposition about the sourness of hard and
110 green apples. But we believe it in such an extensive, thorough, and
unhesitating manner because the universal experience of mankind
verifies it, and we can verify it ourselves at any time; and that is
the strongest possible foundation on which any natural law can rest.

[7] So much, then, by way of proof that the method of estab-
115 lishing laws in science is exactly the same as that pursued in common
life. Let us now turn to another matter (though really it is but another phase of the same question), and that is, the method by which,
from the relations of certain phenomena, we prove that some stand
in the position of causes towards the others.

120   [8] I want to put the case clearly before you, and I will therefore
show you what I mean by another familiar example. I will suppose
that one of you, on coming down in the morning to the parlour of
your house, finds that a tea-pot and some spoons which had been
left in the room on the previous evening are gone—the window is
125 open, and you observe the mark of a dirty hand on the window-
frame, and perhaps, in addition to that, you notice the impress of

a hob-nailed shoe on the gravel outside. All these phenomena have struck your attention instantly, and before two seconds have passed you say, "Oh, somebody has broken open the window, entered the room, and run off with the spoons and the tea-pot!" That speech 130 is out of your mouth in a moment. And you will probably add, "I know there has; I am quite sure of it!" You mean to say exactly what you know; but in reality you are giving expression to what is, in all essential particulars, an hypothesis. You do not *know* it at all; it is nothing but an hypothesis rapidly framed in your own mind. 135 And it is an hypothesis founded on a long train of inductions and deductions.

[9] What are those inductions and deductions, and how have you got at this hypothesis? You have observed, in the first place, that the window is open; but by a train of reasoning involving many 140 inductions and deductions, you have probably arrived long before at the general law—and a very good one it is—that windows do not open of themselves; and you therefore conclude that something has opened the window. A second general law that you have arrived at in the same way is, that tea-pots and spoons do not go out of 145 a window spontaneously, and you are satisfied that, as they are not now where you left them, they have been removed. In the third place, you look at the marks on the window-sill, and the shoe-marks outside, and you say that in all previous experience the former kind of mark has never been produced by anything else but the hand of 150 a human being; and the same experience shows that no other animal but man at present wears shoes with hob-nails in them such as would produce the marks in the gravel. I do not know, even if we could discover any of those "missing links" that are talked about, that they would help us to any other conclusion! At any rate the 155 law which states our present experience is strong enough for my present purpose. You next reach the conclusion, that as these kinds of marks have not been left by any other animals than men, or are liable to be formed in any other way than by a man's hand and shoe, the marks in question have been formed by a man in that 160 way. You have, further, a general law, founded on observation and experience, and that, too, is, I am sorry to say, a very universal and unimpeachable one—that some men are thieves; and you assume at once from all these premises—and that is what constitutes your hypothesis—that the man who made the marks outside 165 and on the window-sill, opened the window, got into the room, and stole your tea-pot and spoons. You have now arrived at a *vera causa*;

you have assumed a cause which, it is plain, is competent to produce all the phenomena you have observed. You can explain all
170 these phenomena only by the hypothesis of a thief. But that is a
hypothetical conclusion, of the justice of which you have no absolute proof at all; it is only rendered highly probable by a series of
inductive and deductive reasonings.

[10] I suppose your first action, assuming that you are a man
175 of ordinary common sense, and that you have established this
hypothesis to your own satisfaction, will very likely be to go off
for the police, and set them on the track of the burglar, with the
view to the recovery of your property. But just as you are starting
with this object, some person comes in, and on learning what you
180 are about, says, "My good friend, you are going on a great deal
too fast. How do you know that the man who really made the marks
took the spoons? It might have been a monkey that took them, and
the man may have merely looked in afterwards." You would probably reply, "Well, that is all very well, but you see it is contrary
185 to all experience of the way tea-pots and spoons are abstracted; so
that, at any rate, your hypothesis is less probable than mine."
While you are talking the thing over in this way, another friend
arrives, one of that good kind of people that I was talking of a
little while ago. And he might say, "Oh, my dear sir, you are cer-
190 tainly going on a great deal too fast. You are most presumptuous.
You admit that all these occurrences took place when you were fast
asleep, at a time when you could not possibly have known anything
about what was taking place. How do you know that the laws of
Nature are not suspended during the night? It may be that there
195 has been some kind of supernatural interference in this case." In
point of fact, he declares that your hypothesis is one of which you
cannot at all demonstrate the truth, and that you are by no means
sure that the laws of Nature are the same when you are asleep as
when you are awake.

200 [11] Well, now, you cannot at the moment answer that kind of
reasoning. You feel that your worthy friend has you somewhat at
a disadvantage. You will feel perfectly convinced in your own mind,
however, that you are quite right, and you say to him, "My good
friend, I can only be guided by the natural probabilities of the case,
205 and if you will be kind enough to stand aside and permit me to
pass, I will go and fetch the police." Well, we will suppose that your
journey is successful, and that by good luck you meet with a police-
man; that eventually the burglar is found with your property on his

person, and the marks correspond to his hand and to his boots. Probably any jury would consider those facts a very good experimental verification of your hypothesis, touching the cause of the abnormal phenomena observed in your parlour, and would act accordingly.

[12] Now, in this suppositious case, I have taken phenomena of a very common kind, in order that you might see what are the different steps in an ordinary process of reasoning, if you will only take the trouble to analyse it carefully. All the operations I have described, you will see, are involved in the mind of any man of sense in leading him to a conclusion as to the course he should take in order to make good a robbery and punish the offender. I say that you are led, in that case, to your conclusion by exactly the same train of reasoning as that which a man of science pursues when he is endeavouring to discover the origin and laws of the most occult phenomena. The process is, and always must be, the same; and precisely the same mode of reasoning was employed by Newton and Laplace in their endeavours to discover and define the causes of the movements of the heavenly bodies, as you, with your own common sense, would employ to detect a burglar. The only difference is, that the nature of the inquiry being more abstruse, every step has to be most carefully watched, so that there may not be a single crack or flaw in your hypothesis. A flaw or crack in many of the hypotheses of daily life may be of little or no moment as affecting the general correctness of the conclusions at which we may arrive; but, in a scientific inquiry, a fallacy, great or small, is always of importance, and is sure to be in the long run constantly productive of mischievous, if not fatal results.

[13] Do not allow yourselves to be misled by the common notion that an hypothesis is untrustworthy simply because it is an hypothesis. It is often urged, in respect to some scientific conclusion, that, after all, it is only an hypothesis. But what more have we to guide us in nine-tenths of the most important affairs of daily life than hypotheses, and often very ill-based ones? So that in science, where the evidence of an hypothesis is subjected to the most rigid examination, we may rightly pursue the same course. You may have hypotheses and hypotheses. A man may say, if he likes, that the moon is made of green cheese: that is an hypothesis. But another man, who has devoted a great deal of time and attention to the subject, and availed himself of the most powerful telescopes and the results of the observations of others, declares that in his opinion

250 it is probably composed of materials very similar to those of which our own earth is made up: and that is also only an hypothesis. But I need not tell you that there is an enormous difference in the value of the two hypotheses. That one which is based on sound scientific knowledge is sure to have a corresponding value; and that which
255 is a mere hasty random guess is likely to have but little value. Every great step in our progress in discovering causes has been made in exactly the same way as that which I have detailed to you. A person observing the occurrence of certain facts and phenomena asks, naturally enough, what process, what kind of operation known to
260 occur in Nature applied to the particular case, will unravel and explain the mystery? Hence you have the scientific hypothesis; and its value will be proportionate to the care and completeness with which its basis had been tested and verified. It is in these matters as in the commonest affairs of practical life: the guess of the fool
265 will be folly, while the guess of the wise man will contain wisdom. In all cases, you see that the value of the result depends on the patience and faithfulness with which the investigator applies to his hypothesis every possible kind of verification.

If you ask a waiter in a restaurant to provide you with some nourishment, you have, perhaps, let him know that you are hungry, but you have not given him any guidance in choosing one or more of the scores of dishes available in the kitchen. To put the matter in another way, you have used an abstract term, "nourishment," when concrete terms—"medium-rare, T-bone steak with onion rings and French-fried potatoes"—were needed.

Ideas, people, places, "things" may be dealt with—in writing and speaking—in the abstract. We can say that democracy is good, that parents love their children, that lakes are good for fishing, that cars travel fast. Though each of these statements communicates some meaning (just as "nourishment" did above), the communication is essentially vague, ineffective, even possibly inexact and inaccurate. Just what is "democracy" and just what does "good" mean? "Good" for whom? Economically "good" or socially "good"? "Good" for all time or only under certain circumstances? Do cars travel "fast" compared with jet planes? Do parents who spoil their children and give them a skewed view of reality "love" them?

It should be obvious—but writers too often overlook the point—that concreteness is a necessary ingredient in exact, accurate, and efficient communication. In organizing his material, a writer must be constantly aware of abstractions that need to be made concrete, of general statements that need to be made specific. Huxley had the problem of making certain abstractions meaningful and Shaler of making a man real and believable; each solved his problem, though in somewhat different ways.

1. Part of the interest in this excerpt from Shaler's autobiography comes from the fact that Agassiz was a famous scientist and teacher; the teaching technique of such a person is inherently interesting. But Agassiz must be made to come alive, to be real and believable. Make a list of the specific details about Agassiz supplied in paragraphs 1, 2, and 3. Which are devoted to his appearance and manner, which to him as a teacher? Which additional details fit into neither of these categories? Are you satisfied with your knowledge of Agassiz by the end of paragraph 3? If so, which details did you find most revealing? If not, what additional information do you think Shaler should have included? Why do you think he did not include it? Are any of the details he did include in the first three paragraphs irrelevant to your understanding of Agassiz?

2. What is the purpose of paragraph 4? Which details are most significant in carrying out the purpose? Why? Should the other details in the paragraph have been omitted? Why or why not?

3. The problems assigned to Shaler by Agassiz must be understood by the reader, who is presumably a layman not wishing to be deluged with scientific details beyond his comprehension. What three problems did Agassiz set for Shaler? What specific details does Shaler supply to explain the first problem? the second? Are enough details supplied to make both problems clear to the reader? Why or why not? Why is the second problem handled so much more briefly than the first?

4. How can you justify the technical details in paragraph 6 about the order of ctenoids and ganoids? Should Shaler have supplied more technical details in dealing with the third problem? Why or why not?

5. What additional insights into Agassiz the man and the teacher do you get from paragraphs 5, 6, and 7? From what specific details do your insights stem?

6. In each of the following paired statements, show which is the better statement and why; use as your criteria the fullness, relevance, and effectiveness of specific details.

    a. (1) "I had, however, picked up several acquaintances among his pupils, learned what they were about, and gained some notion of his methods."

       (2) I had, however, picked up several acquaintances among

his pupils—a tall blonde girl from Indiana and two brothers, both of whom were hoping to become physicians—
learned what they were about, and gained some notion
of his methods.

b. (1) "I shall never forget even the lesser incidents of this meeting, for this great master by his presence gave an importance to his surroundings. . . ."

   (2) I shall never forget even the lesser incidents of this meeting—the graciousness with which he offered me a cigar,
his insistence that I sit while he paced up and down before
me, his suddenly turning to look at me and then looking
just above my head as though he expected me to grow
taller—for this great master by his presence gave an importance to his surroundings.

c. (1) ". . . Agassiz brought me a small fish, placing it before
me with the rather stern requirement that I should study
it, but should on no account talk to anyone concerning
it, nor read anything relating to fishes. . . ."

   (2) Agassiz brought me a small fish and told me to study it
entirely independently.

d. (1) "At length, on the seventh day, came the question, 'Well?'
and my disgorge of learning to him as he sat on the edge
of my table puffing his cigar."

   (2) At length, on the seventh day, came the question, "Well?"
and my disgorge of learning to him as he sat on the edge
of my table puffing his cigar, the tip of his left foot tap-
tapping impatiently on the worn but spotlessly clean oak
floor.

e. (1) "I tried to follow Agassiz's scheme of division into the
order of ctenoids and ganoids, with the result that I found
one of my species of side-swimmers had cycloid scales on
one side and ctenoid on the other."

   (2) I tried to follow Agassiz's scheme of division into the
order of ctenoids and ganoids, with the result that I found
one of my species didn't fit his scheme.

7. In what paragraph do you learn Huxley's purpose? Why is (or
isn't) this an appropriate point in the selection for indicating the
purpose? In order to achieve his purpose, what three abstractions
must Huxley make real in this selection?

8. Explain, even though you may not have read the Molière play, the incident from it to which Huxley refers. How is it relevant as part of the introduction to this selection?

9. Which of the abstractions mentioned in question 1 does the circumstance of the apples exemplify? How? What is a syllogism? Give an example other than the one Huxley gives. What is "an experimental verification"? How does Huxley make this clear?

10. Explain what Huxley means by the statement "The method by which men of science establish the existence of that law [gravitation] is exactly the same as that by which we have established the trivial proposition about the sourness and hardness of green apples."

11. Huxley devotes four rather long paragraphs to the incident of the stolen teapot and spoons. Do you consider this a disproportionate amount of space to allocate to so seemingly trivial a subject? Justify your answer.

12. Give ten illustrations of Huxley's statement that "in nine-tenths of the most important affairs of daily life" we are guided by hypotheses. Why are you being asked to do this?

13. This selection is taken from one of a series of lectures which Huxley delivered to working men. Knowing this, tell whether and why you think his method of defining abstractions in concrete terms is apt. Why has he also included paragraphs 6 and 12, in which he relates his concrete examples back to the abstractions? Do you think the selection would have benefited had he omitted these paragraphs? Why or why not? What is the function of paragraph 7?

Alternate selections for the study of Concreteness: Rutherford Platt, from *The River of Life*; Clarence Day, "Mother and Our Wicked Mare"; Hilaire Belloc, from "The Mowing of a Field."

Theme Assignment: Choose a teacher from any of the schools you have attended to whom you reacted strongly. You may have liked him intensely or disliked him intensely. You may have been fascinated or repelled by his mannerisms or dress or attitude toward his students. You may have thought him your best teacher or your worst. In order to explain your reaction, write a theme describing the teacher in action; remember that avoiding vague generalities and including relevant specific details can make your reaction credible and the teacher alive to the reader—that is, can make your theme an example of mature college writing.

or

In our daily communication with other people, we are constantly using abstractions, words which stand for broad concepts, intangible emotions, or elaborate processes. Some of these terms are "beauty," "harmony," "academic freedom," "centrifugal force," "love," "teleology," "patriotism," "equation," "atomic energy," and "provincialism." If we were called upon to explain these terms and to make them meaningful to people who had never heard them, we could do so only by drawing upon concrete details familiar to these people.

Select one of these terms or another of your own choosing. Write a theme in which you explain it to your readers in specific, concrete terms. In formulating your guiding purpose, clarify in your own mind and, if it seems appropriate to you, include in your theme some delineation of the audience you are addressing.

Relevance

Philosophy in Wartime —
An Apologia

MORRIS R. COHEN

[1] DEAR FRIEND: Your letter gently but unmistakably intimates that I am a slacker, a slacker in peace as well as in war;
that when the World War was raging bitterly I dawdled my time
with subjects like symbolic logic, and that now when the issues of
reconstructing a bleeding world demand the efforts of all who care   5
for the future of the human race, I am shirking my responsibility
and wasting my time with Plato and Cicero. Your sweetly veiled
charge is true, but I do not feel ashamed of it. On the contrary,
when I look upon my professional colleagues who enlisted their
philosophies in the war, who added their shrill voices to the roar   10
of the cannons and their little drops of venom to the torrents of
national hatreds, I feel that it is they who should write apologies
for their course. For philosophers, I take it, are ordained as priests
to keep alive the sacred fires on the altar of impartial truth, and
I have but faithfully endeavored to keep my oath of office as well   15
as the circumstances would permit. It is doubtless the height of the
unheroic to worship truth in the bombproof shelter of harmless

"Philosophy in Wartime—An Apologia," from *The Faith of a Liberal,* by
Morris R. Cohen (New York: Henry Holt and Company, Inc., 1946). (Pub-
lished in *The New Republic,* XXI [December 3, 1919], 19, under the title,
"A Slacker's Apology," by Philonous.) Copyright 1946 by Henry Holt and
Company, Inc. By permission of the publishers.

mathematics when men are giving their lives for democracy and
for the public order which is the basis of civilization. But it would
20 be sad if all the priests deserted their altars and became soldiers, if
the Sermon on the Mount were utterly erased to give place to manu-
als of bayonet practice or instructions on the use of poison gas.
What avails it to beat the enemy if the sacred fires which we are
sworn to defend meanwhile languish and die for want of attendance?
25   [2] Impartial Truth is a goddess whose worship is not without
its difficulties even in a bombproof shelter behind the lines. She is
hated by the great multitude of the impatient and despised by those
superior persons who disdain her as old-fashioned. But as her sworn
votary I cannot deny her. When the Germans sank the *Lusitania*
30 I could not deny the women and children starved by the blockade.
As a citizen I should have been glad, if conditions permitted, to
volunteer for military service. But though I could conscript my body
I could not conscript my mind. As a philosopher I could never
assert that the war was a clear issue between the powers of light
35 and the powers of darkness—or, as Bergson put it, between the
mind or spirit on one side and brute matter on the other. I could
never get myself to say that Japan had a better right to Shantung
than Germany, or that it was better that Poles should oppress Russians and Germans than that the latter should be the oppressors.
40 I could never believe that the world's iniquity would end the moment
the Kaiser (or any other "boss") should be overthrown. Some there
were who insisted that it was my duty to shout these doubts of
mine from the roof tops. But I could not do this any more than I
could shout them to the Germans across the barbed-wire entangle-
45 ments. I believe in the division of labor. I am a priest or philosopher,
not a soldier or propagandist. I yield to none in my admiration for
the brave fellows who gave their all on the bloody fields of Flanders,
but I have no respect for the bigots who cannot realize that "in my
Father's house are many mansions," and that it would be a poor
50 world if there were no diversity of function to suit the diversity of
natural aptitudes. And when people begin to admonish me that if
everyone did as I did, etc., I answer that humanity would probably
perish from cold if everyone produced food, and would certainly
starve if everyone made clothes or built houses. I admit the desperate
55 need of men to defend the existence of our country, but I cannot
ignore the need of men to maintain even in war the things that
make the country worth defending. Purely theoretic studies seem to

me to be of those fine flowers which relieve the drabness of our
existence and help to make the human scene worth while.

[3] I am aware, dear friend, that in my high valuation of purely
theoretic pursuits I have the weight of contemporary authority
against me. My fellow philosophers for the most part are too ready
to assert that theoretic philosophy can justify itself only by its practical applications. But why the fundamental human desire to know
the world is any less entitled to satisfaction than the desire for
kodaks, automobiles, india-paper, or upholstered furniture, they do
not tell us. Indeed, exactly what is practical, and what is the good
of being practical at all, are just the kind of theoretic studies that
they frantically refuse to undertake. I strongly suspect that in this
they are influenced not only by the Puritanic aversion for the arts
of free play, but also by the unenlightened prejudice that the bare
necessities of life are more important than the "luxuries" which by
giving life beauty and dignity make the struggle for it worth while
to free men.

[4] Our excessive specialization tends to make us blind to that
which is outside our interests, and, hence, fiercely intolerant. I have
seen lumberjacks laugh to scorn an artist who was trying to fix on
canvas some of the haunting beauty in the gloaming of the woods;
and we have on public record the contempt of the aluminum manu-
facturers for those sentimentalists who want to preserve the scenic
sublimity of Niagara Falls. It is just as natural for statesmen and
journalists absorbed in the problems of the war and the League of
Nations to scorn those who have other interests. But there are plenty
of historic precedents to justify some skepticism as to the infalli-
bility of the prevailing judgment on what is fundamentally important.
Don't you now think the discovery of certain mathematical propo-
sitions by Archimedes to be more important than the siege and
capture of Syracuse? They used to scorn Hegel for being concerned
with his *Phenomenology* while the fate of Germany was being sealed
at Jena almost at his very door. Yet history has shown the appearance of Hegel's unearthly book to have been of greater importance
than the battle of Jena. The results of the latter were wiped out
within seven years, while the results of Hegel's thought will for
good or evil last for many years to come. When Darwin published
his *Descent of Man* at the end of the Franco-Prussian War, the
authoritative London *Times*, I think, took him severely to task!
When the foundations of property and the established order are

threatened by the fires of the Paris Commune, how can a patriotic
gentleman concern himself with inquiries that are in no wise calcu-
100 lated to help or comfort those who have a stake in the country?
Would anyone today defend that attitude?

[5] If I had your persuasive talent, dear friend, and cared to
exalt one human interest above others, I would contend that the
really important issue before the American people today is not eco-
105 nomic or political but moral and vital—the issue of Puritanism. It
is the Puritanic feeling of responsibility which has blighted our art
and philosophy and has made us as a people unskilled in the art
of enjoying life. (No one who witnessed our victory celebrations
will here ask for proof.) By making daily existence dreary and
110 depressed it drove people to strong drink, and now it deprives people
of their drink without inquiring into its cause or function. But I have
no desire to brand as slackers those who will not enlist in the fight
against Puritanism. What I wish to suggest is some modicum of
doubt as to the complacent assumption that only by absorption in
115 some contemporary social problem can the philosopher justify his
existence. The great philosophers, like the great artists, scientists,
and religious teachers, have all, in large measure, ignored their contemporary social problems. Aristotle, Leonardo da Vinci, Shakespeare, Newton, Buddha, Jesus of Nazareth, and others who have
120 done so much to heighten the quality of human life have very little
to say about the actual international, economic, and political read-
justments which were as pressing in their day as in ours. The great
service of Socrates to humanity was surely not in his somewhat
superficial criticism of the Athenian electoral machinery of his day,
125 but rather in developing certain intellectual methods, and suggesting
to Plato certain doctrines as to the nature of the soul and ideas—
doctrines which in spite of all their impracticality have served for
over two thousand years to raise men above the groveling, clawing
existence in which so much of our life is sunk. I know that Plato's
130 otherworldliness is decidedly out of fashion. We believe nowadays
that by progressive mechanical inventions and by some happy eco-
nomico-political device we can bring about the reign of complete
justice and happiness. Far be it from me to disparage this modern
faith. As a great hope sanctified by the supposed evidence of "scien-
135 tific" evolution, it is to many a real sustaining force in the presence
of otherwise intolerable evil. But to fix all our hope on some
temporal affair like the League of Nations is to leave us helpless
when we come to the inevitable harvest of disappointment. We hold

the benefits of civilization not in fee simple, to our heirs forever,
but by knights' service. Much as we may leave to our successors, 140
we can never manage it so that they shall be entirely free from toil,
pain, and the agonies of death. Let us not, therefore, willfully
impoverish their life by throwing away any of the things that have
served as consolations to so many since the ancient days—among
which are the writings of the divine Plato and even of the altogether 145
unheroic Cicero, who so tragically illustrates the failure of scholars
in politics.

[For treatment of this selection, see p. 91.]

Two Letters, Both Open

E. B. WHITE

New York, N.Y.

12 April 1951

The American Society for the Prevention of Cruelty to Animals
York Avenue and East 92nd Street
New York 28, N.Y.

Dear Sirs:

[1] I HAVE your letter, undated, saying that I am harboring an unlicensed dog in violation of the law. If by "harboring" you
mean getting up two or three times every night to pull Minnie's
blanket up over her, I am harboring a dog all right. The blanket
keeps slipping off. I suppose you are wondering by now why I 5
don't get her a sweater instead. That's a joke on you. She has a
knitted sweater, but she doesn't like to wear it for sleeping; her
legs are so short they work out of a sweater and her toenails get
caught in the mesh, and this disturbs her rest. If Minnie doesn't get
her rest, she feels it right away. I do myself, and of course with 10

this night duty of mine, the way the blanket slips and all, I haven't
had any real rest in years. Minnie is twelve.

[2] In spite of what your inspector reported, she has a license.
She is licensed in the State of Maine as an unspayed bitch, or what
is more commonly called an "unspaded" bitch. She wears her metal
license tag but I must say I don't particularly care for it, as it is
in the shape of a hydrant, which seems to me a feeble gag, besides
being pointless in the case of a female. It is hard to believe that
any state in the Union would circulate a gag like that and make
people pay money for it, but Maine is always thinking of something.
Maine puts up roadside crosses along the highways to mark the
spots where people have lost their lives in motor accidents, so the
highways are beginning to take on the appearance of a cemetery,
and motoring in Maine has become a solemn experience, when one
thinks mostly about death. I was driving along a road near Kittery
the other day thinking about death and all of a sudden I heard the
spring peepers. That changed me right away and I suddenly thought
about life. It was the nicest feeling.

[3] You asked about Minnie's name, sex, breed, and phone number. She doesn't answer the phone. She is a dachshund and can't
reach it, but she wouldn't answer it even if she could, as she has
no interest in outside calls. I did have a dachshund once, a male,
who was interested in the telephone, and who got a great many
calls, but Fred was an exceptional dog (his name was Fred) and I
can't think of anything offhand that he *wasn't* interested in. The
telephone was only one of a thousand things. He loved life—that
is, he loved life if by "life" you mean "trouble," and of course the
phone is almost synonymous with trouble. Minnie loves life, too,
but her idea of life is a warm bed, preferably with an electric pad,
and a friend in bed with her, and plenty of shut-eye, night and day.
She's almost twelve. I guess I've already mentioned that. I got her
from Dr. Clarence Little in 1939. He was using dachshunds in his
cancer-research experiments (that was before Winchell was running
the thing) and he had a couple of extra puppies, so I wheedled
Minnie out of him. She later had puppies by her own father, at
Dr. Little's request. What do you think about *that* for a scandal?
I know what Fred thought about it. He was some put out.

Sincerely yours,

E. B. White

New York, N.Y.
12 April 1951

Collector of Internal Revenue
Divisional Office
Bangor, Maine

Dear Sir:

[1] I HAVE your notice about a payment of two hundred and some-odd dollars that you say is owing on my 1948 income tax. You say a warrant has been issued for the seizure and sale of my place in Maine, but I don't know as you realize how awkward that would be right at this time, because in the same mail I also re- 5 ceived a notice from the Society for the Prevention of Cruelty to Animals here in New York taking me to task for harboring an unlicensed dog in my apartment, and I have written them saying that Minnie is licensed in Maine, but if you seize and sell my place, it is going to make me look pretty silly with the Society, isn't it? 10 Why would I license a dog in Maine, they will say, if I don't live there? I think it is a fair question. I have written the Society, but purposely did not mention the warrant of seizure and sale. I didn't want to mix them up, and it might have sounded like just some sort of cock and bull story. I have always paid my taxes promptly, and 15 the Society would think I was kidding, or something.

[2] Anyway, the way the situation shapes up is this: I am being accused in New York State of dodging my dog tax, and accused in Maine of being behind in my federal tax, and I believe I'm going to have to rearrange my life somehow or other so that everything 20 can be brought together, all in one state, maybe Delaware or some state like that, as it is too confusing for everybody this way. Minnie, who is very sensitive to my moods, knows there is something wrong and that I feel terrible. And now *she* feels terrible. The other day it was the funniest thing, I was packing a suitcase for a trip home 25 to Maine, and the suitcase was lying open on the floor and when I wasn't looking she went and got in and lay down. Don't you think that was cute?

[3] If you seize the place, there are a couple of things I ought to explain. At the head of the kitchen stairs you will find an awfully 30 queer boxlike thing. I don't want you to get a false idea about it, as it looks like a coffin, only it has a partition inside, and two small

doors on one side. I don't suppose there is another box like it in
the entire world. I built it myself. I made it many years ago as a
35 dormitory for two snug-haired dachshunds, both of whom suffered
from night chill. Night chill is the most prevalent dachshund disorder, if you have never had one. Both these dogs, as a matter of
fact, had rheumatoid tendencies, as well as a great many other tendencies, specially Fred. He's dead, damn it. I would feel a lot better
40 this morning if I could just see Fred's face, as he would know
instantly that I was in trouble with the authorities and would be all
over the place, hamming it up. He was something.

[4] About the tax money, it was an oversight, or mixup. Your
notice says that the "first notice" was sent last summer. I think that
45 is correct, but when it arrived I didn't know what it meant as I am
no mind reader. It was cryptic. So I sent it to a lawyer, fool-fashion,
and asked him if *he* knew what it meant. I asked him if it was a
tax bill and shouldn't I pay it, and he wrote back and said, No, no,
no, no, it isn't a tax bill. He advised me to wait till I got a bill,
50 and then pay it. Well, that was all right, but I was building a small
henhouse at the time, and when I get building something with my
own hands I lose all sense of time and place. I don't even show up
for meals. Give me some tools and some second-handed lumber and
I get completely absorbed in what I am doing. The first thing I
55 knew, the summer was gone, and the fall was gone, and it was
winter. The lawyer must have been building something, too, because
I never heard another word from him.

[5] To make a long story short, I am sorry about this non-pay-
ment, but you've got to see the whole picture to understand it, got
60 to see my side of it. Of course I will forward the money if you
haven't seized and sold the place in the meantime. If you have, there
are a couple of other things on my mind. In the barn, at the far
end of the tieups, there is a goose sitting on eggs. She is a young
goose and I hope you can manage everything so as not to disturb
65 her until she has brought off her goslings. I'll give you one, if you
want. Or would they belong to the federal government anyway, even
though the eggs were laid before the notice was mailed? The cold
frames are ready, and pretty soon you ought to transplant the young
broccoli and tomato plants and my wife's petunias from the flats
70 in the kitchen into the frames, to harden them. Fred's grave is down
in the alder thicket beyond the dump. You have to go down there
every once in a while and straighten the headstone, which is nothing
but a couple of old bricks that came out of a chimney. Fred was

restless, and his headstone is the same way—doesn't stay quiet. You have to keep at it.   75

[6] I am sore about your note, which didn't seem friendly. I am a friendly taxpayer and do not think the government should take a threatening tone, at least until we have exchanged a couple of letters kicking the thing around. Then it might be all right to talk about selling the place, if I proved stubborn. I showed the lawyer your 80
notice about the warrant of seizure and sale, and do you know what he said? He said, "Oh, that doesn't mean anything, it's just a form." What a crazy way to look at a piece of plain English. I honestly worry about lawyers. They never write plain English themselves, and when you give them a bit of plain English to read, they say, 85
"Don't worry, it doesn't mean anything." They're hopeless, don't you think they are? To me a word is a word, and I wouldn't dream of writing anything like "I am going to get out a warrant to seize and sell your place" unless I meant it, and I can't believe that my government would either.   90

[7] The best way to get into the house is through the woodshed, as there is an old crocus sack nailed on the bottom step and you can wipe the mud off on it. Also, when you go in through the wood-shed, you land in the back kitchen right next to the cooky jar with Mrs. Freethy's cookies. Help yourself, they're wonderful.   95

Sincerely yours,

E. B. White

In a unified piece of writing, all items of content must be relevant to the guiding purpose. Often enough, however, the relevance of material may not be immediately apparent unless the writer—aware of the necessity for letting his reader in on the "secret"—makes it apparent. Occasionally, seemingly irrelevant material may be introduced for humor or even surprise: when the seemingly irrelevant suddenly becomes relevant, the reader may be amused or shocked. But in expository writing, the main intent is normally not to be funny or shocking; the student writer will do well not only to exclude the irrelevant but also to keep his reader aware at all times of the relevance of the material included.

1. In a single sentence, state the central thesis of Cohen's essay. Which sentence in the first paragraph conveys much of the sense of your sentence? Which sentence deals with the opposite of Cohen's position? What light does it shed on his position?

2. When Cohen says that philosophers "are ordained as priests to keep alive the sacred fires on the altar of impartial truth" (paragraph 1), he is writing figuratively rather than literally. How does the figurative statement affect the reader's response to Cohen's central thesis? How does so affecting the reader's response constitute part of the development of the central thesis?

3. In paragraph 2, Cohen indicates certain ideas and doubts he had about World War I. Are these ideas and doubts relevant to his central thesis? Explain. Are they, for example, the major factor in support of his thesis? In the light of his doubts, is Cohen being hypo-critical when he says, "I yield to none in my admiration for the brave fellows who gave their all on the bloody fields of Flanders . . ."? Why or why not?

4. How is the statement "in my Father's house are many man-sions" relevant to Cohen's thesis? What is Cohen's own "mansion"? How does he justify its value?

5. In which paragraph of the essay does Cohen deal most fully with the position that opposes his own? What is the chief means he uses to support his position? Is refutation of an opposing position an effective method of arguing or of developing an idea? Explain.

6. Which sentence in paragraph 5 most explicitly states the pur-pose of the paragraph? How is this purpose relevant to the central thesis of the essay? Does Cohen use Socrates and Plato in this para-graph for the same purpose as that for which he used Archimedes, Hegel, and Darwin in paragraph 4? Justify your answer.

7. Explain in some detail what you feel is the difference between your statement of Cohen's central thesis and his reasonably full devel-opment of his thesis. Are you convinced that the thesis is valid? If so, which parts of its development do you think most effective? Why? If not, which parts did you find ineffective or fallacious?

8. Why do you suppose Cohen cast his essay into the form of a letter addressed to "Dear Friend"?

9. In one sentence for each, summarize what E. B. White is really saying in both of his letters.

10. What is the relevance of one letter to the other?

11. Why does he choose a jocular method of rambling on from one seemingly irrelevant detail to another? What does this presentation tell you about his mood? How does he feel about Minnie? Fred? his house in Maine? How do you know? What is he making fun of?

12. Trace his train of thought in each letter. In the first, justify his mentioning

> Minnie's sleeping habits
> the roadside markers in Maine
> Minnie's inability to answer the phone
> Fred.

In the second letter, justify his mentioning

> Minnie and the suitcase
> the "dormitory for dachshunds"
> the lawyer
> the henhouse
> his wife's petunias
> the crocus sack.

13. Find some additional details in both letters which seem at first glance irrelevant to the subject. Show that they are not.

14. Which details serve to unify the two letters?

15. Why are the two letters in juxtaposition much funnier than either would have been without the other?

16. Henri Bergson, a well-known aesthetician, has defined humor as the juxtaposition of incongruities. Defend this definition, making use of the letters presented.

Alternate selections for the study of Relevance: Carl Sandburg, "Getting Education"; John H. Randall, "Eternally Old, Eternally New."

Theme Assignment: Each of the adages below has withstood the test of time presumably because each contains some element of truth; at the same time, the validity of each is open to serious question. Though a hasty marriage, for example, may result in leisurely repentance, it is far from inevitable that it do so.

Write a theme dealing with the idea embodied in one of the adages. You may focus on the validity of the idea or its lack of validity; you may show the applicability of the idea to a significant problem; or you may deal with a not-so-obvious implication of the idea. Be sure that your central thesis is so adequately developed that your reader will fully realize its significance and perhaps even be convinced of its validity. Be sure, also, to make the most of specific, concrete, and relevant details.

> Marry in haste and repent at leisure.
> A bird in the hand is worth two in the bush.
> He who hesitates is lost.
> Penny wise, pound foolish.
> Fine words butter no parsnips.
> A stitch in time saves nine.
> The early bird gets the worm.
> Pride goeth before destruction.
> A shoemaker should stick to his last.
> Nothing ventured, nothing gained.

or

Draw up a list of as many sets of incongruities as occur to you. For example, a fat man on ice skates, *Alice in Wonderland* in a medical library, a professor of archaeology seated next to a jockey at a dinner party, the football hero in theatrical make-up for the Varsity Show, two people of different countries with only a smattering of each other's language attempting to communicate.

Write a theme developing one of the incongruities on your list, making use of as much relevant detail as you can to point up the humor.

The Paragraph

Topic
Sentence

FROM *The River of Life*

RUTHERFORD PLATT

[1] THE tree outside my window is mottled with shadows which, from a little distance, look like entrances to dark caves behind the sunlit surfaces of the leaves. I just saw a chickadee vanish in a split second by shooting in between two leaves with a flip of his wings.   5

[2] When I stand under the crown of the tree and look up, I see, instead of black caves, a space beautifully lighted with a sun-flecked glow, formed like a big upside-down basket behind the tapestry of leaves. This is a curious sort of place, suspended above the ground, crisscrossed with branches and twigs, protected from   10 wind and rain, filled with fresh air of moderate and steady temperature. It would be hard to imagine a place in the world more pleasant to live in. And it would be hard to find a creature more suitable than the chickadee to be an inhabitant of such a place.

[3] The chickadee is perfectly designed to fly around in the basket   15 of the tree crown, where there is by no means clear flying space. The chickadee body is bullet-shaped, with a round head snuggled

From pages 283–289, *The River of Life*, by Rutherford Platt, published by Simon & Schuster, Inc. The chapter first appeared in a slightly different version in the 1955 *Book of Knowledge Annual.* Reprinted here by permission of the copyright owners, The Grolier Society, Inc.

into it instead of projecting on a neck. A compact tail is attached
to powerful muscles at the hind end of the body by an amazing
20 hinge that flips it through half a circle. This fast-acting rudder steers
the chickadee more quickly than thought, so the chickadee avoids
collision with twigs when flying inside the basket of the tree. Very
short wings snap closed and hug the body, without the tips sticking
out, then spring out to vibrate for an instant of flight. Other birds
25 must come in with momentum from the outer air and shoot through
the canopy with folded wings, or glide to a perch on outer branches.

[4] Because of the peculiar nature of this happy hunting ground
of the chickadee, there is no right side up or upside down for him.
The paths between branches are twisted labyrinths. To swim through
30 them calls for diving down or rocketing up at steep angles: whirling,
somersaulting, describing figure eights, turning suddenly at right
angles. The chickadee defies the law of gravity with a nervous system planned with short communication lines, rotary blood circula-
tion, and a spherical arrangement of organs. Whether perching on
35 a branch or clambering on the trunk, the chickadee may be head
up or head down or sidewise.

[5] For the same reason, storms with high winds that upset the
equilibrium of other birds do not upset chickadees. People out in
the rain see the acrobatic chickadee always headed into the wind to
40 prevent rain or snow from being blown under his feathers from
behind. In winter, when other birds have taken refuge, he comes
out of his nesting hole in the trunk and frolics in a snowstorm. He
will zip over to a dripping icicle and, without any support except
the sensitive mechanism of wings and tail, catch the drops as they
45 fall off the end of the icicle more neatly than you and I can drink
from a fountain.

[6] The chickadee looks like a "little darling," instead of the
crafty hunter that he is. He can snap up an insect while turning a
somersault in mid-air; he has a trick of whipping a caterpillar over
50 a twig and then, ducking under, he takes hold of both ends of the
caterpillar and does a giant swing. He can scrape up and swallow
caterpillars at the rate of three per minute—that is, he can do that
with smooth, moist caterpillars, while caterpillars with stiff bristles
take a little longer. The problem of a bristly caterpillar, like the
55 woolly bear, is solved in typical chickadee fashion. When a python
swallows a porcupine head-first, it glides down the alimentary canal
with quills folded toward the tail. But caterpillar bristles don't fold,
so the chickadee puts a foot on him to hold him down while he

picks out the meat with his nut-pick beak and leaves the bristles, like bones of a shad on the plate.   60

[7] The busiest, fastest-moving inhabitant of the tree basket needs an enormous supply of energy. Indeed, when the chickadee is about to lay eggs, she eats her body weight in meat every day. At such a time, instead of saying "chickadee," she says "phoebe," with the high clear note of a boy soprano.   65

[8] To the chickadee, the tree basket is a beautiful arrangement exclusively for chickadee living. But the deeper we look the more we discover countless nations and cultures everywhere in the tree world. Hidden within this familiar object of our everyday world dwell stranger and more unbelievable beings than any we can imagine.   70

THE NATION IN THE ROOT JUNGLE

[9] The nation of the tree which is least known or suspected lives in a weird white jungle deep in the blackness of the ground. Both jungle and inhabitants, bathed in the vital essences of the soil, are terrifically animated.

[10] The tip of a root consists of a few tough cells welded to-   75
gether to form a spike that wedges, pushes, and twists its way between tightly packed pebbles and soil particles. This thing that looks so flabby and tender possesses immense power. The cells of the spike do not move forward, although, by expanding back of the point, they act like a wedge. They move by elongating the way   80
a rubber balloon moves forward from your lips when you inflate it. While the irresistible spike is winning new ground, its power is constantly renewed through its cells, which divide to keep ever fresh cells out in front pushing farther and farther. As older cells are stalled and left behind, the inherent power that had thrust them   85
forward now causes them to grow in a peculiar way. Each bulges out with a nipple at right angles to the forward movement of the whole root. The nipple lengthens swiftly, becomes a long, slender, white hair. This is unlike an ordinary hair on a leaf or an animal body—it is an extension of the body of the living cell itself and   90
has protoplasm flowing within it. This marvelous hair is a finger that can explore and absorb nourishing fluids in the neighborhood.

[11] In this way, just back of the growing tip of every root the white jungle appears like a puff of felt. This is the fastest-growing part of the tree. The dense thickets of these hairs bubble out for-   95
ward and get taller and deeper aft. Then suddenly they shrivel and vanish, while fresh ones are springing out up in front. The mass

and height of a tree betokens the immensity of this operation, of
food gathering by astronomical numbers of microscopic hairs.

100   [12] It is impossible even to guess at how fast the roots of a
tree grow or what their total length is. If you tried to heave up a
great tree out of solid ground with a bulldozer you would never,
with all the clamor and confusion, be able to find and separate the
vast root system with which that tree has so quietly permeated the
105 soil. By watching them in a microscope you can see the great speed
of root hairs.

[13] A single grass plant of winter rye was grown from seed in
a wooden box a foot square and twenty-two inches deep. This gave
it a little less than two cubic feet of dirt all to itself. At the end of
110 four months it produced a plant about twenty inches tall. When
its roots were painstakingly measured with the most accurate instruments, they were found to have grown at the rate of more than
three miles per day. But that is only a small part of the story—
the grass roots were outstripped by their root hairs with fifty miles
115 of new length per day. The total score for the four months of this
single plant reveals (with traumatic effect) how strenuously and
intimately a living thing can explore its portion of the earth's surface for food to live by. The winter rye reached out with two million
feet of roots, and these bubbled out with six thousand miles of
120 root hairs—*sic*!

[14] Countless numbers of fanciful, tiny creatures live in this
white root jungle and travel with it through the ground. Thread
worms tie themselves in knots, millipedes run through soil tunnels
on two hundred and thirty legs, earthworms swell and extend their
125 muscular bodies. The most populous and important inhabitants of
the place are the minute units of life which we call bacteria, beings
invisible to the eyes of men, insects, and birds. They are utterly
different from other animals and plants in the way they eat raw
elements and convert these almost instantly into the droplets of their
130 living bodies.

[15] The bacterium during its life incessantly soaks up minerals
locked up in the soil and brews them in its body juices. Bacteria
are being born and dying every twenty minutes, so their generations
are like ripples of life. The white threads of the roots of the tree
135 world pick up the elixirs in the bodies of the dead generations of
bacteria and pass them into the river of sap, to become mysterious
life forces we call proteins, enzymes, and hormones. Thus the
nations in the root hairs make living chemicals that are the corner-
stone of all the life of the tree world.

THE NATION IN THE LEAVES

[16] A vast distance away from the white jungle, at the other 140
end of the tree world, a green leaf flutters in the sun. It seems as
though any inhabitants of that leaf would find themselves in a situation similar to that of a dinghy tossed in a rough sea. But there
is a population living snugly in a wide, vast, low-ceiling room between the upper and lower surfaces of the leaf. Green, sausage-shaped 145
cells hang in great numbers from a transparent ceiling, and the
light that filters through lends the place a soft, emerald glow. Below
these hanging sausage-shaped cells, the room is loosely filled with
spongy cells, between which fresh air circulates from vents in the
floor. This is the food factory, where the tree makes energy out of 150
water, air, and sunlight, for root elongating, bud opening, seed packing, trunk expanding. This energy is made in such quantities that
there is plenty left over to power all the animal life of the tree world.

[17] A unique nation have moved into this lush, air-conditioned
place where they are closer to the source of food all processed and 155
ready to eat than all other beings on earth. They are invisible to
outsiders, well sheltered, and have no food transportation problem,
no water shortage. They are called leaf miners because they spend
their lives running tunnels inside the leaf.

[18] Leaf miners are the specters of certain kinds of beetles, 160
moths, and flies who look so different from one another in the
outer world, where we see them buzz, flutter, or streak like sparks
of sunlight. But the specters of these beetles, moths, and flies that
live inside leaves all look and act in about the same way, because
conditions in the leaf are the same for all of them.   165

[19] They got inside after their mothers had laid eggs about the
leaf. The fly mother used a saw to slit the edge of the leaf and put
in her eggs. Another used a hypodermic needle to puncture a hole
and shoot in the eggs. A third sowed rows of eggs along a vein,
and when they hatched, the babies bit a hole and climbed in.   170

[20] Leaf miners are flat or slender cylinders. They are moist so
that they may slip along easily. They often have wedge-shaped heads
to push open a path among the sponges and sausages. Legs, if any,
are reduced to knobs on which the creature slides. The specter of
the fly inside the leaf has a plastic body of no definite shape. It   175
can take the form of a ribbon to squeeze through narrow places
between leaf veins and compress its body flat to pass through a
shallow place between the juicy cells of the leaf room, becoming
round again when pressure is removed. One leaf miner has stiff

180 bristles mounted in ball sockets scattered over its body which can
be moved individually in any direction by strong muscles in the
skin. This animal poles its way, with its body in any position at
all, through the sponges and sausages that fill the room.

185 [21] Eating equipment of leaf miners is remarkable. Some have
sharp, hollow needles to puncture the cells and suck the juice freshly
made that instant out of air, water, and sunshine. Others are
equipped with scissors on their jaws and hedge-clip a path, swallow-
ing cells whole as they go. Another wears a sharp, curved blade
with which it cuts a swath through the green cells like a reaper.
190 Hedge clippers and scythes cannot cut with broad strokes up and
down in such a shallow place, so the larvae which use them turn
their heads at a right angle and reap the harvest with horizontal
strokes.

[22] I have often been fascinated by the sinuous, serpentine paths
195 of leaf miners, as you see these paths traced in white on the outside of the leaf, when the green cells have been eaten for the tunnels
underneath the surface of the leaf. This indicates extremely lazy
miners who do not bother to cut the hard, woody cells of the veins,
but wander around without direction among the softest and juiciest
200 cells in the paradise of delight.

A paragraph may be defined as a group of sentences which develop
a single idea. In spite of the definition, there are occasionally reasons
for using a one-sentence paragraph: the idea may need merely to be
stated rather than developed, or a writer may want to give an idea
special emphasis and so lets it stand alone, with its development in
a following paragraph. A one-sentence paragraph may serve as a
transition between sections of an essay; dialogue frequently contains
one-sentence paragraphs, a new paragraph being used to indicate each
change of speaker. Normally, however, a paragraph contains a group
of sentences.

The topic sentence states the idea developed in the paragraph. (For
a discussion of methods of paragraph development, see p. 108.) Although most often it is the first sentence, it may be placed anywhere
in the paragraph, depending on the method or methods of development. For example, a writer may give certain bits of evidence leading
inescapably to a logical conclusion; the statement of the conclusion
at the end of the paragraph would be the topic sentence. Or he might
prefer to state his conclusion first and then supply the supporting
evidence or even give some of the evidence, state the conclusion, and
then give the rest of the evidence. Judicious placement of the topic

sentence is one factor in writing good paragraphs; some variety in placement from paragraph to paragraph lends variety to a piece of writing as a whole.

The development of an idea in some paragraphs may make the actual statement of the idea unnecessary; the idea emerges, then, by implication. Such paragraphs are said to have implied topic sentences. A paragraph with an implied topic sentence should be so carefully organized and developed that a reader would have no difficulty in formulating an explicit topic sentence.

1. Which of the paragraphs in the first section of Platt's chapter has an implied topic sentence? Formulate a topic sentence for the paragraph. What is the function of this paragraph in terms of the section as a whole?

2. Identify the topic sentences of the rest of the paragraphs in the first section. Justify the placement of each topic sentence in terms of the content and function of each of the paragraphs.

3. Which of the paragraphs use comparison as part of the method of developing main ideas? Are the comparisons effective? Why or why not?

4. Point out all the means by which Platt achieves coherence in this first section. In particular, how do his topic sentences help to achieve coherence?

5. Which of the paragraphs in the second section have implied topic sentences? Formulate the topic sentences for each such paragraph. Would these paragraphs have been more or less effective if they had had explicit topic sentences? Why?

6. Identify the topic sentences of the rest of the paragraphs in the second section. Which of these topic sentences is further developed in a paragraph other than its own? Should the two paragraphs have been combined into one? What would have been gained or lost?

7. What is the function of paragraph 9? How can you justify the shortness of this paragraph?

8. Paragraphs 18, 19, and 20 all have implied topic sentences; what is the relation between these paragraphs and paragraph 17?

9. Paragraphs 17 through 21 are all devoted to leaf miners. Are any of these paragraphs too short and choppy? Could any be combined without violating unity? If so, which? Why do you suppose Platt paragraphed this section as he did?

Alternate selections for the study of Topic Sentence: Allan Nevins, from "Henry Ford—A Complex Man"; Washington Irving, "Ready-Money Jack."

Assignment: You may have enjoyed this piece by Platt (natural history is the favorite reading matter of many people) or you may have been bored by it or you may even have been repulsed by it. Try to determine just why your reactions were whatever they were: remember that your reactions come from qualities in the writing as well as qualities in you. Write a well-developed paragraph in which you analyze your reactions; be exact and specific enough so that your reader will be convinced of the honesty of your reactions and impressed by your insights into yourself and by your critical acumen. Organize the paragraph so that the topic sentence appears at or near the beginning. Then rewrite the paragraph so that the topic sentence logically belongs at or near the end. Avoid a mere mechanical rearrangement; there is a considerable difference in structure between a paragraph which opens with a topic sentence and one which closes with a topic sentence.

Methods of
Development

ACCUMULATION OF DETAIL

A Coating of
Cold Chocolate Sauce

LLOYD MORRIS

[1] AS the second half of the nineteenth century began, New York became a metropolis. The "Empire City," strangers called it. They were awed by the splendor of its hotels and theaters, its costly, magnificent stores. They were astonished by the incessant torrent of traffic, the day-long, night-long surge and roar of more than 5 five hundred thousand people. To many of them, New York seemed a city of crowds and carnival—breezy, recklessly extravagant, perpetually bent on pleasure. The bright gaslights of bars and restaurants and hotels threw a glare over Broadway until well toward dawn. The rumble of omnibuses and the clatter of hackney-coaches was 10 never stilled. New York was a city where men made such incredible fortunes that a new word, "millionaire," was on everybody's lips. Two things gave it a quality, a flavor that was unique, and New Yorkers were proud of both. Nowhere else was the tempo of life

15 as fast. And the only permanent characteristic of New York was
continuous change. From week to week, almost from day to day,
the look of the city was constantly being transformed.

[2] To give you the feeling of the city, a New Yorker might
take you to the balcony of Barnum's Museum, a large flag-decked
20 building on Broadway and Ann Street, just south of the City Hall.
From there, you could see Broadway from its beginning at Bowling
Green as far north as Astor Place. Along the wide, straight avenue
the white tops of omnibuses, moving swiftly yet densely packed,
looked like a millrace churning into foam. The sidewalks on both
25 sides of Broadway were thronged, and though it seemed as if these
massive rivers of people must sometime stop flowing, they did not;
at certain hours they merely rose to flood tide. Traffic on the avenue
never halted. To cross from the "shilling side" to the "dollar side"—
from east to west—sometimes took half an hour, and you attempted
30 it at the peril of your life or limbs. So hazardous was the crossing
that John N. Genin, the fashionable hatter whose shop was at the
corner of Fulton Street, petitioned the Common Council for permission to build an iron footbridge over Broadway to protect his
customers from accident.

35 [3] Only twenty years earlier Broadway, from City Hall Park
northward, was a residential avenue. But now scarcely a private
home remained below Bleecker Street. "The mania for converting
Broadway into a street of shops is greater than ever," old Philip
Hone noted in the spring of 1850. "There is scarcely a block in
40 the whole extent of this fine street of which some part is not in a
state of transmutation." Hone, one of New York's wealthiest citizens, was a former mayor, a man of fashion, a celebrated host and
diner-out. He had resided on Broadway opposite City Hall Park,
but business had driven him north a dozen years earlier. He bought
45 land on the east side of Broadway and Great Jones Street—then
near the upper limit of the city—and built himself a fine house.
And already his new home was being surrounded by shops and
hotels and theaters. "The improvements here are wonderful," James
Fenimore Cooper, the novelist, told his wife. "They build chiefly
50 brown free stone, and noble edifices of five and six stories, with a
good deal of ornamental pretension." The brownstone era, which
was to cover New York with a coating of cold chocolate sauce,
had begun.

•   •   •   •   •

[4] All during the eighteen-fifties, summer and winter, New York-
55 ers as well as visitors to the city found pleasure in driving out of

town to the upper reaches of Manhattan. On warm, sunny days the Croton Reservoir, on the west side of Fifth Avenue between Fortieth and Forty-second Streets, was a favorite destination. Its high walls gave it the look of a vast Egyptian temple, and their top formed a broad promenade from which you had fine views of the city to the south, the Hudson and East Rivers, and the rolling country that stretched northward to the villages of Yorkville, Manhattanville and Harlem. In 1853, New York held a World's Fair for which a replica of London's celebrated Crystal Palace was erected behind the Reservoir, and President Franklin Pierce came from Washington to inaugurate it. Thousands flocked to see the wonders of the Fair, and afterward crossed to the north side of Forty-second Street to visit a curious tower hastily built by an enterprising businessman. This tower was Latting's Observatory and Ice Cream Parlor, and after eating on the ground floor you could be lifted, by an experimental and often balky steam elevator, to the top of the structure for a spectacular view. A few years later, people drove further north on Fifth Avenue to see the site chosen by Archbishop Hughes for the future St. Patrick's Cathedral, and the vast tract of rocky hills and scrubby woods which the city had bought to transform into a public park—already optimistically named Central Park, although still far out of town.

[5] In summer and in winter, New Yorkers who kept fast pacers and trotters exercised them on Third Avenue. The center of this wide boulevard was paved for one mile north of Astor Place, but there were dirt roads left at the sides, and beyond the pavement it was all open road to Harlem Bridge, five miles north. On a winter afternoon, with hard-packed snow underfoot, Third Avenue was a swarm of sleighs of all sorts and sizes, their bells jangling as they sped along. There were gaily painted cutters driven by fur-capped gentlemen, who draped the backs of their seats with bearskin robes that flaunted out behind. Some of these cutters were extremely elaborate—notably one with a body carved in the form of a sea-green shell lined with crimson velvet. There were large, roomy family sleighs, decked out with buffalo, black-bear and gray-lynx robes bound in red ribbon and equipped with sham eyes and ears, in which pretty girls and their parents took the air behind pacers that stepped along at the rate of twelve miles an hour. There were omnibus sleighs, lumbering along behind four or six horses. Out beyond the city Third Avenue climbed and descended many hills. At the bottom of several of these hills there were taverns where, after a stiff brush on the descent, the "fast crabs" could "take a

horn" and rest their horses. One of the most frequented of these taverns was Wintergreen's in Yorkville, a straggling suburb in the East Eighties. Wintergreen's was famous for its sherry flips, its cobblers, grogs and hot buttered rum.

It has been pointed out that a paragraph contains one basic idea and consists of sentences which develop this basic idea as it is expressed in a topic sentence or as it emerges by implication throughout the paragraph. However, there are many methods of developing an idea. Some paragraphs combine two or more methods of development; others seem to defy analysis. But several methods have emerged (or perhaps simply have been observed) as most useful and therefore most frequently employed; among these methods are accumulation of detail, exemplification, definition, comparison (which may include the use of contrast), and relating cause to effect.

It should be noted that professional writers do not sit at their desks and ask themselves, "Now what type of paragraph shall I use today?" any more than philosophers ask themselves what school of thought they belong to. But students of writing are not "writers." It is useful to study the methods of paragraph development and even, at first, to employ them consciously, to understand and master them.

Furthermore, it is well to keep in mind that ideas need not be fully developed within a single paragraph, but that the methods of development used for single paragraphs apply as well to larger units— a group of paragraphs, perhaps, or even a whole theme or essay. So you will find that you may apply these principles of development in the planning and executing of themes as well as single paragraphs.

Probably the most common method of paragraph development is accumulation of detail. The multiple details may support a central thesis; describe a person, place, or thing; make a general statement specific and concrete; or in any other way substantiate the topic sentence.

1. In the first paragraph of his piece, Morris states that by 1850 New York was becoming a metropolis. He then develops this idea by presenting a number of details. Do these details support the central thesis? Justify your answer.

2. What is the topic sentence of paragraph 2? In what way is the central thought different from the central thought expressed in the first paragraph? Although these thoughts are different, explain and justify the use of the same method of development—accumulation of detail.

3. You will notice that the details in paragraph 2 are arranged in a particular order. What is this order, and why is it appropriate to the topic sentence? Do you find any principle underlying the order of details in paragraph 1? Explain.

4. Notice that paragraph 3 is not primarily developed through accumulation of detail. What central idea does it present? What method of development can you find? What seems to you to be the function of this paragraph in relation to the others? Is the paragraph unified? Why or why not?

5. Paragraphs 4 and 5 form a unit. Explain this statement, analyzing the two paragraphs for topic sentence and method of development. How are the two paragraphs joined?

6. How do all the details used in this selection reflect its point of view and contribute to its unity? What is the over-all plan as reflected in the individual paragraphs? as reflected in the order of these paragraphs?

7. What makes the piece successful or, if you think otherwise, unsuccessful?

[For assignment, see p. 128.]

EXEMPLIFICATION

Eternally Old, Eternally New

JOHN HERMAN RANDALL

THE visitor to Rome who leaves the Corso and wanders westward toward the Tiber, through the maze of narrow streets that swarm with the youth and age of the capital of modern Italy, takes inexhaustible delight in tracing on this ever-changing palimpsest in stone the work of the successive generations of Romans whose 5 descendants are to-day in possession of their dwellings. Leave the tram-line, dodge that big Fiat, turn a corner, and there before you is a picturesque and dilapidated pile framed in the pillars of an old amphitheater, erected in the age when this was the Campus Martius, the pleasure-ground of the subjects of Hadrian. Between 10 the columns are walls of great blocks of travertine, quarried from

From *The Making of the Modern Mind*, by John Herman Randall (rev. ed.; Boston: Houghton Mifflin Company, 1940). Reprinted with the permission of the publisher. Selection title by the Editors.

some Imperial edifice, and builded here into a gloomy fortress in the days when the feudal families of the Orsini and the Colonna were at swords' points over the election of a Leo or a Gregory as
15 Pope. Above is a fine Renaissance cornice from the time of Bramante and Michelangelo; while here and there the stucco of the Ottocento is peeling off under the hard usage of the red shirts of Garibaldi and the black shirts of Mussolini. Cross a crowded piazza, thread that narrow way between two palaces famed in story, and
20 there is a Fascist celebration before the tomb of Vittorio Emanuele in the church of Santa Maria Rotonda, better known as that Pantheon erected by Hadrian to commemorate the conquest by Roman legions of all the Oriental gods. For century after century the men of one age have adapted to their purposes the buildings of another,
25 sometimes preserving them almost entire, merely altering the use, sometimes adding new stones and new forms, sometimes tearing down and building up again with the old material. And still the life goes on, teeming with new activity, oblivious of what went before, the round of birth and hope and failure and death, under
30 emperor or baron, pope, king, or dictator. Of a truth Rome is the Eternal City, eternally old in its forms and walls, eternally new in its hopes and aspirations—a fitting symbol of the humanity that has for so long looked upon it as its center.

[For treatment of this selection, see p. 113.]

A Ferocious Metaphysical Dispute

WILLIAM JAMES

[1] SOME years ago, being with a camping party in the mountains, I returned from a solitary ramble to find everyone engaged in a ferocious metaphysical dispute. The *corpus* of the dis-

From *Pragmatism*, by William James. Reprinted with the permission of Longmans, Green & Company, Inc. Selection title by the Editors.

pute was a squirrel—a live squirrel supposed to be clinging to one side of a tree-trunk; while over against the tree's opposite side a human being was imagined to stand. This human witness tries to get sight of the squirrel by moving rapidly round the tree, but no matter how fast he goes, the squirrel moves as fast in the opposite direction, and always keeps the tree between himself and the man, so that never a glimpse of him is caught. The resultant metaphysical problem now is this: *Does the man go round the squirrel or not?* He goes round the tree, sure enough, and the squirrel is on the tree; but does he go round the squirrel? In the unlimited leisure of the wilderness, discussion had been worn threadbare. Everyone had taken sides, and was obstinate; and the numbers on both sides were even. Each side, when I appeared, therefore appealed to me to make it a majority. Mindful of the scholastic adage that whenever you meet a contradiction you must make a distinction, I immediately sought and found one, as follows: "Which party is right," I said, "depends on what you *practically mean* by 'going round' the squirrel. If you mean passing from the north of him to the east, then to the south, then to the west, and then to the north of him again, obviously the man does go round him, for he occupies these successive positions. But if on the contrary you mean being first in front of him, then on the right of him, then behind him, then on his left, and finally in front again, it is quite as obvious that the man fails to go round him, for by the compensating movements the squirrel makes, he keeps his belly turned towards the man all the time, and his back turned away. Make the distinction, and there is no occasion for any farther dispute. You are both right and both wrong according as you conceive the verb 'to go round' in one practical fashion or the other."

[2] Although one or two of the hotter disputants called my speech a shuffling evasion, saying they wanted no quibbling or scholastic hair-splitting, but meant just plain honest English "round," the majority seemed to think that the distinction had assuaged the dispute.

[3] I tell this trivial anecdote because it is a peculiarly simple example of . . . *the pragmatic method.* The pragmatic method is primarily a method of settling metaphysical disputes that otherwise might be interminable. Is the world one or many?—fated or free?—material or spiritual?—here are notions either of which may or may not hold good of the world; and disputes over such notions are

unending. The pragmatic method in such cases is to try to interpret
45 each notion by tracing its respective practical consequences. What
difference would it practically make to any one if this notion rather
than that notion were true? If no practical difference whatever can
be traced, then the alternatives mean practically the same thing,
and all dispute is idle. Whenever a dispute is serious, we ought
50 to be able to show some practical difference that must follow from
one side or the other's being right.

[For treatment of this selection, see p. 113.]

Automation Everywhere

CARL RIESER

HONEYWELL, in effect, is the Big Brother of all the
robots of automation. In the world of modern technology, Honeywell's eyes are literally everywhere, watching—from the depths of
the sea clear up into outer space. And so are its ears and fingers.
5 A Honeywell sonar device for fishing boats spots and tracks schools
of fish. A remarkable ultraviolet-sensitive tube, no bigger than a
finger, with the uncanny ability to distinguish vapor, smoke, or
flame, guards mines against disasters. A radar type of device, which
detects even the slightest movement in a pitch-black room, traps
10 intruders. A newly refined Honeywell thermostat for the outside of
buildings can measure the combined effects of sun, wind, and temperature and reset the furnace controls down in the basement. In
a year or so, the entire power grid of the Philadelphia Electric Co.
will be operated by Honeywell automatic load controls tied in to a
15 digital computer; the system will calculate demand, apportion the
work load for each generator in the most economic manner—and

From "Minneapolis-Honeywell, 'The Dern Thing Works,'" by Carl Rieser,
Fortune, LIX, No. 5 (May, 1959), 113. Courtesy of Fortune Magazine. Selection title by the Editors.

even determine who owes whom how much when Philadelphia Electric exchanges power with neighboring power companies. And in a few years it is quite likely that the first American travelers in space will be kept from tumbling about in nothingness in their tiny capsule,   20 and will be fetched back to earth, by stabilizing and guidance equipment Honeywell is now designing for the Air Force's Project Mercury (better known by the unfortunate name of "MISS"—Man in Space Soonest).

Another method of developing the central thesis expressed in a paragraph is exemplification. In practice, this method is sometimes difficult to distinguish from the method of accumulation of detail. In fact, they overlap in structure and function. The only meaningful distinction between the two is that details elaborate upon or embellish the central thesis, whereas examples illustrate it.

A paragraph may be devoted to a single example or may present several examples. The topic sentence may appear before the examples or after them; it may, particularly if the entire paragraph is a single example, be implied rather than stated.

1. In the Randall selection, what is the topic sentence? How many examples illustrate it? Why do you suppose Randall decided to place the topic sentence where he did in relation to the examples?

2. In what way or ways is this paragraph similar to paragraphs 1 and 2 of "A Coating of Cold Chocolate Sauce"? In what ways is it different from these paragraphs? How do you explain these similarities and differences?

3. Compare the first paragraph of the selection from "A Ferocious Metaphysical Dispute" with the Randall paragraph, pointing out both their similarities and dissimilarities. Notice that James delays telling you the meaning of the squirrel anecdote until paragraph 3. Why do you think he does this?

4. Do you agree that the anecdote is "a peculiarly simple example"? Justify your answer. Why do you think James used it? Why does (or doesn't) it serve his purpose?

5. Give an example from your own experience of the kind of "ferocious metaphysical dispute" James found his friends engaged in.

6. What major writing problem faced the writer of the paragraph "Automation Everywhere"? How has his method of paragraph development helped him to solve it?

[For assignment, see p. 128.]

DEFINITION

History

CARL L. BECKER

[1] STUDENTS often say to me: "I don't know any history; I think it would be a good thing to learn some." What they seem to mean is that they have never had a "course" in history, or have never read Gibbon's *Decline and Fall of the Roman Empire,*
5   or Mr. Rhodes's *History of the United States from the Compromise of 1850,* or other books similar to these. But they are greatly mistaken if they think they "don't know any history." Every man, woman, and child knows some history, enough at least to stumble along in the world.
10   [2] Suppose, for example, that you had awakened this morning totally unable to remember anything—all your other faculties working properly, but memory entirely gone. You would be in a bad way indeed! You wouldn't know who you were, or where; what you had done yesterday, or what you intended or other people
15   expected you to do today. What could you do in that case? Wander about helplessly, seeing and hearing things, taking them in as altogether new, not at all knowing what they might mean in relation either to the past or the future. You would have to discover your little world all over again, much as you discovered it in childhood;
20   you would have to "re-orient" yourself and get a new running start. In short, you would be a lost soul because you had ceased to have any knowledge of history, the history of your personal doings and associations in the past.

[3] For history is no more than things said and done in the past.
25   It is as simple as that; and we might as well omit the word "past," since everything said and done is already in the past as soon as it is said or done. Done, but not done *with.* We have to remember many things said and done in order to live our lives intelligently; and so far

as we remember things said and done we have a knowledge of history, for that is what historical knowledge is—*memory of things said and* 30 *done*. Thus everyone has some knowledge of history, and it is quite essential that everyone should have, since it is only by remembering something of the past that we can anticipate something of the future. Please note that I do not say *predict* the future. We cannot predict the future, but we can *anticipate* it—we can look forward to it and in 35 some sense prepare for it. Now if memory of some things said and done is necessary, it seems that memory of more things ought to be better. The more we remember of things said and done (if they be the right things for our purpose), the better we can manage our affairs today, and the more intelligently we can prepare for what is coming 40 to us tomorrow and next year and all our lives.

[For treatment of this selection, see p. 116.]

The Born Teacher

FRED B. MILLETT

TO be distinguished alike from the scholarly and the artistic types is the "born" teacher, the person who flourishes only in his relations with students in and out of the classroom, who expresses himself most potently in his devotion to the fine art of teaching, who, at his best, achieves something of the artist's creativeness in his skill 5 in bringing about a vital relationship between the student and what the student is learning or being taught. If the esthete is marked by some of the characteristics of the artist, the "born" teacher is distinguished by some of the characteristics of the actor on the one hand, and the preacher on the other. Like the actor, he is gifted in platform skills: 10 his personality is so plastic that it is possible for him to achieve a temporary and more or less perfect identification of himself with the subject or person that he is discussing. He handles his voice effectively; he may even become famous—as "Copey" of Harvard did—as a public reader. He is sensitive to the reactions of his audience, knows 15

From *The Rebirth of Liberal Education*, by Fred B. Millett. Copyright 1945 by Harcourt, Brace and Company, Inc. Reprinted with the permission of the publishers. Selection title by the Editors.

how to play upon them, is able to make effective patterns and juxta-
positions of the personalities in his audience-group. Like the actor,
he has a sense of timing, a flair for the effective use of properties, a
wide range of tones from the casual and inconsequential to the ironical
20 and the dramatic. But the true teacher is less self-centered than the
actor, more genuinely outgoing, more personally distinct. Although,
like the actor with the text of the play, he uses the subject matter of
his field as his raw material for his performance, the born teacher
feels not only an esthetic but a moral responsibility to the subject
25 matter with which he is working and also to the audience to whom
he is presenting this subject matter. In this respect, he more closely
resembles the preacher than the actor. Ultimately, he is concerned with
bringing light and leading to his charges, with saving them from the
sins of ignorance and prejudice, with enriching their lives with knowl-
30 edge and wisdom. Like the true pastor, he is a "cure of souls." He is
concerned with his students not as minds, but as men, not as points
on the sliding scale of intellectual achievements, but as human beings
with personalities that are curiously complex blends of assets and
liabilities, that are bundles of potentialities. Like the pastor, he fur-
35 nishes—sometimes unwittingly—a kind of norm for behavior and
manners, a model, however imperfect, of devotion to the nobler ends
of which the human animal dreams and in the attainment of which he
is—perhaps fitfully—engaged.

Definition is a fairly formularized process. In order to define a
term, it is necessary to place it in its proper category (*genus*) and
then delineate it from other members of that category by giving its
unique qualities or characteristics (*differentiae*). For example, the
American College Dictionary defines a dive bomber as "an airplane
[*genus*] of the pursuit type which drops its bombs while diving at
the target [*differentiae*]."

1. Students often find it difficult to define terms and thus fall into
the trap of defining merely by giving an illogically formulated illustration: "a democracy is when. . . ." Show how Becker's definition of
history does or does not include both *genus* and *differentiae*. Explain
why Becker's definition does or does not fall into the trap of illogical
illustration.

2. Definition frequently appears in combination with other methods
of paragraph development. Why do you think it does? Which of the
methods you have studied do you think would combine effectively
with the method of definition? Why?

3. Does the paragraph in which Becker defines history employ a
combination of methods? Explain.

4. What is the guiding purpose of the selection? What is the relevance of the example in paragraph 2 to this guiding purpose? What is the logical relation between paragraphs 2 and 3?

5. What other methods of paragraph development does Becker employ?

6. Point out several ways in which he obtains coherence throughout this selection.

7. In his definition of the born teacher, Millett supplies a rather large number of *differentiae*. List them and suggest what may have determined the order which Millett has established for them.

8. What other method or methods of paragraph development does he employ?

[For assignment, see p. 128.]

COMPARISON AND CONTRAST

The Country Squire

THOMAS BABINGTON MACAULAY

[1] WE should be much mistaken if we pictured to ourselves the squires of the seventeenth century as men bearing a close resemblance to their descendants, the county members and chairmen of quarter sessions with whom we are familiar. The modern country gentleman [in the nineteenth century] generally receives a liberal edu- 5 cation, passes from a distinguished school to a distinguished college, and has ample opportunity to become an excellent scholar. He has generally seen something of foreign countries. A considerable part of his life has generally been passed in the capital; and the refinements of the capital follow him into the country. There is perhaps no class 10 of dwellings so pleasing as the rural seats of the English gentry. In the parks and pleasure grounds, nature, dressed yet not disguised by art, wears her most alluring form. In the buildings, good sense and good taste combine to produce a happy union of the comfortable and the graceful. The pictures, the musical instruments, the library, would in 15 any other country be considered as proving the owner to be an

From *The History of England from the Accession of James II*, by Thomas Babington Macaulay, 1848, Chap. 3. Selection title by the Editors.

eminently polished and accomplished man. A country gentleman who witnessed the Revolution [in the seventeenth century] was probably in receipt of about a fourth part of the rent which his acres now yield to his posterity. He was, therefore, as compared with his posterity, a poor man, and was generally under the necessity of residing, with little interruption, on his estate. To travel on the Continent, to maintain an establishment in London, or even to visit London frequently, were pleasures in which only the great proprietors could indulge. It may be confidently affirmed that of the squires whose names were then in the Commissions of Peace and Lieutenancy not one in twenty went to town once in five years, or had ever in his life wandered so far as Paris. Many lords of manors had received an education differing little from that of their menial servants. The heir of an estate often passed his boyhood and youth at the seat of his family with no better tutors than grooms and gamekeepers, and scarce attained learning enough to sign his name to a Mittimus. If he went to school and to college, he generally returned before he was twenty to the seclusion of the old hall, and there, unless his mind were very happily constituted by nature, soon forgot his academical pursuits in rural business and pleasures. His chief serious employment was the care of his property. He examined samples of grain, handled pigs, and, on market days, made bargains over a tankard with drovers and hop merchants. His chief pleasures were commonly derived from field sports and from an unrefined sensuality. His language and pronunciation were such as we should now expect to hear only from the most ignorant clowns. His oaths, coarse jests, and scurrilous terms of abuse, were uttered with the broadest accent of his province. It was easy to discern, from the first words which he spoke, whether he came from Somersetshire or Yorkshire. He troubled himself little about decorating his abode, and, if he attempted decoration, seldom produced anything but deformity. The litter of a farmyard gathered under the windows of his bed-chamber, and the cabbages and gooseberry bushes grew close to his hall door. His table was loaded with coarse plenty; and guests were cordially welcomed to it. But, as the habit of drinking to excess was general in the class to which he belonged, and as his fortune did not enable him to intoxicate large assemblies daily with claret or canary, strong beer was the ordinary beverage. The quantity of beer consumed in those days was indeed enormous. For beer then was to the middle and lower classes, not only all that beer now is, but all that wine, tea, and ardent spirits now are. It was only at great houses, or on great occasions, that foreign drink was placed on the board. The ladies of the house, whose business it had commonly been to cook the repast,

retired as soon as the dishes had been devoured, and left the gentlemen to their ale and tobacco. The coarse jollity of the afternoon was   60
often prolonged till the revellers were laid under the table.

[2] It was very seldom that the country gentleman caught glimpses
of the great world; and what he saw of it tended rather to confuse
than to enlighten his understanding. His opinions respecting religion,
government, foreign countries and former times, having been derived,   65
not from study, from observation, or from conversation with enlightened companions, but from such traditions as were current in his own
small circle, were the opinions of a child. He adhered to them, however, with the obstinacy which is generally found in ignorant men
accustomed to be fed with flattery. His animosities were numerous and   70
bitter. He hated Frenchmen and Italians, Scotchmen and Irishmen,
Papists and Presbyterians, Independents and Baptists, Quakers and
Jews. Towards London and Londoners he felt an aversion which more
than once produced important political effects. His wife and daughter
were in tastes and acquirements below a housekeeper or a stillroom   75
maid of the present day. They stitched and spun, brewed gooseberry
wine, cured marigolds, and made the crust for the venison pasty.

[3] From this description it might be supposed that the English
esquire of the seventeenth century did not materially differ from a
rustic miller or alehouse keeper of our time. There are, however, some   80
important parts of his character still to be noted, which will greatly
modify this estimate. Unlettered as he was and unpolished, he was
still in some most important points a gentleman. He was a member of
a proud and powerful aristocracy, and was distinguished by many both
of the good and of the bad qualities which belong to aristocrats. His   85
family pride was beyond that of a Talbot or a Howard. He knew the
genealogies and coats of arms of all his neighbors, and could tell which
of them had assumed supporters without any right, and which of them
were so unfortunate as to be great grandsons of aldermen. He was a
magistrate, and, as such, administered gratuitously to those who dwelt   90
around him a rude patriarchal justice, which, in spite of innumerable
blunders and of occasional acts of tyranny, was yet better than no
justice at all. He was an officer of the trainbands; and his military
dignity, though it might move the mirth of gallants who had served a
campaign in Flanders, raised his character in his own eyes and in the   95
eyes of his neighbors. Nor indeed was his soldiership justly a subject
of derision. In every county there were elderly gentlemen who had
seen service which was no child's play. One had been knighted by
Charles the First, after the battle of Edgehill. Another still wore a
patch over the scar which he had received at Naseby. A third had   100

defended his old house till Fairfax had blown in the door with a petard. The presence of these old Cavaliers, with their old swords and holsters, and with their old stories about Goring and Lunsford, gave to the musters of militia an earnest and warlike aspect which would
105 otherwise have been wanting. Even those country gentlemen who were too young to have themselves exchanged blows with the cuirassiers of the Parliament had, from childhood, been surrounded with the traces of recent war, and fed with stories of the martial exploits of their fathers and uncles. Thus the character of the English esquire of the
110 seventeenth century was compounded of two elements which we seldom or never find united. His ignorance and uncouthness, his low tastes and gross phrases, would, in our time, be considered as indicating a nature and a breeding thoroughly plebeian. Yet he was essentially a patrician, and had, in large measure, both the virtues and the
115 vices which flourish among men set from their birth in high place, and used to respect themselves and to be respected by others. It is not easy for a generation accustomed to find chivalrous sentiments only in company with liberal studies and polished manners to image to itself a man with the deportment, the vocabulary, and the accent
120 of a carter, yet punctilious on matters of genealogy and precedence, and ready to risk his life rather than see a stain cast on the honor of his house. It is however only by thus joining together things seldom or never found together in our own experience, that we can form a just idea of that rustic aristocracy which constituted the main strength
125 of the armies of Charles the First, and which long supported, with strange fidelity, the interest of his descendants.

[For treatment of this selection, see p. 122.]

FROM *On the Crown*

DEMOSTHENES

[1] AESCHINES says that my individual fortune is paramount to that of the commonwealth, the small and mean to the good and great. How can this possibly be? However, if you are determined,

From *Demosthenes' Orations*, translated by C. Rann Kennedy. Everyman's Library edition. Reprinted by permission of E. P. Dutton & Co., Inc.

Aeschines, to scrutinise my fortune, compare it with your own, and, if you find my fortune better than yours, cease to revile it. Look then from the very beginning. And I pray and entreat that I may not be condemned for bad taste. I don't think any person wise who insults poverty, or who prides himself on having been bred in affluence: but by the slander and malice of this cruel man I am forced into such a discussion; which I will conduct with all the moderation which circumstances allow.

[2] I had the advantage, Aeschines, in my boyhood of going to proper schools, and having such allowance as a boy should have who is to do nothing mean from indigence. Arrived at man's estate, I lived suitably to my breeding; was choirmaster, ship-commander, ratepayer; backward in no acts of liberality public or private, but making myself useful to the commonwealth and to my friends. When I entered upon state affairs, I chose such a line of politics that both by my country and many people of Greece I have been crowned many times, and not even you, my enemies, venture to say that the line I chose was not honourable. Such, then, has been the fortune of my life: I could enlarge upon it, but I forbear, lest what I pride myself in should give offense.

[3] But you, the man of dignity, who spit upon others, look what sort of fortune is yours compared with mine. As a boy you were reared in abject poverty, waiting with your father on the school, grinding the ink, sponging the benches, sweeping the room, doing the duty of a menial rather than a freeman's son. After you were grown up, you attended your mother's initiations, reading her books and helping in all the ceremonies: at night wrapping the noviciates in fawn-skin, swilling, purifying, and scouring them with clay and bran, raising them after the lustration, and bidding them say, "Bad I have scaped, and better I have found;" priding yourself that no one ever howled so lustily—and I believe him! for don't suppose that he who speaks so loud is not a splendid howler! In the daytime you led your noble orgiasts, crowned with fennel and poplar, through the highways, squeezing the big-cheeked serpents, and lifting them over your head, and shouting Evœ Sabœ, and capering to the words Hyes Attes, Attes Hyes, saluted by the beldames as Leader, Conductor, Chest-bearer, Fan-bearer, and the like, getting as your reward tarts and biscuits and rolls; for which any man might well bless himself and his fortune!

[4] When you were enrolled among your fellow-townsmen—by what means I stop not to inquire—when you were enrolled, however,

45 you immediately selected the most honourable of employments, that of
clerk and assistant to our petty magistrates. From this you were removed after a while, having done yourself all that you charge others
with; and then, sure enough, you disgraced not your antecedents by
your subsequent life, but hiring yourself to those ranting players, as
50 they were called, Simylus and Socrates, you acted third parts, collect-
ing figs and grapes and olives like a fruiterer from other men's farms,
and getting more from them than from the playing, in which the lives
of your whole company were at stake; for there was an implacable
and incessant war between them and the audience, from whom you
55 received so many wounds, that no wonder you taunt as cowards people
inexperienced in such encounters.

[5] But passing over what may be imputed to poverty, I will
come to the direct charges against your character. You espoused such
a line of politics (when at last you thought of taking to them) that,
60 if your country prospered, you lived the life of a hare, fearing and
trembling and ever expecting to be scourged for the crimes of which
your conscience accused you; though all have seen how bold you were
during the misfortunes of the rest. A man who took courage at the
death of a thousand citizens—what does he deserve at the hands of the
65 living? A great deal more that I could say about him I shall omit:
for it is not all I can tell of his turpitude and infamy which I ought to
let slip from my tongue, but only what is not disgraceful to myself to
mention.

[6] Contrast now the circumstances of your life and mine, gently
70 and with temper, Aeschines; and then ask these people whose fortune
they would each of them prefer. You taught reading, I went to school:
you performed initiations, I received them: you danced in the chorus,
I furnished it: you were assembly-clerk, I was a speaker: you acted
third parts, I heard you: you broke down, and I hissed: you have
75 worked as a statesman for the enemy, I for my country. I pass by the
rest; but this very day I am on my probation for a crown, and am
acknowledged to be innocent of all offense; whilst you are already
judged to be a pettifogger, and the question is, whether you shall
continue that trade, or at once be silenced by not getting a fifth part
80 of the votes. A happy fortune, do you see, you have enjoyed, that you
should denounce mine as miserable!

In the method of comparison and contrast, two or more units may
be compared in the same paragraph, or separate paragraphs may be

devoted to each unit. Strictly, the purer example of the form is the single paragraph which combines the units.

There is a meaningful distinction between the terms "comparison" and "contrast"; comparison implies similarity, while contrast suggests dissimilarity between or among the units. Of course, items may be both similar in certain ways and dissimilar in others. For example, a plum and a peach are both fruits, both round, both sweet, both juicy. But they have striking dissimilarities: one has smooth skin and the other has fuzzy; one is red and the other is multicolored—green and yellow and "peach." Both comparison and contrast, then, may be relevant to the development of the same topic sentence.

1. In the first paragraph of the Macaulay selection, what points of dissimilarity are there between the "hero" of the piece and his nineteenth-century counterpart?

2. Account for the difference in space allotted to the two gentlemen in paragraph 1.

3. Are they compared, contrasted, or both? Explain, in the light of the whole essay, why you think Macaulay chose the method he uses in his opening paragraph. What would have been gained or lost had Macaulay used two paragraphs instead of one?

4. Macaulay presents an implied contrast, in paragraph 3, between the English squire and "a rustic miller" of the nineteenth century. Explain what he means by

   a. "From this description it might be supposed that the English esquire of the seventeenth century did not materially differ from a rustic miller or alehouse keeper of our time."

   b. "There are, however, some important parts of his character . . . which . . . greatly modify this estimate."

5. In your own words, what is Macaulay saying about the seventeenth-century squire?

6. Demosthenes contrasts two persons. Why does he devote separate paragraphs to himself and Aeschines and then combine Aeschines and himself in one paragraph?

7. Why does he devote so much more space to Aeschines than to himself? Are the reasons he gives to answer this question the same as yours? Why or why not?

8. In paragraph 6, why does he make his contrast point for point instead of following the structure Macaulay employs in the first paragraph of his essay?

9. What are the differences in tone and point of view between the two selections? How are these differences reflected in the writing?

[For assignment, see p. 128.]

CAUSE AND EFFECT

FROM *Triumph over Pain*

RENÉ FÜLÖP-MILLER

[1] FATE lifts one among thousands into prominence; one among thousands finds biographers—and clinicians—to tell the story of his pain.

[2] But pain visits also the inconspicuous, the millions who are
5 neither heroes nor saints and have no title to greatness, for man is born unto trouble as the sparks fly upward. No one asks about it, no one records it. Pain streaks the lives of millions who go down to death unwept, unhonored and unsung.

[3] The sufferings of these become a historical event only when
10 they occur in persons who are under the scourge of pestilence and are, therefore, raised to the rank of a mass phenomenon. Classical historians and medieval chroniclers deign in such cases to give heart-rending reports. In the triumphs of imperators, during the festivals held to honor the gods, amid the pomp of crusading knights, on the
15 merchantmen and the war-galleys, athwart the solemnity of processions, around the wells and in the market places, and at the groaning boards of the hospitable rich, this dread specter may walk. Then pain racks the bowels, the skin and the limbs of all and sundry; by tens and hundreds and thousands people are speeded to death, whole armies of
20 them, the populations of town and countryside, perhaps of an entire continent. Its might will in a trice transform banquet or crusade, galley or triumph or procession, into the spectacle of myriads of pain-fraught visages, heaps of contorted bodies, into cries of pain and terror forced from unnumbered throats, clamoring down the centuries into our own
25 time, to be stilled only when death commands silence.

[4] Since no description suffices, analysts and statisticians have tried to show forth the temporal and spatial dimensions of the evil by a huge aggregate of figures. Here pain—that of bubonic plague,

leprosy, anthrax, cholera, syphilis, smallpox, typhus, and typhoid—has
ravaged intestines and blood, skin and limbs, laying whole districts 30
low; there the epidemic has spread from Persia to the Rhine. Now
and again a third of the inhabitants have perished in such a visitation,
inaugurating new epochs and filling a century with lamentation. Thirteen millions perished thus in Greece. Athens was devastated in her
prime. Byzantium suffered from the Plague of Justinian in the days 35
of her greatest glory. The proudest cities of the Middle Ages became
places of fruitless mourning.

[5] Descriptive medicine was almost unknown before the eighteenth
century. Pinel made a beginning at the Salpêtrière. Thenceforward
symptoms were carefully noted in the hospitals, and clinical histories 40
were kept. Thus originated the archives—Archives of Pain.

[6] The body, to whatever epoch it may belong, no matter whether
it be the body of someone with undying fame or of a nameless unit
of the masses, is a perpetual source of pain. The blood inherits or may
acquire the poison of all diseases, the bones are liable to soften or 45
to be broken or to be eaten away, the nerves may thrill to every ache.
With few exceptions, any organ can give rise to pain, which is an
almost inseparable accompaniment of illness, is present during the
sacred act of birth and attends our dying. "This is the noble truth of
suffering," announced Sâkya Muni in one of his sermons at Benares, 50
"that to be born is to suffer, to die is to suffer, and to fall sick is to
suffer"; while François Villon, the strolling minstrel, exclaimed:
"Whom death strikes down, must die in pain."

[7] The forces of the outer world are in league with those of the
living body; natural catastrophes, earth and sky, weather and war, 55
dead matter and our fellow creatures, all, all can wound us, can sow
the seeds of pain.

A fifth method of paragraph development is that of cause and
effect. There may be one cause with many effects or many causes of
a single effect. Thus either the cause or the effect may be the central
thought of the paragraph and may be placed either at the beginning
or at the end.

1. In paragraphs 6 and 7 of the Fülöp-Miller selection, pain is
the effect. It has many causes. List them. Justify their division into
two paragraphs.

2. Justify the specific quotations in paragraph 6. Do you think
they violate the unity of the paragraph? Why or why not?

3. Why is paragraph 7 only one sentence long?

4. What are the topic sentences of paragraphs 3 and 4? By what method or methods is each developed? Explain your answer in detail.

5. What reasons can you think of to explain why Fülöp-Miller's paragraphs are so varied in length?

6. Indicate possible subjects for paragraphs in which there might be one cause with many effects (the reverse of the paragraphs in this selection).

[For assignment, see p. 128.]

COMBINED METHODS

FROM *The Comic*

JOHN JAY CHAPMAN

[1] IT is easy for us today to see that comedy is in its nature the same sort of thing as tragedy. They arise out of the same need, convey the same truth, depend upon the same talent. The English drama interwove comedy and tragedy in the same play, and Shake-
5 speare's greatness in one is of a piece with his greatness in the other. Indeed there are scenes in Lear, [The Merchant of Venice], and Henry IV where tragedy and comedy are overlaid—where the same scene is both tragic and comic and we laugh and cry at the same time. But for a Greek to have seen this identity is very remarkable; because
10 Greek tragedy and Greek comedy represented distinct professions and were totally different in their methods of appeal. A Greek tragedy was a drama of fate, based on a familiar bit of religious folk-lore. The plot was known, the interest lay in the treatment. A Greek comedy, however, was a farrago of licentious nonsense, developed in the course
15 of a fantastic narrative-play: it was what we should call a musical extravaganza. Greek comedy is gigantesque buffoonery, interspersed with lyric and choral passages of divine beauty—the whole, following a traditional model as to its arrangement.

From "The Comic," reprinted by permission of Dodd, Mead & Company, Inc., from *Learning and Other Essays,* by John Jay Chapman.

[2] With this machinery Aristophanes proceeds to shake the stones of the Greek theatre with inextinguishable laughter. He will do any- 20 thing to raise a laugh. He introduces Socrates hung up in a basket and declaring that he is flying in the air and speculating about the sun. He makes the god Dionysus—the very god in whose honour the theatre and festival exist—to leap from the stage in a moment of comic terror, and hide himself under the long cloak of his own high-priest, 25 whose chair of state was in the front row of the pit. Is it possible to imagine what sort of a scene in the theatre this climax must have aroused? There has been no laughter since Aristophanes. There is something of the same humor in Rabelais; but Rabelais is a book, and there each man laughs alone over his book, not in company with 30 his whole city or tribe, as in the Greek theatre.

[3] Now what is it they are laughing at? It is sallies of wit, personal hits, local allusions, indecencies, philosophical cracks, everything from refined satire to the bludgeons of abuse—and the whole thing is proceeding in an atmosphere of fun, of wild spirits, of irre- 35 pressible devilry. Compared to Aristophanes, Shakespeare is not funny; he lacks size. He is a great and thoughtful person, of superabundant genius and charm, who makes Dutch interiors, drenched in light. But Aristophanes splits the heavens with a jest, and the rays of truth stream down from inaccessible solitudes of speculation. 40 He has no epigram, no cleverness, no derivative humor. He is bald foolery. And yet he conveys mysticism: he conveys divinity. He alone stands still while the whole empyrean of Greek life circles about him.

It has been pointed out that paragraphs may combine several methods of development; they may employ any number of methods not analyzed here. Some of these additional methods are repetition, division into components (for example, a step-by-step description of a process), and analogy. The number of possible combinations begins to be astronomical and had best be left to the realm of the computing machine. It will be enough to sample these combinations of methods in the selection from John Jay Chapman's essay; you will, in your own writing, employ many other of the possible combinations.

1. For each of the three paragraphs, explain which methods of development have been combined.

2. What one method is employed in all three paragraphs? Explain why you think this method combines well with the other methods Chapman uses.

3. Is it necessary to have read Shakespeare and Aristophanes to understand this selection? Why or why not?

4. Point out the sentences, words, or phrases in this selection which explain or explicitly state the methods of development employed. List other such words or phrases which might appear in paragraphs combining methods of development.

5. Bring to class three paragraphs which you find in print. Be prepared to explain which method or methods of development each employs and to suggest another possible method for developing the topic sentence of each paragraph.

6. List six topics which lend themselves well to a combination of methods, and indicate what these combinations might be.

Alternate selections for the study of Methods of Development: Alistair Cooke, "It's a Democracy, Isn't it?"; Gilbert Highet, "The Study of Style"; Jacques Barzun, " 'Say, Bud!' . . . 'Hiya, Baby!' "

Assignment: The following topic sentences lend themselves to any number of possible methods of paragraph development. Suggest alternate methods for developing each of the sentences into paragraphs, indicating what material of your own invention you would include for each method selected.

Select one of the sentences, and write three separate paragraphs developing it three different ways.

or

Write one paragraph for each of three of the sentences, employing different methods of development for each.

"In the caverns of our nature lie hid various emotions like beasts in a lair."—Chapman, "The Comic"

"The stuff of which tragedy and comedy are made is the same stuff."—*Ibid.*

"What is the secret mesmerism which friendship possesses, and under the operation of which a person ordinarily sluggish, or cold, or timid, becomes wise, active, and resolute, in another's behalf?"— Thackeray, *Vanity Fair*

"The discipline of the family, in those days, was of a far more rigid kind than now."—Hawthorne, *The Scarlet Letter*

"A new era of splendor had set in."—Morris, *Incredible New York*

"They sat in adjoining windows of the same room . . . looking out upon the . . . animated scene."—Hardy, *The Mayor of Casterbridge*

"The morning came."—*Ibid.*

"It is pleasant to turn from contemplating the strife and turmoil of political existence, to the peaceful repose of private life."—Dickens, *Pickwick Papers*

"It is very possible that at some earlier period in his career . . . [his] profile might have presented a bold and determined outline."— *Ibid.*

"There are certain queer times and occasions in this strange mixed affair we call life when a man takes this whole universe for a practical joke . . . and more than suspects that the joke is . . . [at] nobody's expense but his own."—Melville, *Moby Dick*

"But desire of knowledge, like the thirst of riches, increases ever with the acquisition of it."—Sterne, *Tristram Shandy*

"In her person and her dress she was perfect, and well she knew her own perfection."—Trollope, *Barchester Towers*

"The old woman was a gnarled and leathery personage, who could don at will an expression of great virtue."—Crane, *Maggie: A Girl of the Streets*

"There is absolutely nothing new in the pragmatic method."—James, *Pragmatism*

"A human figure emerged from behind the door."—Dumas, *The Count of Monte Cristo*

Unity

Around-the-World Grouch

NICHOLAS MONSARRAT

[1] I'VE recently spent four months traveling 42,000 miles, zigzagging my way round the world from my home in Canada, visiting twenty-one different countries. You think it was fun? Gather round. The whole thing was a terrible mistake; I should have stood
5 in bed, which is where I am now. Here is my list of world-wide complaints. Any omissions will be the subject of a later article.

[2] To begin at the beginning: *Don't go to England.* They're in a real mess there. It rains all the time, especially upon the Rolls-Royces which stand listlessly, three deep in the traffic blocks. And people—
10 even normally decent folk—are getting far too talkative; you can't spend two hours in a railway carriage without some pushful fellow saying "Nice weather" and rattling his newspaper at you. Hereditary peers, long-time champions of the monarchy, now turn around and snap at its ankles, like curs or weasels. Mr. Khrushchev
15 actually stayed at Claridge's, on the very next floor. The British seem to have lost their heads altogether.

[3] *Don't go to Scandinavia.* If you fulfill even half your social obligations, your liver will never recover. Someone says, "Skoal!" and you say, "Skoal!" and the man next to you says, "Did you say
20 skoal?" and you say, "Yes—skoal!" In no time at all you have aquavit running out of your ears. If you fail to raise your glass toward

every single woman in the party, you are a social pariah; if you make the gross error of toasting your hostess, a kindly man will say: "In this country we do not toast our hostess. It is deeply forbidden. Skoal!" Your host, an enormous blond man, will knock you nearly senseless 25 with a friendly blow between your shoulder blades and say, "You insult my wife, yes? Skoal!"

[4] Skoal.

[5] *Do not fly to Paris* by the Hotshot Lunchtime Special or what-ever it is called. By the time you reach Le Bourget you will be 30 permanently felled by indigestion. The airline is in honor bound to serve you a nine-course meal with three different kinds of wine, in the space of sixty-five minutes; and by gosh they do it! As soon as the "fasten your seat belts" sign is flicked off, the whole place is in a gastronomic uproar. Food and drink are thrown at you as if in a 35 lunatic cafeteria; they seem to pour down the stewards' arms. Above all, they are compulsory. If you don't wolf everything in sight, and wash it down with tiny individual bottles of Martini, sherry, white wine, red wine, champagne, brandy, Drambuie, and Cointreau, you're just wasting the company's time and foully betraying their boasted 40 atmosphere of an exclusive airborne London club.

[6] Striving for a touch of individuality in my flight, I asked the steward (after snagging him firmly by the trousers) why he hadn't opened my bottle of champagne. "Sir," he said, tugging for his free-dom, "the company don't allow it! If we opened even half the bottles, 45 we'd never get through on time. Would you care for coffee?" "Coffee?" I said, appalled. "I haven't even finished my soup!" "One coffee," he said, and disappeared like a flash through a door labeled KEEP OUT.

[7] In fact, *don't go to Paris at all.* You will be asked to appear on television. You will explain that your French is not good enough. 50 The man will say: "*Alors*, we will do it in English," but thirty sec-onds before zero, under the blinding lights and the equally blinding stares of the technicians, he will announce: "*Alors,* we will do it in French, after all." You do it in French, after all. *Ma foi!*

[8] *Don't go to Nigeria or Ghana.* Hot rain falls all the time. There 55 are far too many foreigners, actually running their own country. Under blinding skies, the temperature soars to 105 degrees. In Lagos, the causeway is sinking into the sea, cutting off the capital from the mainland, but only the taxi drivers are worried—the climate defeats everyone else. In Ghana a man will thrust a microphone 60 under your nose and ask you what you think of this glorious epoch, which has at last brought freedom from the hated British. As a

British immigrant to Canada, your personality is hopelessly split, which, in a temperature of 105 degrees (humidity 98), hurts.

65   [9] *Don't go to Johannesburg.* They have a crime wave there which has to be seen to be believed; they also have a government, somewhat ditto. In the game reserve, hired lions snarl at you, while elephants walk away in studied reproof. You will lose a fortune at poker. The bookmakers are positive robbers. A simple little dinner party for
70 twenty people (just caviar, guinea fowl, and *cerises au* something-or-other, with a bare twenty-one bottles of champagne) will set you back four hundred and ten dollars.

[10] *Do not dream of going to Bombay.* It is hot, it is dirty, it has three million Indians, most of them milling round the door of
75 your hotel. To add further confusion, people gather under peepul trees, spitting betel juice onto wandering—yes, you've guessed it. A handmade silk tropical suit will cost all of twenty dollars, and the tailor takes a whole twenty-four hours to make it. A personal bearer, who squats permanently outside your door and does everything from
80 pressing your clothes to painting your toenails, gouges you a full sixty cents a day. Above all, Bombay is *dry.* An ingenious government racket will compel you to pay a rupee to fill in a form to apply for a liquor permit (five rupees) in order to buy (one per week) a bottle of Scotch whisky costing sixty-five rupees. Total disbursements,
85 fifteen dollars. There are no polite words to describe the taste of the whisky, when you finally get it.

[11] Alternatively, you can buy on your permit twenty-seven quart bottles of fermented liquors of a strength not exceeding 2 per cent of alcohol by volume. Brother, you'll need them all.

90   [12] *Don't fly across India.* Enormous crowds gather at the airport to bid farewell to every plane. The whole place is crammed with relatives, dogs, children, well-wishers, and professional mourners. You cannot get anywhere near the plane, and pretty soon you don't want to. For all these people are in tears, all of them absolutely
95 inconsolable; there is a crescendo of wailing sobs as your departure is announced, and a final rush toward the counter labeled "Flight Insurance." It is not reassuring; and the journey itself completes a process of aerial demoralization. All Indian air crews sport large black curling mustaches, like the more reckless type of Battle of
100 Britain pilot. Life in hand, curry in throat, you zoom and dip toward the eastern horizon.

[13] *Don't go anywhere near Calcutta,* if you want to hold on to your breakfast. This, the premier city of a country which has the effrontery to lecture the West on how to conduct its affairs, is a

positive monument to disease, dirt, and mismanagement. The main 105
streets must be the filthiest in the world. Outside the city, malodorous
acres of shacks, indescribably squalid, deface the landscape, worse
than any Johannesburg native location. Beggars, and hawkers selling
every conceivable kind of trash, pester you from morning till night.

[14] On a short nighttime walk of a mile or so, in the center 110
of the city, I counted one hundred and seventy people asleep on
steps and sidewalks, like bundles of rags left to be picked up in the
morning. They have been left there by the Indian government, and
they are without hope. Next time you read a vaunting headline, "Mr.
Nehru on the Reorganization of the Entire Globe," just bear all this 115
in mind. Mr. N. would do better to run for mayor of Calcutta, and
begin his global charity at home.

[15] *Don't go to Rangoon*; it might accidentally spoil the rest of
the trip. You will start a wonderful forty-eight hours with a party,
which develops into a screwball singing festival: Americans singing 120
Rule Britannia, English singing *Way Down upon the Wabash*, Burmese singing Gilbert and Sullivan. It ends, with regret, at 3:30 A.M.
Bright and early next morning, you will be afloat in the British
ambassador's pride and joy, his newly acquired Chinese junk, designed, built, and canvased according to a plan at least one thousand 125
years old. You will eat à la Burmese, not faked-up European food.
You will examine exquisite prints of the Burma of a hundred and
fifty years ago. In the evening you will meet half the Burmese air
force, and then an old school friend who, taking you home for dinner,
confides that he has the hi-fi set to end all hi-fis. You will listen to 130
Dvořák's cello concerto, and most of *La Forza del Destino*. You
will wake up next morning thoroughly disgruntled, with the conviction that in Burma, though only half way round the world, you've
enjoyed yourself in a way that won't be duplicated in the future.

[16] There are just a couple of things to offset all this. You will 135
need a slide rule for the currency, which is in rupiahs, a kind of
ruptured rupee. If you visit a Buddhist pagoda, you will wade bare-
foot through betel juice, while large sneering gongs are struck to
signalize other people's almsgiving.

[17] *Have nothing to do with Hong Kong*. It is a free port; you 140
will certainly invest in a mink coat (female, Siberian, very cheap)
which later disintegrates and earns you a reputation for frugality
which was *not* your original intention. Earlier, flying in, you will
roar past hills and even buildings which are within touching distance
of either hand; looking back, pale, shaking all over, you will think, 145
"Heavens! Did we really do that?" The women wear the ugliest

clothes in the world; washed-out tunics, shapeless trousers, all the mysterious glamour of the East wrapped up in one dreary shake of the head. The rickshaw boys, passing you, call out, "Rickshaw?"
150 Then they sidle up and say, "Nice girl?" Then they take a closer look at you and say: "*Young* girl?" The streetwalkers make loud kissing noises as they pass you. It is about as intriguing as a muffled sneeze.

[18] *Avoid Singapore like the plague.* It is hot. It is humid. Its
155 guns still point the wrong way. In your hotel, the note paper has your full name printed on it. You can't even write an anonymous letter.

[19] *Djakarta. Ah, Djakarta.* Never make a stop there, however short, however inadvertent. You don't have to be Dutch to feel like
160 a leper. Here the Indonesians have contracted the prime disease of nationalist fervor: the filling in of forms, and then the cancellation of them, unseen, with enormous rubber stamps. They have a currency form for transients that is positively brutal in its particularity. When you have filled out all thirty-two items, racking your brains
165 to remember how many frozen yen you had in 1929, a man will seize the form, stamp it, and hand it back to you, his face a bored inscrutable mask. And that is all. No one reads it, no one wants it, either now or later. It is your own do-it-yourself souvenir of Indonesia.

170 [20] The man ahead of me in the queue, a cynical fellow with three cameras, completed the item "Traveler's Checks" with "$6,000-000." Of course, it could have been true; after all, we were traveling first class. But no one blinked an eyelash, anyway.

[21] *Leave Australia completely out of your itinerary*, for there
175 you will receive the bitterest disappointment of your life. You will have heard terrible tales of Australia; how you can only get a drink between five and six in the evening, how there isn't any service at all, how you'll have to sleep four in a hotel room, how if you ask to be called at 7 A.M. with a cup of tea, they will hand you an alarm
180 clock and a thermos flask.

[22] None of this is true at all, and you will experience an undoubted sense of loss as you drink all day, relax in your air-conditioned hotel suite at night, ring the bell at three in the morning and order your friends their four final Scotch-and-sodas. True, you
185 can complain about finding such daunting dishes as rump steak and lamb chops on the breakfast menu, but it's not really much to get worked up about. The trouble is, Australia is not what it was (if it ever was).

[23] *Never fly across the Pacific*, from Sydney to San Francisco, at one gulp. It takes nearly two days suspended in mid-air, and visions 190 of *The High and the Mighty* will plague you all the way. Point of No Return, They Died with Their Seat Belts Fastened—there is no end to the intimations of disaster. You will have a short stopover of five hours in Honolulu, but what can you do in Honolulu in five hours, if you are forty-seven years of age and married? The fact is, 195 the Pacific is a very big ocean, and anyone may quote me on the point.

[24] *Please don't go to San Francisco.* Does the road wind uphill all the way? Yes, to the very end. San Francisco is the *very* end, a city insanely tacked onto an overhanging cliff. I suppose if you 200 were tired, or afraid, you could lean against it.

[25] *Finally, never fly nonstop from San Francisco to New York.* You will arrive nine hours late (engine trouble), having spent the morbid period of 2 A.M. to 7 A.M. at Denver airport, and a further educational two hours at Chicago. At Denver, a man in the full-dress 205 uniform of Santa Claus, rather intoxicated, will board the plane and, inexplicably, complete the journey with you. Who is he? An eccentric? A vice president on the run? A nightclub reject? Who can tell?

[26] My literary agent, a perceptive New Yorker, suggests that the company always installs a jolly Santa Claus on any plane that 210 is over two hours late, to distract the customers. On that scale, we should have had four or five of them, all loaded to the gills.

[27] *All in all, don't go round the world.* Come and stay with me in Ottawa instead. East Wing, Ward G. Knock and enter. But softly.

[For treatment of this selection, see p. 140.]

Myths and Dreams

ERICH FROMM

[1] IF it is true that the ability to be puzzled is the beginning of wisdom, then this truth is a sad commentary on the wisdom of modern man. Whatever the merits of our high degree of literary and

From *The Forgotten Language*, by Erich Fromm. Copyright 1951 by Erich Fromm. Reprinted by permission of Rinehart & Company, Inc. Selection title by the Editors.

universal education, we have lost the gift for being puzzled. Every-
5 thing is supposed to be known—if not to ourselves then to some
specialist whose business it is to know what we do not know. In
fact, to be puzzled is embarrassing, a sign of intellectual inferiority.
Even children are rarely surprised, or at least they try not to show
that they are; and as we grow older we gradually lose the ability
10 to be surprised. To have the right answers seems all-important; to
ask the right questions is considered insignificant by comparison.

[2] This attitude is perhaps one reason why one of the most
puzzling phenomena in our lives, our dreams, gives so little cause
for wonder and for raising questions. We all dream; we do not
15 understand our dreams, yet we act as if nothing strange goes on
in our sleep minds, strange at least by comparison with the logical,
purposeful doings of our minds when we are awake.

[3] When we are awake, we are active, rational beings, eager to
make an effort to get what we want and prepared to defend our-
20 selves against attack. We act and we observe; we see things outside,
perhaps not as they are, but at least in such a manner that we can
use and manipulate them. But we are also rather unimaginative,
and rarely—except as children or if we are poets—does our imagination go beyond duplicating the stories and plots that are part of
25 our actual experience. We are effective but somewhat dull. We call
the field of our daytime observation "reality" and are proud of our
"realism" and our cleverness in manipulating it.

[4] When we are asleep, we awake to another form of existence.
We dream. We invent stories which never happened and sometimes
30 for which there is not even any precedent in reality. Sometimes we
are the hero, sometimes the villain; sometimes we see the most
beautiful scenes and are happy; often we are thrown into extreme
terror. But whatever the role we play in the dream *we* are the
author, it is *our* dream, *we* have invented the plot.

35 [5] Most of our dreams have one characteristic in common: they
do not follow the laws of logic that govern our waking thought. The
categories of space and time are neglected. People who are dead, we
see alive; events which we watch in the present, occurred many years
ago. We dream of two events as occurring simultaneously when in
40 reality they could not possibly occur at the same time. We pay just
as little attention to the laws of space. It is simple for us to move
to a distant place in an instant, to be in two places at once, to fuse
two persons into one, or to have one person suddenly be changed
into another. Indeed, in our dreams we are the creators of a world

where time and space, which limit all the activities of our body, 45
have no power.

[6] Another odd thing about our dreams is that we think of events
and persons we have not thought of for years, and whom, in the
waking state, we would never have remembered. Suddenly they
appear in the dream as acquaintances whom we had thought of 50
many times. In our sleeping life, we seem to tap the vast store of
experience and memory which in the daytime we do not know
exists.

[7] Yet, despite all these strange qualities, our dreams are real
to us while we are dreaming; as real as any experience we have in 55
our waking life. There is no "as if" in the dream. The dream is
present, real experience, so much so, indeed, that it suggests two
questions: What is reality? How do we know that what we dream is
unreal and what we experience in our waking life is real? A Chinese
poet has expressed this aptly: "I dreamt last night that I was a 60
butterfly and now I don't know whether I am a man who dreamt
he was a butterfly, or perhaps a butterfly who dreams now that he
is a man."

[8] All these exciting, vivid experiences of the night not only dis-
appear when we wake up, but we have the greatest difficulty trying 65
to remember them. Most of them we simply forget, so completely
that we do not even remember having lived in this other world.
Some we faintly remember at the moment of waking, and the next
second they are beyond recall. A few we do remember, and these
are the ones we speak of when we say, "I had a dream." It is as if 70
friendly, or unfriendly, spirits had visited us and at the break of
day had suddenly disappeared; we hardly remember that they had
been there and how intensely we had been occupied with them.

[9] Perhaps more puzzling than all the factors already mentioned
is the similarity of the products of our creativeness during sleep with 75
the oldest creations of man—the myths.

[10] Actually, we are not too much puzzled by myths. If they
are made respectable as part of our religion, we give them a conventional and superficial acknowledgment as part of a venerable
tradition; if they do not carry such traditional authority, they are 80
taken for the childish expression of the thoughts of man before he
was enlightened by science. At any rate, whether ignored, despised,
or respected, myths are felt to belong to a world completely alien
to our own thinking. Yet the fact remains that many of our dreams
are, in both style and content, similar to myths, and we who find them 85

strange and remote when we are awake have the ability to create
these mythlike productions when we are asleep.

[11] In the myth, too, dramatic events happen which are impossible in a world governed by the laws of time and space: the hero
90 leaves his home and country to save the world, or he flees from his
mission and lives in the belly of a big fish; he dies and is reborn;
the mythical bird is burned and emerges from the ashes more beautiful than before.

[12] Of course, different peoples created different myths just as
95 different people dream different dreams. But in spite of all these
differences, all myths and all dreams have one thing in common,
they are all "written" in the same language, *symbolic language.*

[13] The myths of the Babylonians, Indians, Egyptians, Hebrews,
Greeks are written in the same language as those of the Ashantis or
100 the Trukese. The dreams of someone living today in New York or
in Paris are the same as the dreams reported from people living
some thousand years ago in Athens or in Jerusalem. The dreams of
ancient and modern man are written in the same language as the
myths whose authors lived in the dawn of history.

105 [14] Symbolic language is a language in which inner experiences,
feelings and thoughts are expressed as if they were sensory experiences, events in the outer world. It is a language which has a different logic from the conventional one we speak in the daytime, a logic
in which not time and space are the ruling categories but intensity
110 and association. It is the one universal language the human race has
ever developed, the same for all cultures and throughout history. It
is a language with its own grammar and syntax, as it were, a language one must understand if one is to understand the meaning of
myths, fairy tales and dreams.

115 [15] Yet this language has been forgotten by modern man. Not
when he is asleep, but when he is awake. Is it important to understand this language also in our waking state?

[16] For the people of the past, living in the great cultures of both
East and West, there was no doubt as to the answer to this question.
120 For them myths and dreams were among the most significant expressions of the mind, and failure to understand them would have
amounted to illiteracy. It is only in the past few hundred years of
Western culture that this attitude has changed. At best, myths were
supposed to be naïve fabrications of the prescientific mind, created
125 long before man had made his great discoveries about nature and
had learned some of the secrets of its mastery.

[17] Dreams fared even worse in the judgment of modern enlight-

enment. They were considered to be plain senseless, and unworthy of the attention of grown-up men, who were busy with such important matters as building machines and considered themselves "real- 130 istic" because they saw nothing but the reality of things they could conquer and manipulate; realists who have a special word for each type of automobile, but only the one word "love" to express the most varied kinds of affective experience.

[18] Moreover, if all our dreams were pleasant phantasmagorias 135 in which our hearts' wishes were fulfilled, we might feel friendlier toward them. But many of them leave us in an anxious mood; often they are nightmares from which we awake gratefully acknowledging that we only dreamed. Others, though not nightmares, are disturbing for other reasons. They do not fit the person we are sure we are 140 during daytime. We dream of hating people whom we believe we are fond of, of loving someone whom we thought we had no interest in. We dream of being ambitious, when we are convinced of being modest; we dream of bowing down and submitting, when we are so proud of our independence. But worse than all this is the fact that 145 we do not understand our dreams while we, the waking person, are sure we can understand anything if we put our minds to it. Rather than be confronted with such an overwhelming proof of the limitations of our understanding, we accuse the dreams of not making sense.

[19] A profound change in the attitude toward myths and dreams 150 has taken place in the past few decades. This change was greatly stimulated by Freud's work. After starting out with the restricted aim of helping the neurotic patient to understand the reasons for his illness, Freud proceeded to study the dream as a universal human phenomenon, the same in the sick and in the healthy person. He 155 saw that dreams were essentially no different from myths and fairy tales and that to understand the language of the one was to understand the language of the others. And the work of anthropologists focused new attention on myths. They were collected and studied, and some few pioneers in this field, like J. J. Bachofen, succeeded 160 in throwing new light on the prehistory of man.

[20] But the study of myths and dreams is still in its infancy. It suffers from various limitations. One is a certain dogmatism and rigidity that has resulted from the claims of various psychoanalytic schools, each insisting that it has the only true understanding of 165 symbolic language. Thus we lose sight of the many-sidedness of symbolic language and try to force it into the Procrustean bed of one, and only one, kind of meaning.

[21] Another limitation is that interpretation of dreams is still con-

170 sidered legitimate only when employed by the psychiatrist in the treatment of neurotic patients. On the contrary, I believe that symbolic language is the one foreign language that each of us must learn. Its understanding brings us in touch with one of the most significant sources of wisdom, that of the myth, and it brings us in
175 touch with the deeper layers of our own personalities. In fact, it helps us to understand a level of experience that is specifically human because it is that level which is common to all humanity, in content as well as in style.

[22] The Talmud says, "Dreams which are not interpreted are
180 like letters which have not been opened." Indeed, both dreams and myths are important communications from ourselves to ourselves. If we do not understand the language in which they are written, we miss a great deal of what we know and tell ourselves in those hours when we are not busy manipulating the outside world.

In order to achieve unity, a paragraph must contain one central thesis—specific, carefully delineated, and capable of development—and that thesis must be fully and methodically developed. But there is more to the problem. Perhaps the easiest approach to the subject of paragraph unity is a negative approach. A unified paragraph does not contain material irrelevant to the central idea; it does not veer off on tangential material, however interesting that material may be; it does not get so wound up in one of the subdivisions of the topic or in one of the methods of development that it never completes the development of the central thesis.

1. What artificial device emphasizes—even exaggerates—the unity of the paragraphs in the Monsarrat essay? Why is this device excusable here, although admittedly it is entirely too monotonous for most writing? Why do you think Monsarrat used it? Do you think he overdoes it? What does he gain by the sameness of the paragraphs? What does he lose? What other means does he use to achieve paragraph unity?

2. Define what is meant by "slick" writing. Why do you think the term is applicable to "Around-the-World Grouch"? How do the means of achieving paragraph unity contribute to the slickness?

3. Select five paragraphs from "Myths and Dreams," and determine whether they do or do not violate unity. Explain your conclusions in terms of

   a. the guiding purpose
   b. the method or methods of development.

4. What are the topic sentences of paragraphs 5 to 8 of the Fromm selection? What words or groups of words are used to achieve coherence in these paragraphs?

5. Are paragraphs 13 and 19 of "Myths and Dreams" unified? Explain your answer by showing either the relevance or the irrelevance of every sentence to the form and topic sentence of each paragraph.

6. When might an author deliberately violate paragraph unity? Does either Monsarrat or Fromm do so? Where? Why?

Alternate selections for the study of Unity: Georges Blond, "Chuan and the Wild Geese"; Thomas H. Huxley, "Thinking like a Scientist."

Assignment: Write a one-paragraph summary of either selection. Be sure that your paragraph, although it covers the contents of the essay you select, does not violate paragraph unity. Thus you must formulate a guiding purpose of your own and determine upon a method of developing it. You must also be prepared to omit many minor points made in the essay and avoid the dangers of introducing irrelevant material or veering off on your reactions to the piece.

Coherence

An Ulcer, Gentlemen,
Is an Unwritten Poem

JOHN CIARDI

[1] THE poet in our times is a figure of estrangement and he knows it. He not only knows it, he has grown used to the fact and does not much mind it. The truth seems to be, for that matter, that the poet—outside those Golden Ages of folk-poetry now long
5 gone—never did reach more than a few special people in any culture.

[2] In the past, however, poets have managed to persuade themselves that they were some sort of social force. Elizabethan poets liked to claim that their sonnets conferred immortality on the ladies they wrote about. The seventeenth century satirists were especially
10 fond of the idea that by "holding folly up to ridicule" they purified the intellect of their ages. More recently Shelley found it possible to assert that "Poets are the unacknowledged legislators of the world." And even within the last twenty-five years, the social poets of the 'thirties may be cited as having seriously believed that their poems
15 of social protest had a measurable effect on the government of nations.

[3] Stephen Spender, looking back on the mood of poetry in the 'thirties from the vantage point of 1950, summarized the poet's then-sense of himself as very much a warrior of the practical world:

It was still possible then to think of a poem as a palpable, overt, 20
and effective anti-fascist action. Every poetic assertion of the dignity
of the individual seemed to be a bullet fired in the war against
human repression.

[4] I know of no sane poet today who persuades himself that the
action of his art and imagination has any significant consequence in 25
the practical reality of Dow-Jones averages, election returns, and
state of the nation. Wherever the practical world may be, Auden
has defined the position of poetry in our time:

> For poetry makes nothing happen: it survives/In the valley of its
> saying where executives/Would never want to tamper; it flows 30
> south/From ranches of isolation and the busy griefs,/Raw towns
> that we believe and die in; it survives,/A way of happening, a
> mouth.

[5] But no—perhaps to prove that poets are no prophets—the
executives have wanted to tamper. Under the auspices of the College 35
English Association a group of leading business executives have been
meeting regularly with writers and teachers of the liberal arts; and
from their problems in the practical world of business management,
they seem to be asking seriously what meeting there can be between
the arts and the practicalities of industry. 40

[6] The answer to these questions may well be that the poets and
the practical men would be mutually happier in leaving one another
strictly alone, the poets on their ranches of isolation practising a
way of happening, and the practical men in their cities of numbered
and lettered glass doors busily pushing the buttons of the world. 45

[7] For the gap that divides the poet from the practical man is
real. Nor will it be measurably closed by pointing out that some men
have functioned with distinction in both the poetical and the practical
imagination. There was a director of public works named Chaucer,
there was a bricklayer named Ben Jonson, there was a good soldier 50
named Richard Lovelace—one could compile endlessly. But all that
such a list would prove is that some men are ambidextrous: it would
not eliminate the distinction between the right hand and the left.

[8] A poem is a kind of human behavior. Plowing a field, running a chemical experiment, and analyzing the character of a job- 55
applicant are also kinds of human behavior. The poem may, of
course, be about any one of these human actions; but when the
poem deals with them, it does so in non-practical ways. The poet
who writes about plowing a field may find significance in the *idea*

60 of plowing, or he may describe plowing so richly that the riches of
the description become a self-pleasing idea in themselves. He does
not, however, turn physical soil, plant an actual crop, and take it
to the literal human diet by way of a negotiable cash market. In the
same way, the poet may create a powerfully penetrating picture of
65 the character of the man the business executive is interviewing for
a job. But when the poet has finished his analysis, he has no need
to make a payroll decision and to assign the man to a specific job
in a specific department.

[9] Poetry and practicality are in fact two different worlds with
70 two different workers of experience and of imagination. The poet
enters his world as an *as if*: he writes *as if* he were analyzing a real
man seated before him. He is free with a stroke of the pen to change
the lineaments of the world he has imagined. The worksheets of a
poem by Karl Shapiro contain a monumental example of this free-
75 dom to *as if* at will.

[10] Setting out to describe the [*as if*] dome of darkness that settles over a city at night, he writes in his first draft: "Under the
fatherly dome of the universe and the town." Now "fatherly dome"
cannot fail to imply a theological universe in the mind of God the
80 Father. For reasons that need not be examined here, Shapiro, in
his second draft, rephrased the idea "under the dome of zero."
Simply by changing one central word, Shapiro swung the universe
itself from the theological concept of "father" to the scientific concept of "zero." And the poem continued to follow itself as if the
85 process of reversing thirty centuries of human attitudes in a single
word amounted to nothing whatever.

[11] The practical man has no such large freedom. He enters a
world called *is*. When he is at work, he *is* plowing a field, he *is*
assembling chemical apparatus, he *is* interviewing an actual man
90 whose name appears on the census listings and who *is* offering his
services in return for real and taxable wages.

[12] It is only natural, moreover, that men who give their attention to either of these two worlds should not be especially well disposed to the other. Poets tend to think very little of stock-brokers,
95 and stock-brokers tend to think even less—if at all—of poets. And
the fact is that some of the best poetry of our times has been written
on what may be called an inverted sense of reality, an order of
imagination that asserts openly or by implication that what the practical men do is meaningless and that only the *as if* of the vicarious
100 imagination has a place in the final mind of man. So Wallace

Stevens, in a poem significantly titled "Holiday in Reality," lists a series of things seen and says of them: "These are real only if I make them so," and concludes: "Intangible arrows quiver and stick in the skin/ And I taste at the root of the tongue the unreal/ Of what is real." 105

[13] It may be very much to the point that Wallace Stevens, in another part of his imagination, is a vice-president of the Hartford Accident and Indemnity Company and a specialist in claims on surety bonds. Obviously, however, Wallace Stevens cannot look into his surety bond claims and send in a report that "These are real only 110 if I make them so." That difference between the world of practical solutions and the world of the vicarious imagination must not be blinked away.

[14] What must be borne in mind, rather, is the fact that no sane human being is exclusively a practical man. The plant manager may 115 be the most mechanically efficient of calculators during his waking hours; and still his dreams or his nightmares will be human and impractical. What is his order of reality and of business efficiency when he first holds his newborn child? Or when, as some men must in time, he stands by his child's grave? What is his order of reality 120 when he steps out of a late conference and finds a hurricane shaking the earth? Or his wife is ill and the telephone rings: In one ear he hears his assistant howling that the sub-contractor sent the wrong parts and that a rush order is delayed, while with the other he hears the doctor close the bedroom door and start down the stairs to tell 125 him his wife will or will not recover. Which of these realities is more real than the other to live to?

[15] The poem does not care and cannot care what happens to that rush order. The poem is of the humanity of the man. And despite the tendency . . . [to respect] only those men who "do things" and 130 to scorn "dreamers," the fact is that no man can be wholly practical or wholly impractical, and that the humanity of any man's life requires some, at least, of both orders of the imagination.

[16] There is no poetry for the practical man. There is poetry only for the mankind of the man who spends a certain amount of 135 his life turning the mechanical wheel. But let him spend too much of his life at the mechanics of practicality and either he must become something less than a man, or his very mechanical efficiency will become impaired by the frustrations stored up in his irrational human personality. An ulcer, gentlemen, is an unkissed imagination taking 140 its revenge for having been jilted. It is an unwritten poem, a neglected

music, an unpainted watercolor, an undanced dance. It is a declaration from the mankind of the man that a clear spring of joy has not been tapped, and that it must break through, muddily, on its own.

145   [17] Poetry is one of the forms of joy, the most articulate, the most expanding, and, therefore, the most fulfilling form. It is no separation from the world; it is the mankind of the world, the most human language of man's uncertain romance with the universe.

Much of the discussion of coherence in the whole theme is relevant to the paragraph. The ideas in a paragraph must be ordered so that their logical relations are immediately clear to the reader; when necessary, transitional words or expressions may be used to point up relations.

1. What is the basic idea in the first paragraph? In what sentence is it stated? What contribution does the second sentence make to the basic idea? What justification is there for Ciardi's repeating in the second sentence the fact that the poet knows he is "a figure of estrangement"? What would be changed if the repetition were omitted? In the third sentence, what does the expression "for that matter" tell the reader about the direction the thought is going to take?

2. The basic idea of the second paragraph is in sharp contrast to that of paragraph 1. What means does Ciardi use to prepare the reader for the contrast, to help him bridge the gap between the paragraphs? Point out all the means used to achieve coherence in the paragraph.

3. By what means is a transition effected between paragraphs 2 and 3? What does the word "today" in the first sentence of paragraph 4 contribute to coherence? Point out two devices of coherence in the first sentence of paragraph 5.

4. Paragraph 6 indicates one answer to the questions raised by business executives in paragraph 5. Paragraph 6, then, might be considered as developing the basic idea of paragraph 5; it could have been made part of paragraph 5. How would you justify having paragraph 6 —containing a single sentence—stand as a separate paragraph?

5. What function is served by the word "for" in the first sentence of paragraph 7? What is the topic sentence of the paragraph? By what methods is the basic idea of the paragraph developed? What do you need to know about Chaucer, Jonson, and Lovelace to understand their relevance to the basic idea of the paragraph?

6. Paragraph 8 introduces new content into the essay—the nature of a poem. Though Ciardi does not use an explicit transition, the relevance of the paragraph to the preceding paragraphs becomes abundantly clear. Just how has coherence been achieved? What methods of development are used in the paragraph? Point out all the transitional expressions used to achieve coherence within the paragraph.

7. How is paragraph 10 related to paragraph 9? Could the two paragraphs have been combined into one without violating unity (a paragraph develops a single idea) and coherence? What, if anything, is gained by having paragraph 10 stand alone?

8. What is the topic sentence of paragraph 11? By what method is the basic idea developed? What one word in the first sentence of the paragraph is transitional?

9. If the first sentence of paragraph 12 is the topic sentence, how can you justify inclusion of the quotation from Wallace Stevens' "Holiday in Reality"?

10. What is the function of paragraph 13 in relation to the rest of the essay? What statement made earlier in the essay does paragraph 13 echo and develop?

11. What is the topic sentence of paragraph 14? What method or methods of development are used in the paragraph? Point out all means of achieving coherence in the paragraph.

12. What justification is there for the repetition in paragraph 15 of material developed in paragraph 14?

13. What basic idea is developed through paragraphs 16 and 17?

Alternate selections for the study of Coherence: Learned Hand, "A Plea for the Freedom of Dissent"; Margaret Leech, "General Winfield Scott."

Theme Assignment: In Ciardi's terms, consider what you have done thus far in your life to avoid becoming "something less than a man," to avoid the "frustrations stored up in . . . [your] irrational personality." Have the radio, the TV, the motion picture played a part in helping you to realize your "humanity," or have these been additional sources of frustration? Has literature or painting or music entered significantly into your life? Have you created anything comparable to a good poem? Do you feel that life as a businessman or an engineer or a teacher or a lawyer will be rewarding enough so that you won't have to worry about getting an "ulcer"?

Write a theme of three adequately developed, coherent paragraphs—paragraphs whose basic ideas are made clear and convincing through adequate development—answering any one of the questions above or any other one suggested to you by Ciardi's essay. Underline with a single line the topic sentence of each paragraph (an implied topic sentence will not do for this assignment); with a double line, transitional devices that help achieve coherence within each paragraph; and with a triple line, transitional devices that achieve coherence between paragraphs. In the margin next to each paragraph, indicate the method or methods of paragraph development you have used.

Adequacy

FROM *Atoms and People*

RALPH E. LAPP

[1] ORDINARY or natural uranium is quite harmless for it will not, by itself, sustain chain reaction. Only when it is embodied in an enormous matrix of some light element like graphite or heavy water does it sustain a slow chain reaction. Were this to be allowed
5 to run out of control, it would not in general produce anything like an explosion. Heat would be produced and some inner parts of the reactor might melt, but it would not qualify as a bomb.

[2] Enriched uranium or plutonium is quite different from ordinary uranium. Assemble too much of it in one place, and the chain
10 reaction will automatically run away. Thus, it was rather important for the people at Oak Ridge and at Hanford to know how much was "enough" so that safety precautions could be taken. At Los Alamos the experts refined their calculations as to the size of the critical mass, but it was essential to have experimental measurements.
15 [3] The man who headed up the "critical assembly" group was a good friend of mine. I knew Louis Slotin while an undergraduate at the University of Chicago and liked him very much for his pleasant manner and friendly advice. He was never too busy to help out a Ph.D. aspirant, and I remember that he gave me valuable pointers
20 on making Geiger counters. On my visits to Los Alamos I used to stop by to see Slotin and give him the news of Chicago. He was a short, wiry youth with dark hair and soft sad eyes. Somehow or other, he always ended up doing jobs nobody else wanted. He never

complained, and I respected the cheerful way that Slotin did dirty work. 25

[4] Slotin had nerves of iron and he needed them for his critical experiments with the "nukes." Here is essentially what he did in making a critical assembly, or in "tickling the dragon's tail," as we called it. He would set up a table with a neutron counter and a rack. On the rack he would place two pieces of bomb stuff, each one 30 being somewhat less than a critical amount. Then he would push the two pieces, often in the form of hemispheres the size of a split baseball, toward each other. As the gap narrowed between the pieces, he would measure the buildup of the chain reaction inside the assembly. He used a small source of neutrons to amplify the effect, 35 rather than waiting for stray neutrons to come from cosmic rays or from the material itself. He determined the tempo of the buildup by listening to the clicks in an amplifier connected to the neutron counter and in watching a recorder trace out a jagged red line on a moving roll of graph paper. 40

[5] As the hemispheres came closer and closer, more and more of the neutrons would tend to be caught within the bomb stuff and fewer would be lost through the narrowing air gap. The chain reaction would build up, and, just before it was ready to rip, Slotin would calmly stop the experiment, measure the separation and deduce 45 just how big the critical mass was. He grew quite adept at the experiment for he repeated it fifty times or more. His nonchalance amazed Fermi who once warned him, "Keep doing that experiment that way and you'll be dead within a year." Some of Slotin's colleagues tried to get him to build in automatic safety devices, like 50 powerful springs, which could be triggered to hurl the two hemispheres apart when the neutrons built up too fast. He turned aside this suggestion with this retort: "If I have to depend upon safety devices I am sure to have an accident."

[6] Slotin was asked to repeat the experiment "just one more 55 time" to demonstrate the technique to others in the laboratory. So he gathered the group of six people behind him in the sunlit room where he did his work. One man, Dr. Alvin Graves, had his hand almost on his shoulder as Slotin proceeded to demonstrate his technique. He used two hemispheres that he had worked with before 60 and holding a screwdriver he moved the two pieces of bomb material together to form a "nuke" or nuclear core. Slowly, at first, then more quickly the counters clicked away and the red line moved upward on the white paper chart.

[7] Suddenly the counters screamed and the red ink indicators 65

swung off scale. There had been an accident! The chain reaction was running away. Almost as if by reflex action Slotin hurled himself forward and tore the reacting mass apart with his bare hands. The others gasped and, turning around, Slotin, his face whitely
70 reflecting his terror, motioned them to leave the room.

[8] Slotin telephoned the hospital and said that there had been an accident. Then he telephoned his close friend, Phil Morrison. He was nauseated but, always the true scientist, paused in the hallway and drew a pencil sketch of the room and marked everyone's
75 position, putting a big X for himself. Then he scribbled the time, 3:20 P.M., and hustled the group off to the hospital, all of them jamming into two jeeps.

[9] The big question in the mind of everyone was: how much dose did Slotin get? The neutrons and X-rays which flashed through
80 his body before he tore the assembly apart caused biological damage to his body. This we measure in certain units—called roentgens or r-units. A total of about 400 r over the entire body is considered the lethal amount for most people. This deadly amount does not produce immediate effect but takes time . . . weeks . . . or days . . .
85 depending on the dose.

[10] Phil Morrison, gifted theoretical physicist, worked feverishly to reconstruct the accident and to learn how serious was his friend's plight. Slotin's very blood had been made radioactive by the burst of neutrons which riddled his body, and a small sample of his blood
90 gave a clue to the dose. Of course, Slotin was hospitalized and became ill rather soon, but during the first few days he was cheerful and would ask when visited by Morrison, "Well, what's the dose?" Nobody really knew and it took a long time to find out. Before they did, the tide had changed in Slotin's reaction to the radiation. His
95 differential blood cell count told the story—a picture so hopeless that the attending Army nurse, hardened to hospital routine, broke down and sobbed when she saw the results.

[11] Slotin had been most severely irradiated around the hands and arms. These parts of his pain-ridden body swelled grotesquely
100 and the skin sloughed off. The nation's best doctors were flown to the Army hospital at Los Alamos but they could do little for the weakening patient. Nor could we do much more today.

[12] Technicians strung a telephone connection into the bare hospital room and Slotin talked with his mother in Winnipeg, Canada.
105 The next day, his parents were flown to New Mexico by special Army plane, and they stayed at their son's bedside until he breathed

his last. The end came early on the morning of the ninth day after the accident.

[13] The man who stood behind Slotin, Dr. Graves, was severely injured by the accident but he recovered and went on to become 110 associate director of Los Alamos in the postwar period. He had this to say of Slotin: "I can perhaps tell you as much about his personality and character as I could in very many words if I merely quote to you his first statement when we were alone together in the hospital room. He said, 'I'm sorry I got you into this. I am afraid 115 that I have less than a fifty-fifty chance of living. I hope you do better than that.'"

[14] Slotin was not destined to be a great or a famous man. He was one of the many scientists who worked devotedly and unselfishly throughout the war. The young scientist gave his life, just as did 120 many of his comrades in arms.

[15] Slotin's experiment was outlawed at Los Alamos. With the development of television and remote-control gadgetry, it became possible to do the critical assembly operations with no one within a quarter of a mile. White-coated technicians, principally women, con- 125 trol the assembly and make all their observations without the slightest danger to themselves.

There is no clear-cut answer to the question, "How long should a paragraph be?" or—to put the matter another way—"When is a paragraph adequately developed?" The writer's judgment must guide him in deciding just how many details or examples to supply, just how far to carry a comparison, or just how many methods of development to combine in dealing with a given topic. Sometimes the question answers itself: the main idea in a paragraph may lend itself to only one type of development and the development comes to its own natural conclusion. At other times, the writer must make decisions. An exceptionally long paragraph may be needed to do justice to a given topic, while another topic can best be handled in a short, crisp paragraph. The writer who is aware of the problem of adequacy—of making his paragraphs just the right length to serve their purpose—will usually solve the problem quite satisfactorily.

1. The first two paragraphs of Lapp's account of the tragedy of Louis Slotin compare ordinary uranium with enriched uranium. The material could easily have been unified into a single paragraph developed by the method of comparison. How can you justify Lapp's decision to use two paragraphs?

2. The third paragraph introduces Louis Slotin, the central character

in the piece. Though it is longer than the first two paragraphs, it is still a relatively short paragraph. Is it adequately developed? Defend your position, making clear the criteria on which you based it.

3. Paragraphs 4 and 5 are devoted to Slotin's "critical experiments." What reasons can you find for Lapp's having ended paragraph 4 where he did? Would "adequacy" have been better served had he combined the two paragraphs into one? Why or why not?

4. Why does Lapp end paragraph 6 where he does? What obvious reason does he have for keeping paragraph 7 short?

5. Except for paragraph 10, the remaining paragraphs in the piece are all relatively short—so short, indeed, as to suggest that the effect they achieve might be unpleasantly choppy writing; on the surface they might seem inadequately developed. Analyze these paragraphs to show whether each adequately does the job it is meant to do in terms of the piece as a whole.

6. No mature reader can fail to be moved by the death of Louis Slotin. Yet Lapp has rigorously avoided sentimentality, "tugging at the heartstrings," overdramatizing for emotional effect. What contribution does the length of what you consider to be key paragraphs make to the total effect of the piece? What other techniques of writing make major contributions to the total effect? Consider particularly organization of the whole, tone, and irony.

Alternate selections for the study of Adequacy: Morris R. Cohen, "Philosophy in Wartime—An Apologia"; Albert Camus, "A Thoroughly Negative Place."

Theme Assignment: As question 6 above suggests, irony is one of the ingredients of the account of Slotin's death. Part of a dictionary definition of irony is "an outcome of events contrary to what was, or might have been, expected" (*The American College Dictionary*). Irony is part of the very texture of life: what seems like a stroke of good luck may turn out to be tragic; a plane missed by a businessman resulted in the loss of a business deal but saved the man's life because the plane exploded in midflight; Louis Pasteur suffered public disgrace and humiliation for medical discoveries which subsequently saved the lives of countless people the world over.

Write a theme in which you support the statement that "irony is part of the very texture of life." You may deal with one or more situations in which irony is evident, or you may treat an idea which has ironic implications, or you may discuss any of the "machines" that make modern living what it is in order to point up the irony inherent in the "machine." Your paragraphs should show that you have learned to solve the problem of adequacy.

Variety

FROM *The Tatler*

RICHARD STEELE

[1] AMONG the many Employments I am necessarily put
upon by my Friends, that of giving Advice is the most unwelcome
to me; and indeed, I am forced to use a little Art in the Manner;
for some People will ask Counsel of you, when they have already
acted what they tell you is still under Deliberation. I had almost 5
lost a very good Friend t'other Day, who came to know how I like
his Design to marry such a Lady, I answered, By no Means; and I
must be positive against it, for very solid Reasons, which are not
proper to communicate. Not proper to communicate! (said he with
a grave Air) I will know the Bottom of this. I saw him moved, and 10
knew from thence he was already determined; therefore evaded it by
saying, To tell you the Truth, dear *Frank*, of all Women living, I
would have her my self. *Isaac*, said he, Thou art too late, for we
have been both one these two Months.

[2] I learned this Caution by a Gentleman's consulting me formerly 15
about his Son. He railed at his damn'd Extravagance, and told me,
In a very little Time, he would beggar him by the exorbitant Bills
which came from *Oxford* every Quarter. *Make the Rogue bite upon
the Bridle, said I, pay none of his Bills, it will but encourage him to
further Trespasses.* He look'd plaguy sour at me. His Son soon after 20
sent up a Paper of Verses, forsooth, in Print on the last publick
Occasion; upon which he is convinced the Boy has Parts, and a Lad

From *The Tatler*, No. 25, Tuesday, June 7, 1709.

of Spirit is not to be too much cramp'd in his Maintenance, lest he
take ill Courses. Neither Father nor Son can ever since endure the
25 Sight of me.

[3] These sort of People ask Opinions, only out of the Fulness of
their Heart on the Subject of their Perplexity, and not from a Desire
of Information.

[4] There is nothing so easy as to find out which Opinion the
30 Man in Doubt has a Mind to; therefore the sure Way is to tell him,
that is certainly to be chosen. Then you are to be very clear and
positive; leave no Handle for Scruple. Bless me! Sir, there's no
Room for a Question. This rivets you into his Heart; for you at
once applaud his Wisdom, and gratify his Inclination. However, I
35 had too much Bowels to be insincere to a Man who came Yesterday
to know of me, with which of two eminent Men in the City he
should place his Son? Their Names are *Paulo* and *Avaro*. This gave
me much Debate with my self, because not only the Fortune of the
Youth, but his Virtue also dependeth upon this Choice. The Men
40 are equally wealthy; but they differ in the Use and Application of
their Riches, which you immediately see upon entring their Doors.

[5] The Habitation of *Paulo* has at once the Air of a Nobleman
and a Merchant. You see the Servants act with Affection to their
Master, and Satisfaction in themselves: The Master meets you with
45 open Countenance, full of Benevolence and Integrity: Your Business
is dispatched with that Confidence and Welcome which always accom-
panies honest Minds: His Table is the Image of Plenty and Generosity, supported by Justice and Frugality. After we had dined here,
our Affair was to visit *Avaro*: Out comes an awkward Fellow with
50 a careful Countenance; Sir, would you speak with my Master? May
I crave your Name? After the first Preamble, he leads us into a
noble Solitude, a great House that seemed uninhabited; but from the
End of the Spacious Hall moves towards us *Avaro*, with a suspicious
Aspect, as if he believed us Thieves; and as for my Part, I approached
55 him as if I knew him a Cut-purse. We fell into Discourse of his
noble Dwelling, and the great Estate all the World knew he had to
enjoy in it; And I, to plague him, fell a commending *Paulo*'s Way
of living. *Paulo*, answered *Avaro*, is a very good Man; but we who
have smaller Estates, must cut our Coat according to our Cloth.
60 Nay, says I, Every Man knows his own Circumstances best; you
are in the right, if you han't wherewithal. He look'd very sowr; (for
it is, you must know, the utmost Vanity of a mean-spirited rich Man

to be contradicted, when he calls himself poor). But I was resolved
to vex him, by consenting to all he said; the main Design of which
was, that he would have us find out, he was one of the wealthiest 65
Men in *London,* and lived like a Beggar. We left him, and took a
turn on the *Change.* My Friend was ravished with *Avaro*: This (said
he) is certainly a sure Man. I contradicted him with much Warmth,
and summed up their different Characters as well as I could. This
Paulo (said I) grows wealthy by being a common Good; *Avaro* by 70
being a general Evil: *Paulo* has the Art, *Avaro* the Craft of Trade.
When *Paulo* gains, all Men he deals with are the better: Whenever
Avaro profits, another certainly loses. In a Word, *Paulo* is a Citizen,
and *Avaro* a Cit. I convinced my Friend, and carried the young
Gentleman the next Day to *Paulo,* where he will learn the Way both 75
to gain and enjoy a good Fortune. And though I cannot say, I have,
by keeping him from *Avaro* sav'd him from the Gallows, I have
prevented him deserving it every Day he lives: For with *Paulo* he
will be an honest Man, without being so for Fear of the Law; as
with *Avaro,* he would have been a Villain within the Protection of it. 80

Variety among the paragraphs of an essay is obtained in several
ways: most obvious is varying the lengths of the several paragraphs
that make up the essay. The placing of a topic sentence at the beginning of one paragraph and at the end of another supplies variety, as
does the occasional use of an implied topic sentence. In addition, the
use of different methods of paragraph development with consequent
differences in the structure of the paragraphs is a major source of
variety.

Part of the success of the selection from the famous early eighteenth-
century periodical, *The Tatler,* lies in the variety in length and structure of its paragraphs.

1. This selection covers a wider range of content than is at first
indicated. What is the large subject to which the whole piece is devoted?
Where is this subject most explicitly stated? What additional subject or
subjects do you find discussed at some length? Where?

2. Because Steele—as indicated in question 1—has discussed more
than one subject, is it your opinion that he has seriously violated unity
of the whole? Justify your opinion in terms of the content of the whole.

3. What is the topic sentence of the first paragraph? What method
of development is used in the paragraph? Is the first sentence of paragraph 2 the topic sentence? Why or why not?

4. What is the relation between the first two paragraphs and the

third? Does your answer explain the shortness of paragraph 3? (If not, your answer is inadequate.) If paragraph 3 had been placed before paragraph 1, what would have been gained or lost?

5. What is the topic sentence of paragraph 4? What three methods of development are used in the paragraph?

6. Paragraphs 1, 2, and 4 all contain material about men who have asked advice of the writer. How does this material in paragraph 4 differ from that in the other two paragraphs, thus enabling Steele to achieve variety in paragraph structure? Could this material in paragraph 4 have been put into a separate paragraph? Why or why not?

7. What is the topic sentence of paragraph 5? What methods of development do you find used? Point out all the means by which Steele achieves coherence in the paragraph.

8. The last paragraph is divisible into four major units; where does each of these units begin? Had Steele broken this paragraph into four paragraphs, he would not only have lost the variety supplied by the long paragraph in contrast to the rest of the paragraphs in the piece but he would also have changed the fundamental relation between this paragraph and the rest of the essay. Explain this statement in detail.

9. Indicate any means used by Steele not touched on in the preceding questions to achieve variety in his paragraphing.

Alternate selection for the study of Variety: Jacques Barzun, " 'Say, Bud!' . . . 'Hiya, Baby!' "

Theme Assignment: Steele makes us aware of some of the problems involved in giving asked-for advice, and there are still others. Assume that your advice has been asked concerning the best ways of getting along during the first few weeks as a student at your college. You may create any type of questioner—one who is intelligent and sincere in his request for advice or one who wants to show off his own knowledge as he asks for advice or one who hears only what he wants to be told. Decide on the type of questioner for whom you are writing, and then write your advice in the form of a theme of several adequately developed, varied paragraphs. Though you need not describe your questioner in so many words, the type he is should emerge clearly in the course of your theme through the kind of advice you give him and the tone you adopt.

Paragraphs in Combination

Inland Navigator

KENNETH ANDLER

[1] I WANT to tell you about a woodsman, what he was like, what his work was, and what it meant. His name was Alfred D. Teare and he came originally from Nova Scotia, but all the time I knew him his home was in Berlin, New Hampshire. Probably the best surveyor of old lines in New England, he was—in his way— 5 a genius.

· · · · · ·

[2] The problem of surveying in the timberland of northern New England is one of the most difficult and fascinating things in the world. It's difficult because it consists largely of re-locating the old lines of original lots and ranges run by pioneers with crude compasses 10 as much as one hundred and seventy-five years ago. The early surveyors blazed or spotted the trees along these lines, and for corners set posts, marked trees, or piled up stones. They also blazed trees about the corners for "witnesses." Succeeding surveyors have re-spotted the lines infrequently, perhaps not oftener than once in twenty 15 years, and in many instances the original lines have not been renewed at all.

[3] When a tree is spotted with an axe the wood grows over the blaze in a few years and leaves nothing on the bark but a scar which
20 only an experienced woodsman can recognize. A novice either notices no spot at all or thinks that every scar he sees is a spot whether it's a hedgehog mark, a wind-gall, or just a natural blemish.

[4] The original lots, laid out by the proprietors of each township, classified by number in ranges and divisions, usually contained about
25 one hundred acres each and were described quite accurately and specifically by the early surveyors, who gave points of compass and definite distances in the title deeds; but as these lots were either split up or amalgamated with other lots, people grew very careless when conveying real estate, and fell into the habit of bounding land
30 by the names of the adjoining owners, as in the classic example Mr. Teare used to quote from a Vermont deed: "Bounded on the North by Brother Jim, on the West by Brother Bill, on the South by Sister Sal, and on the East by Mother."

[5] With the migration of farmers to the West, or to the cities,
35 immense areas of rural farm land reverted to the wilderness. Even many New Englanders do not realize how far this went and how extensively the forests have crept in over once-tilled fields. We have seen sites of villages silent in the woods, crumbling cellar holes through which great trees are growing, once proud highways which
40 are now only dim trails, and even a graveyard in Vermont from which three crops of pulp wood have been cut. Gone are the people who owned these farms, their most lasting works faded like old ink, their names nothing but an echo in the land records.

[6] Consequently, in these abandoned districts, now merely a
45 wilderness, a reference in an old deed such as "bounded on the North by land of Abijah Davis," which may have been perfectly plain to the contracting parties in 1860, means very little now. A surveyor must trace the title deeds in the registry, draw tentative diagrams and fit them together like a jigsaw puzzle, and somehow
50 or other get the chain of title back to the older deeds where references to compass courses and distances provide something definite to work on. By this research one may discover that Abijah Davis owned Lot Number 2 in the 3d Range and 1st Division and that the line in question was originally "North 85° East 88 Rods and
55 17 Links."

[7] To his task Mr. Teare brought very peculiar educational equipment. He never went beyond the seventh grade in school as he had to leave and go to work, but in his early years he had followed the

sea and had become skipper of a three-masted schooner, and thus he had learned navigation. 60

[8] As a surveyor he brought this navigation inland. It was really dead reckoning on land. A college-trained engineer would have thought his methods rule of thumb, but where such an engineer would have seen only woods, Mr. Teare could read them like an open book. For instance, he would go up to some old spruce on 65 which, once he'd pointed it out, you could see a small scar, then taking an axe he'd swing with great true blows; and as large flying chips began to litter the ground he would lay open the white flesh of the tree in a larger and larger gash. After a while he would begin to strike more slowly and carefully, now and then peering into the 70 opening, until finally he had disclosed an old blaze, black and flat with the original axemarks in it.

[9] Then he would fish up his glasses from his shirt and holding them to his eyes would count the annual rings of growth. More than once I have seen him cut out spots made more than a hundred 75 years before, and he once found spots on the old Masonian curved line, run in 1751 by Joseph Blanchard—the first line surveyed in New Hampshire. Mr. Teare had a spiritual affinity with the pioneer surveyors. He saw at a glance what they'd done, what they meant by their marks. He would sometimes look at a spot which definitely 80 had been made with an axe, glance around and growl: "Not a line, just a trapper's trail."

[10] He could follow not only the original spotted lines but the "lines of occupancy" as well, such as the trail of an old brush fence, all obvious remnants of which had disappeared at least twenty-five 85 years before. This he would do by noting the crooked growth of trees here and there along its course, or a stretch of hazel bushes (which are likely to grow up along the remains of a brush fence), or piles of moss-covered stones in which fence posts had once been set. Whenever Mr. Teare, scattering the leaf mould near one of these 90 stone heaps, uncovered a split ash rail, he would pick it up and fondle it lovingly. "They never rot," he would say with a solid approval of the wood itself and of the pioneer farmer who had taken pains to use it.

[11] For equipment he used an open-sight compass with about 95 a five-inch needle. There was no telescope on it but sight vanes instead with slits in them, and this compass rested not on a tripod, which would be too awkward in the woods, but rather on a single staff called a "Jacob staff." That was the kind of compass George

100 Washington and Abraham Lincoln used when they were land surveyors, but Mr. Teare's was considerably more accurate. He referred
affectionately to his compass as "Mary Jane" and almost always
called it an "instrument" instead of a "compass."

[12] When I first went with him he used a Gunter's chain, two
105 rods in length, but in later years a steel tape of the same length.
The Gunter's chain is an actual chain with real links and it can be
folded up instead of rolled. It is very durable; it can be used to help
a man go down over steep ledges, and will perform a hundred and
one odd jobs that it would be sacrilege to force on a tape, which
110 couldn't do them anyhow. He never wanted a chain or tape longer
than two rods because the ground he had to work on was so hilly
and rough. Somehow or other the Gunter's chain seemed to fit him
better than a tape.

[13] This type of surveying, difficult and requiring an analytical
115 mind as well as woodcraft, is a fascinating pursuit—a sort of treasure
hunt for old lines and corners. The problem was posed more than
a century ago by men who marked those lines and corners in the
wilderness and left cryptic directions on how to find them. In deserted
areas it is a search through a forest-buried civilization as dead as
120 the bottom layer of an Egyptian city. The fascination of it for Mr.
Teare never left him.

[14] I can see him now hunched over his compass while the
needle settles on the proper course, then standing behind it and
shouting directions to his axemen, while the two chainers bring up
125 the rear. He is full of anticipation at what he may find at a given
distance where he thinks a corner ought to be. He assiduously
examines the trees alongside the line to see if he is following the
old spotting, and now and then breaks into some rollicking song.
His joy in living radiates around him.

130 [15] Mr. Teare's genius, true to the proverb, consisted largely in
his capacity for taking infinite pains. He would always make sure of
a starting point that could not be questioned. Once he ran twenty-
four miles of trial line to locate one corner. Furthermore, he would
never let an obstacle or a series of them block him. If a swamp were
135 deep and cold he crossed it nevertheless, if towering cliffs barred his
way he scaled them, if blown down trees strewed his path he slashed
his way through, if a swollen river cut across a line he felled a tree
for a bridge and kept on going. He was absolutely indomitable and
he followed an old line as a hound follows a fox.

140 [16] He hated to see the woods cut by the companies for which
he was working, even though he well knew that timber like other

crops must be harvested. Often people asked him what he considered the most beautiful thing he had seen and he always gave them the same reply—sunset over the Adirondacks and Lake Champlain, from Mt. Mansfield. He worked most of a lifetime in the woods of northern New England and in spite of hardships and privation he never lost his love for these wild and wooded hills, for the silence of the deep forest in winter, the splendor of the mountains in the winey tang of autumn days.

[17] The infinite variety of his daily scenes of activity pleased him. One day he might stand among tall spruces high up on some mountain, sighting, far below, an isolated farmhouse on which he could take a "triangulation shot"; another day he might be following a hardwood ridge of beech and maple, or working in the bear-wallow sort of land that often lies atop a mountain, or following the stone walls of abandoned fields. Often he made a traverse survey of the great roaring brooks which come tumbling out of mountain ponds and cut their resounding way down deep ravines; he loved to drive a canoe across a lake or down a river through white water.

[18] Often he would pause at the summit of some hill. Then with his Jacob staff, he would point out to us the mountains and hills as they rolled away into blue distance, calling them by name and referring to certain jobs he had done on each. He knew them all as a father knows his children.

[For treatment of this selection, see p. 167.]

Building a Molecule to Specifications

ROBERT E. ROSE

[1] ALL of us have seen the juggler who entertains by throwing one brightly colored ball after the other into the air, catching each in turn and throwing it up again until he has quite a number moving from hand to hand. The system which he keeps in motion

From *Chemistry in Industry*, courtesy of The Chemical Foundation, Incorporated. Selection title by the Editors.

5 has an orderly structure. He changes it by selecting balls of different colors, altering the course or the sequence of the balls, or by
adding to or diminishing the number with which he plays.

[2] With this figure in mind let us use our imaginations. Before
us we have an assemblage of hundreds of thousands of jugglers vary-
10 ing in their degree of accomplishment; some handle only one ball,
others, more proficient, keep several in motion, and there are still
others of an astounding dexterity who play with an hundred or more
at once. The balls they handle are of ninety different colors and sizes.
The jugglers do not keep still but move about at varying rates; those
15 handling few and light balls move more quickly than those handling
many or heavier ones. These dancers bump into each other and when
they do so in certain cases they exchange some of the balls which they
are handling or one juggler may take all of those handled by another,
but in no case are the balls allowed to drop.

20   [3] Now imagine the moving group to become smaller and smaller
until the jugglers cease to be visible to us, even when they dance
under the highest power microscope. If someone who had not seen
them were to come to you and say that he proposed undertaking the
problem of finding out how the balls were moving and what were the
25 rules of the exchanges made, and further that he proposed utilizing
his knowledge to control what each minute juggler was doing, you
would tell him that his task was hopeless. If the chemist had listened
to such advice there would be no chemical industry and you would
lose so much that you would not be living in the way you are.

30   [4] The jugglers are the electromagnetic forces of matter, the balls
are the atoms, and each group in the hands of the juggler is a molecule
of a substance. In reality, of course, instead of each molecule being
represented by one unit we should multiply our jugglers by trillions
and trillions.

35   [5] The chemist, without even seeing them, has learned to handle
these least units of materials in such a way as to get the arrangements
which are more useful from those less useful. This power he has
acquired as the outcome of his life of research, his desire to understand, even though understanding brought him no material gain, but
40 mere knowledge. Because of his patience and devotion he has built a
number of industries; all have this in common—they serve to rearrange atoms of molecules or to collect molecules of one kind for the
service of man.

[6] The study of the substances of the earth's crust, of the air over
45 and of the waters under earth, which has led us to our present knowl-

edge of the electron, atom, and molecule, has been more adventurous than many a great journey made when the world was young and the frontier of the unknown was not remote from the city walls. Into the unknown world of things upon the "sea that ends not till the world's end" the man of science ventured, and he came back laden with 50 treasure greater than all the gold and precious stones ever taken from the earth. He gave these to others and he fared forth again without waving of flags, without the benediction of holy church, with no more than the courage of him who would win Nature, who had chosen a harder road than that of the great, made famous because of subduing 55 other men. He took no arms upon his quest, scarcely enough food to keep body and soul together, but instead, fire, glass, and that most astounding of all tools, the balance. As he pushed farther and farther on his great venture and as more and more joined his little band, he brought more and more back to those who did not understand in the 60 least what he was doing, until now the lives of all men are made easier if not happier by these strange, most useful, and most potent things of which he is the creator by reason of the understanding his journeys have given him—a power much greater than any mere black magic. 65

[7] This is the story of . . . [one] of the strange treasure[s] found by him in the far lands that are about us—[a] treasure found by learning the secret of the jugglers' dance—the dance of the least little things out of which all we know is fashioned.

[8] In Sicily and other parts of the earth where there are volcanoes, 70 lumps of a yellow crumbly "stone" are found, called brimstone (a corruption of *brennisteinn* or burning stone). This material was regarded as having curative properties; if it was burned in a house the bad odors of the sickroom of primitive times were suppressed. Also the alchemists found that it took away the metallic character of most 75 metals and they considered it very important in their search for the philosopher's stone, the talisman that was to turn all things to gold. The alchemists found also that sulfur, when burned over water, caused the water to become acid, and one of them found further that if the burning took place in the presence of saltpeter the acid which was 80 produced was much stronger; indeed, if concentrated it was highly corrosive. A useless find, it seemed, of interest only to the alchemist who hoped to become rich beyond the dreams of avarice, and immortal as the gods. But the chemist made this discovery of more importance to the condition of the human race than that of Columbus, 85 because by it he gave man a kingdom different from any that could

have been his by merely discovering what already existed upon earth. That is the wonder of the chemist's work; he finds that which is not upon the earth until he discovers it; just as the artist creates so does
90 the chemist. If he did not, there would be no chemical industry to write about.

[9] Having investigated this acid, he found it a most valuable new tool with which many new and interesting things could be made, and much could be done that before had been impossible. It became neces-
95 sary, then, if all men were to profit as the chemist always wishes them to do by his power, that sulfuric acid should be made easily and cheaply in large quantities. The first attempt at commercial manufacture was in 1740; before that each experimenter made what little he needed for himself. The process, that mentioned above, was carried
100 out in large glass balloons. It was a costly method and tedious. Then in 1746 lead chambers were substituted for the glass and the industry progressed rapidly.

•   •   •   •   •

[10] Of the three elements necessary [oxygen, hydrogen, sulphur], oxygen occurs uncombined in the air of which it forms one-fifth by
105 volume; it is also present combined with other elements in very large quantities in water, sand, and generally throughout the earth's crust, which is nearly half oxygen in a combined condition.

[11] The great storehouse of hydrogen on the earth is water, of which it forms one-ninth, by weight. Sulfur is not so widely distributed
110 in large quantities but it is very prevalent, being present in all plants and animals and also in such compounds as Epsom salts, gypsum, and Glauber's salt. In the free condition, i.e., as sulfur itself, it is found in volcanic regions and also where bacteria have produced it by decomposing the products of plant decay. There is one other source of
115 sulfur that is quite important, a compound with iron which contains so much sulfur that it will burn.

[12] The problem then was to take these substances and from them group the elements in such order as to produce sulfuric acid.

[13] Since sulfur burns readily, that is, unites with oxygen to form
120 sulfur dioxide, one might expect it to take up one more atom of oxygen from the air and become sulfur trioxide. It does, but so slowly that the process would never suffice for commercial production. But there is a way of speeding up the reaction which depends on using another molecule as a go-between, thus making the oxygen more active. The
125 principle is that of the relay. Suppose an out-fielder has to throw a ball a very long way. The chances are that the ball will not be very

true and that it may fall short of reaching the base. If there is a fielder between, he can catch the ball and get it to the base with much greater energy.

[14] The chemist uses as a go-between a catalyst (in one process), oxides of nitrogen. Molecules of this gas throw an oxygen atom directly and unfailingly into any sulfur dioxide molecule they meet, then equally certainly they seize the next oxygen atom that bumps into them and are ready for the next sulfur dioxide molecule. Since molecules in a gas mixture bump into each other roughly five billion times a second, there is a very good chance for the exchange to take place in the great lead chambers of approximately a capacity of 150,000 cubic feet into which are poured water molecules (steam), oxygen molecules (air), and sulfur dioxide, to which are added small quantities of the essential oxides of nitrogen.

[15] A corrosive, sour drizzle falls to the floor and this is chamber acid. It is sold in a concentration of 70 to 80 per cent. The weak chamber acid is good enough for a great many industrial purposes and is very cheap. If it is to be concentrated this must be done in vessels of lead up to a certain concentration and then in platinum or gold-lined stills if stronger acid is needed. Naturally this is expensive and every effort was made to find a method of making strong sulfuric acid without the necessity of this intermediate step. Especially was this true when the dyestuffs industry began to demand very large quantities of tremendously strong sulfuric acid which was not only 100 per cent but also contained a considerable amount of sulfur trioxide dissolved in it (fuming sulfuric acid).

[16] The difficulty was overcome by using another catalyst (platinum) in the place of the oxides of nitrogen. If sulfur dioxide and oxygen (air) are passed over the metal the two gases unite to form sulfur trioxide much more rapidly and in the absence of water. Since platinum is very expensive and its action depends on the surface exposed, it is spread on asbestos fibers and does not look at all like the shiny metal of the jeweler. This method is known as the contact process and the product is sulfur trioxide, which represents the highest possible concentration of sulfuric acid and can be led into ordinary oil of vitriol (98 per cent sulfuric acid) and then diluted with water and brought to 98 per cent acid or left as fuming acid, depending on the requirements of the case. The perfection of this process was the result of some very painstaking research because when it was tried at first it was found that the platinum soon lost its virtue as a catalyst, and it was also discovered that the reason for this was the presence

of arsenic in the sulfur dioxide. To get rid of every trace of arsenic is the hardest part of the contact process.

170   [17] Next time you visit a laboratory ask to be shown a bottle of concentrated sulfuric acid. You will see a colorless, oily liquid, much heavier than water, as you will notice if you lift the bottle. A little on your skin will raise white weals and then dissolve your body right away; paper is charred by it as by fire. When it touches water there is
175 a hissing.

[18] A dreadful oil, but its importance to industry is astonishing. If the art of making it were to be lost tomorrow we should be without steel and all other metals and products of the metallurgical industry; railroads, airplanes, automobiles, telephones, radios, reënforced con-
180 crete, all would go because the metals are taken from the earth by using dynamite made with sulfuric acid; and for the same reason construction work of all kinds, road and bridge building, canals, tunnels, and sanitary construction work would cease.

[19] We should have to find other ways to produce purified gaso-
185 line and lubricating oil. The textile industry would be crippled. We should find ourselves without accumulators, tin cans, galvanized iron, radio outfits, white paper, quick-acting phosphate fertilizers, celluloid, artificial leather, dyestuffs, a great many medicines, and numberless other things into the making of which this acid enters at some stage.
190   [20] If at some future date, however, all of our sulfur and all of our sulfur ores are burned up the chemist will yet find ways of making sulfuric acid. Possibly he may tap the enormous deposits of gypsum which exist in all parts of the earth. This has been done to some extent already but is not a process which is cheap enough to compete with
195 sulfuric acid made from sulfur.

•　•　•　•　•

[21] The brief story for which we have space indicates but very dimly the real interest and fascination the chemist has in handling matter. His knowledge has increased to such a point that he can build you a molecule almost to order to meet any specifications. To be with-
200 out any knowledge of chemistry is to go through life ignorant of some of the most interesting aspects of one's surroundings; and yet the acquisition of some knowledge of this subject is by no means hard. There are any number of books which tell the story in simple language if you do not wish to study the science intensively. On the other hand,
205 all that you need is a real interest and a willingness to think as you read.

Although we have been considering the paragraph as a unit, and discussing its attributes and its method or methods of development, it would be virtually impossible to find a piece of writing which is composed exclusively of paragraphs developed according to some one method. Since the topic sentence of each paragraph grows ultimately out of the guiding purpose, it is the guiding purpose which governs the organization of individual paragraphs and the combinations of types of paragraphs. For example, in a piece on how to drive a car, the guiding purpose might well necessitate the use of one or more paragraphs of definition (What is "power steering," an "emergency brake," "automatic transmission"?); paragraphs developed according to the principle of accumulation of detail (What are the minimal tools which every car should have?); paragraphs of comparison or contrast (What constitutes parking which will satisfy the requirements of the road test and what does not?); plus paragraphs which fall outside any rigid pattern but are governed by a step-by-step explanation of the process of driving.

1. Paragraph 1 of the Andler selection states the guiding purpose. What is it? Into how many parts is it divided?

2. Even though the selection you have read is excerpted from the original article, all the parts of the guiding purpose are treated in it. Find examples of paragraphs which deal with one or more of the subdivisions of the guiding purpose. What method or methods of development does each of the paragraphs you have selected employ? Show that these methods are suitable to the topic sentences and to the guiding purpose.

3. The first sentence of paragraph 2 states an effect for which a number of causes are given. How many paragraphs are devoted to these causes? What is the logical relation between the second and third paragraphs and paragraph 1? Justify the brevity of paragraph 3.

4. What two methods of development are combined in paragraph 5? Explain why the paragraph requires both methods. What is the function of the last sentence of the paragraph?

5. What is the relation between the method of development of paragraph 6 and the last sentence of paragraph 5?

6. Explain the statement that the primary purpose of paragraph 7 is to contribute to coherence.

7. Paragraph 8 contains contrast, exemplification, and elaboration of a step-by-step process. Identify each of these in the paragraph. Is paragraph 8 self-contained? If not, what larger unit is it part of? Where else in the selection is contrast used?

8. Which paragraph in the selection uses definition as its primary method of development? Why is it (or is it not) successfully handled?

9. Discuss the unity (or lack of it) in paragraph 13.

10. Justify the order of details in paragraph 14.

11. Paragraph 15 contains exemplification within its internal structure and is itself an example of a statement made in paragraph 1. Explain.

12. In "Building a Molecule to Specifications," find examples of all the major types of paragraph development. Which paragraphs in the selection combine more than one of these methods? What are the methods combined?

13. Which paragraphs in the Rose selection are devoted to or contain elaboration of a process? Discuss the effectiveness of these paragraphs, including in your discussion the criteria of clarity, logical order, and adequacy.

14. Break down the selection into groups of closely related paragraphs. Of these groups, which contain some paragraphs using one method of development and others using another method? What subtitle might be given to paragraphs 10 to 13?

15. Explain why paragraph 11 is adequate to its purpose, although it is only one sentence long.

16. What is the function of the last paragraph?

Alternate selections for the study of Paragraphs in Combination: Joseph Wood Krutch, "The Autobiography of My Friend Mark Van Doren"; Russell Lynes, "Teen-Agers Mirror Their Parents"; Erich Fromm, "Myths and Dreams."

Theme Assignment: Write a theme in which you explain a process familiar to you but assumed to be unfamiliar to the reader. Remember that you will not only take the reader step by step through the process in a logical order but may also have to define some of your terms, give examples and details, explain cause-effect relations. For example, if you are explaining how to make a salad, you will not only tell the reader what to do first, second, third, and so on. You may also want to define the word "chapon" (a slice of bread rubbed with garlic), list some of the trimmings and condiments which may be added to vary a basic dressing, explain the effect of vinegar and salt on lettuce or the effect of tomato slices on the dressing. Thus your theme should utilize several different methods of paragraph development.

The Sentence

Types of
Sentences

Mother and
Our Wicked Mare

CLARENCE DAY

[1] MOTHER never thought of the horse as the friend and companion of man. She looked at all horses suspiciously. Perhaps they were not wild animals, in the sense in which lions and zebras were wild, but still there was something strange about them. They weren't really tame, like our dogs. She loved dogs. She liked ponies too, they 5 were more our own size, but horses were too large to be trusted, and they had ironshod feet.

[2] Once in a while she grew fond of some special horse after she had watched it for years, but even then she never undertook to drive it herself. Driving was a man's job. That didn't mean that she thought 10 men in general were good drivers, however. Mother hadn't any more confidence in men in general than she had in horses. Men were always assuring her that they knew how to do this or that, when they didn't at all. If it had been safe to do so, she would have liked to trust herself in their hands, it would have been so convenient, for as she was a 15

woman she felt that she had to have certain things done for her. But men, although stronger, were childish. They greatly over-estimated their ability as drivers, for instance. All of them firmly believed that they understood horses, whereas Mother knew better. When she saw
20 a horse and a man having trouble, she privately bet on the horse.

[3] In the nineties everybody used horses—if in no other way at least in horse-cars and buses. Our family needed several every summer when we lived in the country. One was reserved solely as a saddle-horse for Father to ride. Father rode early every morning before
25 breakfast and then took a train to the city. The other horses were used for all sorts of things. What with catching trains, mornings, and meeting them again, afternoons, and going for the mail, or taking some of us down to the beach, or trotting along the dusty country roads with Mother when she paid an afternoon call on some friend three or four
30 miles away, or when she went to the village to shop, our horses were kept pretty busy, and when one of them had to be turned out to rest, it was hard on the others.

[4] Mother at last went to Father about it. She said that things had come to a point where we had to have one more horse.

35 [5] Father said, "The trouble with you, Vinnie, is that you don't use enough forethought. You don't plan these things out. With a little careful management you can get along with what we have now."

[6] Mother replied that there wasn't a woman on earth who could plan every minute, and she'd like to see forethought pull the station-
40 wagon when Brownie went lame, but if we used Father's saddle-horse in the dog-cart perhaps that would do.

[7] From Father's point of view this was blasphemous. "Any time that I can't have even one horse in condition to ride," he told Mother, "I'll sell the whole lot of them, hide and hair, and the family can
45 walk. Do 'em good."

[8] He got thinking things over after this conversation however, and made up his mind that he'd better do something about it and look around for some decent animal that could be got cheap. He heard of one soon at the club, a dark brown, muscular mare.

50 [9] The member of the club who owned her had gone abroad and couldn't be reached. He had posted the mare for sale with the cryptic phrase, "Warranted sound." The usual guarantee, when there was any, was "Warranted sound, kind and willing," but we thought that per-haps the omission was inadvertent. The price was low. Father bought
55 her.

[10] This mare's name was Uarda, a strange name, but somehow it

fitted her. We heard later that an Egyptian princess named Uarda, of evil repute, had lived a bad life in some dynasty centuries back. Whether Uarda the mare had come from Egypt too, nobody knew. She looked it, however. She looked like the horse of some genie in the *Arabian Nights*. She was slithery, bony and lean, and her coat had a glitter, and her eyes were unnaturally greenish and wild and unfathomable.

[11] There was plenty of work in her. She never went lame or got tired. She seemed made of steel. Sudden sights or sounds that made other horses shy, Uarda ignored. She was wholly without fear, and there wasn't an ounce of love in her either. She was oblivious of the Day family, and not interested in her surroundings.

[12] O'Dowd the coachman was frankly afraid of her. "She's always brooding, sir," he whispered to Father, as though she could understand what he said and revenge herself on him. She certainly had a remote and contemptuous look.

[13] Uarda's contempt could be seen in her eye. Her hatred she expressed with her tail. All carriage horses were docked in those days, many of them too much, but Uarda from O'Dowd's point of view hadn't been docked enough. She had an extra long bone in her tail, he explained, and it had only been shortened a trifle. And the muscle in her tail, which was strong as steel, hadn't been nicked. The purpose of nicking the under muscle was to weaken it, so that a horse's little bobbed tail would stand cocked up and look stylish, and aside from looks there was a practical advantage to this, because it prevented a horse from catching a rein under his tail and clamping it down. When that happened, he couldn't be reined in or guided, and now and then that led to a runaway or some bad collision.

[14] Humanitarians were always denouncing men who docked horses' tails. A horse with a docked tail was helpless in fly-time, they argued, and when it was chopped off it hurt. Father pished at these arguments. He said that it wasn't his fault if there were flies in the world, and that nobody wept over him when his teeth were chopped by the dentist.

[15] He wouldn't have a horse docked himself though. He simply bought them that way. When O'Dowd wanted Uarda's tail shortened, Father wouldn't allow it. O'Dowd shook his head over this. He said we'd live to regret it.

[16] We came to see what he meant. As Uarda sullenly trotted along, thinking of sin, or black magic, she would flail her tail round and round powerfully, like a propeller. Sooner or later, no matter how

careful O'Dowd was, she'd catch a rein under it, and hold that rein
tight as a vice. With some horses you could watch till the muscle
100 relaxed for a moment and then vigorously yank the rein out, but no
one could do this with Uarda. The only thing to do was to reach over
the dashboard and yank at her tail, and yank hard with all your
strength too, and yank over and over, hoping that she wouldn't lash
out and kick you before you got the rein loose. This was an undigni-
105 fied performance to go through, and O'Dowd felt it shamed him in
public.

[17] What mortified him still more was the way Mother behaved at
such moments. At the very first sign of trouble Mother's one idea was
to get out of the carriage just as quick as she could. She couldn't
110 jump, her skirts were too long and voluminous and there were too
many petticoats under them, but she could and did shout to O'Dowd
to stop, at the top of her voice, and then gather up her dress in one
hand and clutch at the arm of the seat and feel around with her foot
for the inadequate little round metal steps, which always seemed so
115 high from the ground when she hadn't any horse-block to step out
onto, and then while the springy surrey was shaking, and giving a bit
on one side, she would precariously descend in a hurry, getting dust
or mud on her skirts from the wheel, and more on her high buttoned
shoes in the old-fashioned dirt road.

120 [18] Standing there in safety she would stare at O'Dowd while he
yanked. She would also make comments. When this happened way off
on some deserted road it wasn't so bad, but sometimes it happened
on Purchase Street in Rye, where other coachmen were watching, or
outside old Mr. Raser's store opposite the station in Harrison. "Mercy
125 on us, what takes you so *long*, O'Dowd?" Mother would cry. "If you
can't drive any better than that, why don't you say so?"

[19] O'Dowd was a good-natured soul, but he knew he could drive
as well as most coachmen, and he used to get silently exasperated on
these occasions. It was useless for him, though, to attempt to lay the
130 blame upon Uarda, or to say he had never seen such a horse in all
his born days. "Never mind about all your born days, O'Dowd,"
Mother would tell him impatiently. "That horse knows more than you
do, this minute, and I should think that you'd be ashamed to sit there
and admit it."

135 [20] As O'Dowd had never even dreamt of admitting it, this kind
of attack used to stagger him. "I know as much as any horse in the
stable, Mum," he would begin, in confusion.

[21] "But you ought to know *more* than an animal!" Mother would

interrupt swiftly. "That's what we pay you your wages for, O'Dowd. You're a *man*, not a horse. If you don't know any more than our 140 horses you ought not to be driving them. It really isn't safe for me to go out with you."

[22] "Not an accident have I ever had on my soul, Mrs. Day, in all the twenty years that ————"

[23] "You'll have one this very minute if you can't get that rein 145 out," Mother would interrupt sharply.

[24] As O'Dowd knew that this was highly probable he would concentrate upon Uarda, and when he had got her under control again Mother would climb back into the carriage, still talking, and off they would go. 150

[25] Somehow O'Dowd never seemed to feel any resentment toward Mother, after a scene of this sort. He understood Mother. His hostility was all toward that mare. On Uarda's bad days he got into such a bitter state, as he drove her about, that he used to carry on a one-sided conversation with her, in a low growling mutter. "Oho! 155 That's the way of it, is it? Trying it on me again! Ye black-hearted Eye-gyptian! Bad scran to ye, ye limb of the Divil, ye!"

[26] After a while he invented an arrangement of buckles and straps, which moored Uarda's tail to the shafts. This contraption left her tail just leeway enough for her to arch it but kept her from 160 flailing it around or getting it over the reins. She was in a cold fury about it. O'Dowd wore a broad grin.

[27] These moorings were so elaborate that they were unsightly, however. They looked very odd. Mother complained that everyone stared at them, which was perfectly true. People even asked questions. 165 Mr. Read, who was a judge at the horseshow, and who had supposed himself to be familiar with every kind of harness there was, couldn't get his eyes off them when Mother went to call on his wife and when he came forward to help her get out at his door. "Ah," he said, staring fixedly at the bright silver buckle in the middle of Uarda's slick tail, 170 and the leather shrouds and stays that led down from it to either shaft, "Ah! May I ask what this—er—? Why this ————?"

[28] "Oh, don't pay any attention to that, Mr. Read," Mother answered. "Our coachman seems to feel he can't drive without it. It's just some idea of O'Dowd's." And she hurried up the piazza steps, 175 leaving O'Dowd red and speechless, and taking Mr. Read with her, so mystified by what he had seen and so baffled for the moment by Mother that he became speechless too.

[29] As for Father, he said it was a disgusting arrangement, the

180 first time he saw it, and he ordered O'Dowd to "remove that infernal
rigging at once." But the fact remained that when we used them those
straps were effective, and every time we went out without them, we
got into trouble. Uarda never actually ran away when she got a rein
under her tail, but she never would quite admit that she wasn't going
185 to bolt, and she had such a wicked look about her that we knew things
were dangerous. We all gradually came to tolerate letting O'Dowd
strap her up, even Father. There was really only one safe alternative,
when he left O'Dowd home and drove us around in the low surrey
himself, and that was to hold the reins up very high, at the level
190 almost of his nose. Father couldn't and wouldn't do that.

[30] One day Father and Mother and George and I were out in the
surrey. Father was driving of course, and I was sitting beside him on
the front seat. Uarda was in a vile mood. Her tail strained at
O'Dowd's straps and buckles. It writhed like a snake. Two or three
195 miles from home she triumphantly tore it loose. "Oh, oh!" Mother
wailed.

[31] "Be quiet, confound it," said Father. "Clarence, can you strap
it down again?"

[32] I got out and tried but I couldn't strap it securely enough.
200 Only O'Dowd knew the secret. No matter how I adjusted the buckles
and hauled on the straps, Uarda contemptuously flicked her tail out.
"Take it off altogether," Father ordered. "We'll never get home at this
rate."

[33] "I want to get out then," said Mother. "I'd much rather walk."
205 [34] Father gritted his teeth. "Sit still," he said sharply. "I've
driven horses since I was a boy."

[35] Back-seat driving was invented long before motors, and when
Mother was nervous she had a really deadly gift for this art. She tried
to control herself that afternoon, at Father's repeated requests, but she
210 couldn't. Uarda's tail was too much for her.

[36] "I only bought this horse to please your mother," Father said
in a loud, oratorical tone, as though he were making a speech, addressing his sons and the landscape in general as Uarda trotted along, "and
if I ever saw any animal that came straight from hell ———"
215 [37] "She's swishing it, Clare," Mother called to him.

[38] "She can swish and be hanged," Father said, feeling that he
had his hands full, fore and aft, with these two unmanageable females
who were spoiling his drive.

[39] "Look out! Look out, Clare dear!"
220 [40] "Vinnie, will you keep still!"

[41] "I'm trying to, darling," screamed Mother, "but that awful horse ——— Oh! Oh! Look *out!*"

[42] Father cut at Uarda's flanks with the whip.

[43] "Clare! *Do* please be careful!"

[44] "I *am* being careful. Be quiet." 225

[45] "There she goes again! Oh Clare, let me out!"

[46] "See here," Father said to her sternly, turning half-around in his seat, "if you cannot control yourself ———"

[47] Swish! Uarda's tail caught the rein.

[48] Father swore and leaned forward and pulled on it. Uarda 230 came to a stop. We were on our way up a long hill at the moment, and Father had just begun walking her. Luckily for us, she now decided it was a good place to rest.

[49] Father jerked at the rein twice more—once cautiously, and once with more force. Uarda held it clamped tight to her rump. Her 235 ears went back. She snorted.

[50] "Oh mercy! Let me get out of this!" Mother shrieked, and climbed down onto the road. "Come on, Georgie!"

[51] George jumped out beside her. It was a narrow road with a ditch on each side. She scrambled across the ditch to safety, and stood 240 on the steep, grassy bank.

[52] Father felt deeply insulted at this lack of confidence in him. His blood surged to his face, his eyes popped with passion. He stood up, facing a little sidewise, took the rein in both hands, set his jaws, and gave one mighty yank. At that very instant Uarda, with the skill 245 of a demon, let go. Father fell over backward out of the surrey and crashed into the ditch.

[53] Mother screamed.

[54] I leaned over the dashboard and got the reins. George ran to help Father. Uarda tossed her head and stood still. 250

[55] Father rose from the ditch, muddy yet somehow majestic, and said to us, "It was your mother."

[56] "Why, *Clare!*" Mother shouted indignantly from the opposite bank.

A piece of writing may be well organized and adequately paragraphed, but if its sentences are not both grammatically correct and rhetorically effective, the writing cannot be said to meet a reasonable college standard. The ability to write grammatically correct sentences—sentences in which the subject agrees with the verb in number, sentences in which independent clauses are correctly connected, sentences in which verbals are not used as though they were finite verbs, and so on—is idealistically considered to be a minimum requirement for college entrance; realistically, college handbooks have sections devoted to the problems of grammatical correctness of sentences.

But grammatically correct sentences are not enough to make good writing. The individual sentence should communicate clearly and efficiently. Words should not be wasted, for, as Alexander Pope says in his "Essay on Criticism,"

> Words are like leaves; and where they most abound,
> Much fruit of sense beneath is rarely found.

The relations among the parts of the idea expressed should be reflected in the structure of the sentence. The parts of the sentence should follow normal English order, and there should be variety in structure from sentence to sentence. In addition, sentence rhythms should be not only pleasing to the reader but also, when relevant, functional as well.

One of the advantages of English as a language for the communication of ideas of some complexity is the flexibility of its sentence structure. This very flexibility, however, presents the writer with the constant necessity of having to decide which of the several possible ways of saying something—of constructing a sentence—is best for his purposes. For example, each of the following sentences communicates essentially the same idea, but notice the considerable differences in structure, and consequently, in effect among them.

a. The president of the college wanted to help the students and he wanted to please the faculty too and consequently he decided to appoint several highly trained student counselors who would guide students and in this way relieve faculty members of some of their heavy work programs.

b. Wanting to give students good guidance and to reduce the work load of the faculty, the president of the college appointed several highly trained student counselors.

c. Several highly trained student counselors were appointed by the president of the college to give students guidance and thus take the counseling burden off the overworked faculty.

d. The overworked faculty was relieved of the burden of student counseling when the president of the college appointed several highly trained student counselors, much to the delight of the student body.

1. Which of the sentences communicates most efficiently? least efficiently? What are the specific differences in content among the sentences? In which sentence or sentences is the relation among the various parts of the idea communicated not explicitly clear? On what grounds would you decide which of the sentences is best?

For the purposes of rhetorical analysis of sentences, that is, the close study of the structure of sentences to understand their over-all effectiveness (or lack of effectiveness), it is helpful to know the following standard classification of sentences.

Simple: a sentence consisting of a single main clause:

    a. The train left.

    b. The book fell from the man's hands.

    c. The duke and duchess loved and obeyed their king and queen.

Compound: a sentence consisting of two or more main clauses:

    a. The woman walked, but the man ran.

    b. There were two chairs and a table in the room; the walls and floor were entirely bare.

    c. "Give me liberty, or give me death."

Complex: a sentence consisting of one main clause and one or more subordinate clauses:

    a. When it rained, we stayed indoors.

    b. Students sometimes fail examinations because they don't read the questions carefully enough.

    c. After the war had ended but before the soldiers had returned from the combat areas, the heads of the warring countries became involved in the beginnings of the "cold war."

Compound-Complex: a sentence consisting of two or more main clauses and at least one subordinate clause:

    a. When dinner was over, the adults settled into somnolent conversation and the children began to play in front of the house.

    b. The clock struck; the man shuddered because this was the moment he had most feared.

    c. Living on a secluded lake shore is rewarding; it gives a man time to take stock of himself when he is closest to nature.

Just as some ideas can be developed in a paragraph by one method rather than another, with the writer scarcely aware of having made a choice of method, so many sentences fall into one or another of the normal English patterns almost automatically. Yet a knowledge of the different types of sentences and an awareness of the differences in effect among them will aid the writer in understanding the effectiveness of prose he reads and in achieving greater effectiveness in his own writing; his very awareness of the potentialities of English sentences can increase his ability to achieve clarity and variety in his own sentences. A writer does not usually decide to write a simple sentence or a compound-complex sentence: he expresses himself in sentences which come naturally to him. In revising his writing, however, to make it clearer or more efficient or more effective, he may well decide to combine two simple sentences into a compound sentence, say, and subsequently to change the compound sentence into a complex sentence both because the content demands the subordination of one of the parts to another and because he may already have too many compound sentences in the paragraph.

2. Four of the six sentences in the first paragraph of the Clarence Day selection are simple; identify them. Why do you suppose so skillful a writer as Day piled up so many simple sentences in his first paragraph? In other words, what effect is achieved through the simple sentences? How do you classify the remaining two sentences in the paragraph?

3. Which sentences in paragraph 2 are simple? Had they been combined with any other sentences in the paragraph, what would have been gained or lost?

4. Classify each of the sentences in paragraph 3, and be prepared to identify main and subordinate clauses where relevant.

5. Combine the sentences in paragraph 4 into a single complex sentence. Which is more effective, your sentence or Day's two sentences? Why?

6. Without changing word order, make the single sentence in paragraph 6 into three complex sentences; how have you changed the effect of the paragraph?

7. What effect or effects are achieved through the simple sentences in paragraphs 7 through 9? (To answer this question adequately, you will have to consider all the sentences in these paragraphs.)

8. Compare the following rewriting of paragraph 10 with the original: precisely what is gained or lost by each of the changes made?

> This mare's name was Uarda, a strange name, which somehow fitted her. We heard later that an Egyptian princess named Uarda, of evil repute, had lived a bad life in some dynasty centuries back; whether Uarda the mare had come from Egypt too, nobody knew, but she looked it. Looking like the horse of some genie in the *Arabian Nights*, she was slithery, bony, and lean. Her coat had a glitter. Her eyes were unnaturally greenish and wild and unfathomable.

9. Make the first three sentences of paragraph 11 into a compound sentence, then into a complex sentence, and then into a compound-complex sentence. What changes has the meaning undergone as a result of each of the changes you have made? Which of the versions (including Day's three sentences) is most effective? Why?

10. It should be acknowledged that Clarence Day's sentence structure is as erratic and unpredictable as Clarence Day's father. For

example, his punctuation of compound (or what at first glance appear to be pure compound) sentences often fails to give even a passing nod to a semicolon. Also, some of his sentences are so long that you might have wondered how your instructor survived reading them. Select three sentences which seem to you to fall into the category of "erratic" in punctuation and structure. Determine the type of each sentence. Decide whether each is effective and appropriate in context; make your criteria clear.

Alternate selection for the study of Types of Sentences: Thor Heyerdahl, "The Storm."

Assignment: The characters of both Mother and Father are clearly etched in "Mother and Our Wicked Mare." Write a paragraph of from eight to ten sentences on your impressions of either Mother or Father or both; presumably you will write your first version without thinking particularly of the various types of sentences you have been studying. Analyze each of your sentences to determine its type; wherever necessary, thoroughly revise your sentences to make them as efficient, clear, and effective as you can. Make a list of the types of sentences you used in your first version and in your revised version. Be prepared to submit both paragraphs and lists to your instructor.

Variety of Structure

The Spirit of Man

WILLIAM FAULKNER

[1] I FEEL that this award was not made to me as a man, but to my work—a life's work in the agony and sweat of the human spirit, not for glory and least of all for profit, but to create out of the materials of the human spirit something which did not exist before.
5 So this award is only mine in trust. It will not be difficult to find a dedication for the money part of it commensurate with the purpose and significance of its origin. But I would like to do the same with the acclaim too, by using this moment as a pinnacle from which I might be listened to by the young men and women already dedicated to the
10 same anguish and travail, among whom is already that one who will some day stand here where I am standing.

[2] Our tragedy today is a general and universal physical fear so long sustained by now that we can even bear it. There are no longer problems of the spirit. There is only the question: When will I be
15 blown up? Because of this, the young man or woman writing today has forgotten the problems of the human heart in conflict with itself which alone can make good writing because only that is worth writing about, worth the agony and the sweat.

Speech of acceptance upon the award of the Nobel Prize for Literature, delivered in Stockholm on December 10, 1950. From *The Faulkner Reader*. Random House, Inc., publishers. Selection title by the Editors.

[3] He must learn them again. He must teach himself that the basest of all things is to be afraid; and, teaching himself that, forget it forever, leaving no room in his workshop for anything but the old verities and truths of the heart, the old universal truths lacking which any story is ephemeral and doomed—love and honor and pity and pride and compassion and sacrifice. Until he does so, he labors under a curse. He writes not of love but of lust, of defeats in which nobody loses anything of value, of victories without hope and, worst of all, without pity or compassion. His griefs grieve on no universal bones, leaving no scars. He writes not of the heart but of the glands.

[4] Until he relearns these things, he will write as though he stood among and watched the end of man. I decline to accept the end of man. It is easy enough to say that man is immortal simply because he will endure: that when the last ding-dong of doom has clanged and faded from the last worthless rock hanging tideless in the last red and dying evening, that even then there will still be one more sound: that of his puny inexhaustible voice, still talking. I refuse to accept this. I believe that man will not merely endure: he will prevail. He is immortal, not because he alone among creatures has an inexhaustible voice, but because he has a soul, a spirit capable of compassion and sacrifice and endurance. The poet's, the writer's, duty is to write about these things. It is his privilege to help man endure by lifting his heart, by reminding him of the courage and honor and hope and pride and compassion and pity and sacrifice which have been the glory of his past. The poet's voice need not merely be the record of man, it can be one of the props, the pillars to help him endure and prevail.

Structures of sentences should make sense, but they are not inviolable. There is always more than one way to say something, usually more than one effective way. And sentences, though they stand alone grammatically, do not literally "stand alone." They appear, most frequently, in combination with other sentences, and they affect one another. Thus, no matter how "right" a simple sentence may be for expressing a particular thought, an unrelieved string of simple sentences is tiresome; each loses some of its effectiveness in combination with so many others like itself—just as an Easter bonnet, strikingly original at home, loses some of its effectiveness in the Easter parade if there are too many others just like it. On the other hand, a simple sentence is heightened in effectiveness if it appears in combination with sentences of more complicated structure. At the same time, the sentences of more complicated structure are more effective if they are well spaced or paced. Too many unrelieved sentences of any one structure call attention away from the thought to the structure itself; too many extremely involved sentences become heavy and cumbersome.

Variety can be achieved not only through the functional mingling of types of sentences but also by varying the order of the parts within the sentence. The most elementary order is subject, verb, object. But if sentence after sentence follows this sequence, the result is singsong, and this is not the only possible sequence of English sentences. (The old man cried, "Fire!" *or* "Fire!" cried the old man.) Note that since inversion affects emphasis it is a useful device for pointing up precise meaning and should be used for this purpose as well as to attain variety. It is also often desirable to defer the main clause and open with a dependent element, such as a phrase or dependent clause; to separate the main elements from one another by the inclusion of a dependent element; or to compound one or another of the major elements. A periodic sentence (in which the basic meaning is not complete until the end or near the end) may supply variety when introduced among several loose sentences (in which the basic meaning is made clear well before the end). Occasionally, where it can logically be introduced without sounding forced or false, an exclamation, question, or even command may help to break the monotony of repeated declarative sentences. But all of these methods of varying the sentence structure must be used judiciously; they must further the meaning, not merely embellish it.

1. William Faulkner has often been criticized for the length and complexity of his sentences. Does this criticism apply to his speech of acceptance of the Nobel Prize for Literature? Why or why not?

2. Determine the type of every sentence in the speech, and comment on your findings with respect to variety.

3. Select a passage (it need not be more than two or three sentences) which you think illustrates the effectiveness of varied sentence structures. Justify your selection.

4. State in your own words the guiding purpose of the speech. What idea or ideas has each paragraph contributed to this guiding purpose? Which sentences are irrelevant to it?

5. Rewrite paragraph 4 of the speech, using only simple sentences. Comment on the relative effectiveness of your paragraph and Faulkner's.

6. Explain why Faulkner is able to use the abstract terms "love and honor and pity and pride and compassion and sacrifice" in paragraph 3 without defining them. Why is or is not this list monotonous? Why does he make another such list in paragraph 4? In what ways does it differ from the list in paragraph 3? In what respects is it the same? Account for these similarities and differences.

7. Do the words "among whom is already that one who will some day stand here where I am standing" (paragraph 1) violate sentence unity? Why or why not?

8. Why did Faulkner say, "He writes not of the heart but of the glands" (paragraph 3) rather than "He writes of the glands and not of the heart"?

9. Why does Faulkner begin the fourth sentence with the word "But"? Isn't this an error?

10. Which is more effective, and why:

   a. "There is only the question: When will I be blown up?"

   b. There is only the question of when each of us will be blown up.

11. In paragraph 3, why does Faulkner say "teaching himself that"? Hasn't he just said that?

12. In the next sentence of the same paragraph, do you think Faulkner put the dependent clause at the beginning merely to vary the sentence structure? What other reasons for doing so can you think of?

Alternate selections for the study of Variety of Structure: Hans Zinsser, "Mamie"; Erich Fromm, "Myths and Dreams"; James Agee, "Knoxville: Summer 1915."

Theme Assignment: ". . . the young man or woman writing today has forgotten the problems of the human heart in conflict with itself which alone can make good writing because only that is worth writing about, worth the agony and the sweat," Faulkner says. The human heart, today as always, is the arena of many conflicts: Should one strive to perfect a talent at the possible sacrifice of personal relations? Should a young person move away from home, go away to study or to live, or remain with or near his parents? Should one give up a love because someone else might be hurt by it? Is it possible to understand and, understanding, to relinquish a self-destructive habit or way of life? Should a student who has embarked upon a premedical course largely because his father is a doctor and who discovers that what he really wants to study is classical Greek change his major? These questions are not easily answered; perhaps some of them have no one right answer. But they involve emotional conflict and are fairly easily illustrated.

Write a theme on a "problem of the human heart in conflict with itself," one of these or another which this list may suggest to you. Be as specific as you can about the conflict; you will surely want to illustrate it by at least one example. (Your whole theme may be devoted to a single example.) You may or may not resolve the conflict, depending upon your own conviction. Be sure to make use of the principle of writing under consideration in this section—variety of sentence structure. And don't forget that you are *expected* to experience "agony and sweat."

Length

FROM *The Mowing of a Field*

HILAIRE BELLOC

WHEN one does anything anew, after so many years, one
fears very much for one's trick or habit. But all things once learnt
are easily recoverable, and I very soon recovered the swing and power
of the mower. Mowing well and mowing badly—or rather not mowing
at all—are separated by very little; as is also true of writing verse, of 5
playing the fiddle, and of dozens of other things, but of nothing more
than of believing. For the bad or young or untaught mower without
tradition, the mower Promethean, the mower original and contemptuous of the past, does all these things: He leaves great crescents of
grass uncut. He digs the point of the scythe hard into the ground with 10
a jerk. He loosens the handles and even the fastening of the blade.
He twists the blade with his blunders, he blunts the blade, he chips it,
dulls it, or breaks it clean off at the tip. If anyone is standing by he
cuts him in the ankle. He sweeps up into the air wildly, with nothing
to resist his stroke. He drags up earth with the grass, which is like 15
making the meadow bleed. But the good mower who does things just
as they should be done and have been for a hundred thousand years,
falls into none of these fooleries. He goes forward very steadily, his
scythe-blade just barely missing the ground, every grass falling; the
swish and rhythm of his mowing are always the same. 20

"The Mowing of a Field," from *Hills and the Sea,* by Hilaire Belloc. By
permission of Methuen and Co., Ltd., London.

There is nothing intrinsically good or bad about sentences of any particular length. Indeed, there are few rules about sentence length that stand up under scrutiny. The most valid rule seems to be "It depends . . . ." It depends on what you have to say; it depends on the purpose for which you are writing; it depends on your audience. The same writer may employ a preponderance of short sentences in one situation and of long ones in another. For example, no sentence in Faulkner's speech runs to more than about sixty-five words, whereas in many of Faulkner's novels occasional sentences run to well over two hundred words. Granted, these are extreme examples. And granted, too, that no piece of writing would be effective with all short or all long sentences. There must be some variety. But this does not mean padding or chopping apart thoughts that belong together. Nor does it follow that simple sentences are always short; and compound, complex, or compound-complex sentences always long. "I came, I saw, I conquered" contains three independent clauses, yet there are few shorter announcements in history.

What *can* be said is that sentences should not be pointlessly or needlessly long or short. There is obviously no point in "The red-headed man driving the old green Ford truck, battered from many trips and many accidents at home or on highways from one coast to another and up and down the seaboard from Canada to Mexico, grasped the broken steering wheel tightly in both his work-roughened but still youthful-looking hands and squinted into the lights of the oncoming car." Or in "The man had red hair. He was driving a Ford truck. It was old and green. It was battered from many trips. It had also been in many accidents. Some of these accidents took place at home. Others occurred on highways. The truck had been across the country many times. It had gone from Canada to Mexico, etc."

Appropriateness, then, is the best rule of thumb for sentence length—appropriateness to meaning, purpose, and audience. Some variety, of course, is desirable.

1. Do you consider the typical sentence length in the Belloc selection short, average, or long? Explain your answer in terms of meaning, tone, and probable audience.

2. Does Belloc achieve variety in the length of his sentences? in their structure? What method or methods does he use to vary the structure?

3. In the sentences which begin "He leaves . . . ," "He digs . . . ," "He loosens . . . ," "He twists . . . ," "He sweeps . . . ," "He drags . . . ," Belloc appears to be disregarding or maybe violating any principle of variety. What do you think is his purpose in doing so? By what means, if any, does he achieve variety among these sentences?

4. What does he mean by "but of nothing more than of believing"?

5. What method or methods of paragraph development has Belloc employed? Explain your answer in some detail.

6. How do you account for the distribution of sentence lengths? Why are the shortest sentences in the middle of the paragraph?

7. Rewrite the sentences about the "bad or young or untaught mower," making them into one compound-complex sentence. Why is this less effective than Belloc's sentences?

Alternate selections for the study of Length: Thomas H. Huxley, "Thinking like a Scientist"; E. B. White, "Two Letters, Both Open."

Assignment: Write separate sets of directions for reaching your home from the center of the nearest town or city for each of the following:

a. a kindergarten class
b. your grandfather, who lived in that town as a child and hasn't been back since
c. a travel folder
d. a sociologist on a field trip

Remember that your sentence lengths will vary from one set of directions to another as your audience and tone vary.

Parallelism

The Happy Valley

SAMUEL JOHNSON

[1] HERE the sons and daughters of Abissinia lived only to know the soft vicissitudes of pleasure and repose, attended by all that were skilful to delight, and gratified with whatever the senses can enjoy. They wandered in gardens of fragrance, and slept in the
5 fortresses of security. Every art was practised to make them pleased with their own condition. The sages who instructed them told them of nothing but the miseries of publick life, and described all beyond the mountains as regions of calamity, where discord was always raging, and where man preyed upon man.

10 [2] To heighten their opinion of their own felicity, they were daily entertained with songs, the subject of which was the *happy valley*. Their appetites were excited by frequent enumerations of different enjoyments, and revelry and merriment was the business of every hour from the dawn of morning to the close of even.

15 [3] These methods were generally successful; few of the Princes had ever wished to enlarge their bounds, but passed their lives in full conviction that they had all within their reach that art or nature could bestow, and pitied those whom fate had excluded from this seat of tranquility, as the sport of chance, and the slaves of misery.

20 [4] Thus they rose in the morning, and lay down at night, pleased with each other and with themselves, all but Rasselas, who, in the

From *The History of Rasselas*, by Samuel Johnson, in *Rasselas, Poems, and Selected Prose*, ed. Bertrand H. Bronson (Rinehart Editions; New York: Rinehart & Company, Inc., 1958). Selection title by the Editors.

twenty-sixth year of his age, began to withdraw himself from their pastimes and assemblies, and to delight in solitary walks and silent meditation. He often sat before tables covered with luxury, and forgot to taste the dainties that were placed before him: he rose abruptly in 25 the midst of the song, and hastily retired beyond the sound of musick. His attendants observed the change and endeavoured to renew his love of pleasure: he neglected their officiousness, repulsed their invitations, and spent day after day on the banks of rivulets sheltered with trees, where he sometimes listened to the birds in the branches, sometimes 30 observed the fish playing in the stream, and anon cast his eyes upon the pastures and mountains filled with animals, of which some were biting the herbage, and some sleeping among the bushes.

[5] This singularity of his humour made him much observed. One of the Sages, in whose conversation he had formerly delighted, fol- 35 lowed him secretly, in hope of discovering the cause of his disquiet. Rasselas, who knew not that any one was near him, having for some time fixed his eyes upon the goats that were browsing among the rocks, began to compare their condition with his own.

[6] "What," said he, "makes the difference between man and all the 40 rest of the animal creation? Every beast that strays beside me has the same corporal necessities with myself; he is hungry, and crops the grass, he is thirsty, and drinks the stream, his thirst and hunger are appeased, he is satisfied and sleeps; he rises again and he is hungry, he is again fed and is at rest. I am hungry and thirsty like 45 him, but when thirst and hunger cease I am not at rest; I am, like him, pained with want, but am not, like him, satisfied with fulness. The intermediate hours are tedious and gloomy; I long again to be hungry that I may again quicken my attention. The birds peck the berries or the corn, and fly away to the groves where they sit in seem- 50 ing happiness on the branches, and waste their lives in tuning one unvaried series of sounds. I likewise can call the lutanist and the singer, but the sounds that pleased me yesterday weary me to day, and will grow yet more wearisome to morrow. I can discover within me no power of perception which is not glutted with its proper pleasure, 55 yet I do not feel myself delighted. Man has surely some latent sense for which this place affords no gratification, or he has some desires distinct from sense which must be satisfied before he can be happy."

[7] After this he lifted up his head, and seeing the moon rising, walked towards the palace. As he passed through the fields, and saw 60 the animals around him, "Ye," said he, "are happy, and need not envy me that walk thus among you, burthened with myself; nor do I, ye

gentle beings, envy your felicity; for it is not the felicity of man. I have
many distresses from which ye are free; I fear pain when I do not
65 feel it; I sometimes shrink at evils recollected, and sometimes start at
evils anticipated: surely the equity of providence has ballanced peculiar sufferings with peculiar enjoyments."

[8] With observations like these the prince amused himself as he
returned, uttering them with a plaintive voice, yet with a look that
70 discovered him to feel some complacence in his own perspicacity, and
to receive some solace of the miseries of life, from consciousness of
the delicacy with which he felt, and the eloquence with which he
bewailed them. He mingled chearfully in the diversions of the evening, and all rejoiced to find that his heart was lightened.

[For treatment of this selection, see p. 195.]

The Study of Style

GILBERT HIGHET

[1] STYLE is an extraordinary thing. It is one of the subtlest
secrets of all art. Through a sensitive appreciation of style, we can
actually understand a creative artist more deeply than through weigh-
ing his subjects, dissecting his themes, or reading his biography. In
5 painting, it is composition, colour-sense, and brushwork. In sculpture,
it is the treatment of depths and surfaces and the choice of stones and
metals. In music, it is surely the melodic line, the tone-colour, and the
shape of the phrase—who could fail to recognize the four hammer-
blows in C minor as the very voice of Beethoven? In prose and poetry,
10 it is the choice of words, their placing, and the rhythms and melodies
of sentence and paragraph. The work of a really good writer can be
subjected—from this point of view alone, almost without reference to
his meaning or message—to long and subtle analysis, which does not
deform or deaden our appreciation of his art, but increases it more
15 than we should have thought possible.

[2] For example, when Bernard Berenson estimated a newly dis-

From *Poets in a Landscape*, by Gilbert Highet, by permission of Alfred A.
Knopf, Inc. Copyright 1947 by Gilbert Highet. Selection title by the Editors.

covered picture, which might be by a master such as Botticelli, he used to arrange, first of all, to see it rapidly and all at once, without preparation. Next came the detailed study. And in that, one of the most difficult and rewarding investigations was his examination of the brushwork. In those two movements, by which he first subjected himself to the total impression of the picture, and then reconstructed the very movements of the artist's hand, the very quality of his paint and brushes, Berenson penetrated as close as possible to the soul of the painter.

[3] In the same way, students of music can spend months of profitable work simply on analysing a single composer's use of the varied instruments of the orchestra—how he loves groups of horns, with their strange, muffled, distant voices, how he will balance them with clear, high violins, shimmering like fountain-spray at the top of their range, how he maintains command over his audience by recurrent and insistent drums. It is possible, similarly, to learn much about Plato by studying something apparently so insignificant as his use of particles— the little, almost meaningless words of emphasis and qualification like "of course," "certainly," "at least," in which the Greek language is so rich, and which (in written prose) perform the same function as gestures, voice-tones, and facial expressions in conversation. Much can be told about the date and the emotional tone of any play by Shakespeare, simply from an examination of the endings of the lines. A great artist impregnates every detail of his work.

[4] Not only a man's art, but his temperament, is reflected in his style. Any intelligent reader of Ezra Pound's *Cantos* would know, without further information, that Pound had led a life of spiritual and intellectual excitement, disorganization, and intermittence, and conflict. The random quizzical ethos of Laurence Sterne, and even his rather frail health, are reflected in his punctuation. Chopin's music gradually becomes tubercular.

[5] One of the rewards of reading good writers, not in translation but in their own languages, is that we can learn to appreciate their styles. Translations are deformations, disguises; an original gives us the man's voice as his friends and his first readers heard it: almost as he himself heard it. Only if a Frenchman understands English well and has read much English poetry with ease, can he appreciate Shakespeare. A good Greek scholar can read a Greek poem, explain its meaning, discuss its beauties of rhythm and tone, analyse its structure and its models—and still be left with an important residue of experience which he is usually powerless to explain unless in hints, but which

is none the less a vital moment of his enjoyment, which is indeed one of the chief reasons he devoted himself to the study of Greek.

60   [6] This is much more true of Greek and Latin poetry than the average man realizes. The Greek and Roman poets did not write very much. But they spent a great deal of thought and effort on their styles. Although they worked within a limited range of metres and handled a comparatively small collection of subjects, every one of them who has

65 any claim to be called good developed an entirely individual style—so unmistakable that no careful reader could confuse it with the style of any other poet (even with a poet writing in the same metre on the same subjects), so expressive that it conveyed meanings and nuances of emotion which supplemented and deepened the themes of his

70 poems. Tennyson in his ode on the anniversary of Vergil's birth speaks of

> All the charm of all the Muses
> often flowering in a lonely word.

Without exaggerating, any lover of the Greek and Roman classics will

75 accept this, and go further. He will point to a single syllable, a single cadence, even a single vowel, and say truly that it could have been placed only by one poet, and that it expresses many years of his meditation on life and art, as many centuries of the turbulent history of our planet are expressed in a single diamond.

80   [7] All this comes home to anyone who reads Tibullus in his own words. He might easily be called a decadent. He flaunts his own spiritual weaknesses. He admits that he cannot resist temptation, even when the object is utterly unworthy of him. He cries and complains of small disasters in a surprisingly un-Roman way. All the traditional

85 ideals of his nation he rejects: courage, self-control, self-sacrifice, energy, and a planned career—he boasts that they are all quite meaningless to him, and that he is ready to accept the scorn of others if he can just live his own inert and sensual life. He sounds like a thoroughly despicable young man.

90   [8] And yet his style proves that at heart he was not. There is a positive sweetness in his elegies, there are a gentleness and grace which can only have inhabited a good and sensitive soul. The movement of his thought is calm and orderly, and if his epithets are sometimes a little obvious, even vapid, his verse is always delicately

95 melodious. When read slowly, sympathetically, and meditatively, he is quite clearly an admirable poet. In music, he might be compared to Mendelssohn or Fauré. A gentle, soft-hearted man, he had an exquisitely subtle taste, and the spirit of a fine artist.

One of the devices or variations which may be employed in constructing the sentence is parallelism. Since sentences are composed of various units—the word, the phrase, the clause—these units may be repeated much as a pattern is repeated in a fabric or a design repeated in the façade of a building. Coordinate units of thought, equal in importance and hence in weight, are expressed in parallel constructions.

These parallel constructions are alike in grammatical structure or syntax; they serve the same grammatical function in the sentence. They may be words (He was tall, dark, and handsome); phrases ("that government of the people, by the people, and for the people . . ."); adjective clauses ("Oh how great is thy goodness, which thou hast laid up for them that fear thee; which thou hast wrought for them that trust in thee before the sons of men!"—*Psalms* 31:19); or adverbial clauses ("Hear the voice of my supplications, when I cry unto thee, when I lift up my hands toward thy holy oracle."—*Psalms* 28:2). Each of the parallel grammatical units derives from or modifies or is dependent in some way upon one element within the sentence. The words "tall," "dark," "handsome" all modify "He"; "of the people," "by the people," "for the people" all modify "government"; the clauses "which thou hast laid up for them that fear thee" and "which thou hast wrought for them that trust in thee" modify "goodness"; "when I cry unto thee" and "when I lift up my hands toward thy holy oracle" modify "Hear."

The meaning of parallel structure is frequently extended to include similarly constructed independent clauses (The man walked slowly down the road; the dog limped along at his side) and even sentences (An auto, which travels on the ground, can create an illusion of speed. An airplane, which speeds through the air, can suggest utter motionlessness).

No device should ever be used solely as an end in itself, though *in* itself it may be pleasing. Parallelism is certainly pleasing: discovery of pattern and rediscovery of the familiar have delighted our senses since we learned "Pat-a-cake." But parallelism, like any other device, must also be, and it is, functional. It helps to delineate fine points of meaning; thus it is a device of coherence. It enables the reader to anticipate and then to follow the sense of the sentence; hence it is an aid to clarity. Just because it is patterned, it contributes to the cadences or rhythm of the sentence. And it is a device for avoiding wordiness. Compare, for example, these two units for succinctness:

    a. The family huddled around the fireplace because it was the only warm place in the house. It was light there, too. Also, they were able to enjoy each other's company that way.

    b. The family huddled around the fireplace for warmth, light, and companionship.

1. Examples of parallelism in the first paragraph of "The Happy Valley" are "vicissitudes of pleasure and repose"; "attended by all that were skilful to delight and gratified with whatever the senses can enjoy"; "They wandered in gardens of fragrance, and slept in the fortresses of security"; "where discord was always raging, and where man preyed upon man." Analyze these examples fully, explaining what grammatical units are parallel and how the sense is reflected and enhanced by the use of each parallel construction.

2. In paragraphs 2, 3, and 4 of the Johnson selection, point out and analyze as many examples of parallelism as you can find.

3. Johnson says that Rasselas "began to compare their [the goats'] condition with his own." Show how parallelism is used in the comparison which follows this statement. Why is parallelism an effective device for this purpose?

4. What one sentence sums up the meaning of the selection? With this sentence in mind, explain why there is so much parallelism used throughout the chapter.

5. Parallelism may be effectively used to develop examples or illustrations of a point. Show where and how this is done in the first three paragraphs of the Highet piece.

6. Paragraph 7 of "The Study of Style" contains a sentence which uses parallelism for the accumulation of detail (within the sentence). Determine which sentence this is and justify this statement about it. Why is parallelism an effective method of delineating detail? On the basis of what you have learned about the uses of parallelism in exemplification, comparison, and accumulation of detail, what can you conclude about methods of development of the paragraph and of the sentence?

7. Find and justify the use of one periodic sentence in the Highet selection.

8. Parallelism may be used to show climax—the ascending order which distinguishes among similar objects or ideas. Find and explain a sentence in paragraph 6 of Highet in which parallelism is used for this purpose.

9. Why does Highet begin so many of his sentences in paragraph 7 with "He . . ."?

10. In the last paragraph of "The Study of Style," how is the meaning reflected in the structure of both the entire paragraph and the individual sentences?

Alternate selections for the study of Parallelism: Rutherford Platt, from *The River of Life*; John H. Randall, "Eternally Old, Eternally New."

Theme Assignment: Gilbert Highet says, "A great artist impregnates every detail of his work" and also, "Not only a man's art, but his temperament, is reflected in his style." The use of parallelism is certainly an element of style. Though you may not have read anything else by either Johnson or Highet, if Highet is right you should be able to tell a good deal about both men from these samples of their writing, just as Highet tells about Tibullus—an ancient Greek poet—from the small body of his poetry.

Write a theme in which you discuss the uses of parallelism—an element of style—in either the Johnson or the Highet selection. Then, on the basis of your discussion, generalize to whatever extent you feel justified about the man—his artistry and his temperament. Use as many illustrations from the selection as you can to fortify your conclusions.

Balance

On Luxury

OLIVER GOLDSMITH

[1] FROM such a picture of Nature in primeval simplicity, tell me, my much respected friend, are you in love with fatigue and solitude? Do you sigh for the severe frugality of the wandering Tartar, or regret being born amidst the luxury and dissimulation of the polite?
5 Rather tell me, has not every kind of life vices peculiarly its own? Is it not a truth, that refined countries have more vices, but those not so terrible, barbarous nations few, and they of the most hideous complexion? Perfidy and fraud are the vices of civilized nations, credulity and violence those of the inhabitants of the desert. Does
10 the luxury of the one produce half the evils of the inhumanity of the other? Certainly those philosophers, who declaim against luxury, have but little understood its benefits; they seem insensible, that to luxury we owe not only the greatest part of our knowledge, but even of our virtues.

15 [2] It may sound fine in the mouth of a declaimer when he talks of subduing our appetites, of teaching every sense to be content with a bare sufficiency, and of supplying only the wants of Nature; but is there not more satisfaction in indulging those appetites, if with innocence and safety, than in restraining them? Am not I better
20 pleased in enjoyment than in the sullen satisfaction of thinking that I can live without enjoyment? The more various our artificial necessities, the wider is our circle of pleasure; for all pleasure consists in

From *Letters from a Citizen of the World to His Friends in the East*, by Oliver Goldsmith. Selection title by the Editors.

obviating necessities as they rise; luxury, therefore, as it encreases our wants, encreases our capacity for happiness.

[3] Examine the history of any country remarkable for opulence 25 and wisdom, you will find they would never have been wise had they not been first luxurious; you will find poets, philosophers, and even patriots, marching in Luxury's train. The reason is obvious; we then only are curious after knowledge when we find it connected with sensual happiness. The senses ever point out the way, and reflection 30 comments upon the discovery. Inform a native of the desert of Kobi, of the exact measure of the parallax of the moon, he finds no satisfaction at all in the information; he wonders how any could take such pains, and lay out such treasures in order to solve so use- less a difficulty; but connect it with his happiness, by shewing that 35 it improves navigation, that by such an investigation he may have a warmer coat, a better gun, or a finer knife, and he is instantly in raptures at so great an improvement. In short, we only desire to know what we desire to possess; and whatever we may talk against it, luxury adds the spur to curiosity, and gives us a desire of becom- 40 ing more wise.

[4] But not our knowledge only, but our virtues are improved by luxury. Observe the brown savage of Thibet, to whom the fruits of the spreading pomegranate supply food, and its branches an habi- tation. Such a character has few vices I grant, but those he has are 45 of the most hideous nature, rapine and cruelty are scarce crimes in his eye, neither pity nor tenderness, which ennoble every virtue, has any place in his heart; he hates his enemies, and kills those he sub- dues. On the other hand, the polite Chinese and civilized European seem even to love their enemies. I have just now seen an instance 50 where the English have succoured those enemies whom their own countrymen actually refused to relieve.

[5] The greater the luxuries of every country, the more closely, politically speaking, is that country united. Luxury is the child of society alone, the luxurious man stands in need of a thousand differ- 55 ent artists to furnish out his happiness; it is more likely, therefore, that he should be a good citizen who is connected by motives of self-interest with so many, than the abstemious man who is united to none.

[6] In whatsoever light therefore we consider luxury, whether as 60 employing a number of hands naturally too feeble for more laborious employment, as finding a variety of occupation for others who might be totally idle, or as furnishing out new inlets to happiness, without

encroaching on mutual property, in whatever light we regard it, we
65 shall have reason to stand up in its defence, and the sentiment of
Confucius still remains unshaken; *that we should enjoy as many of
the luxuries of life as are consistent with our own safety, and the
prosperity of others, and that he who finds out a new pleasure is
one of the most useful members of society.*

One of the dictionary definitions of balance is "harmonious arrangement or adjustment, especially in the arts of design." The most ele-
mental concept of balance is based on an equal distribution of weight
or color or mass: in a well-decorated room, chairs and couches are
arranged so that the weightier and larger pieces are distributed fairly
equally through the room. An extremely large or heavy piece of furniture is balanced by several smaller pieces across the room. In automobiles, the longer hoods made necessary by large engines are
balanced by large rear fins. Balance plays a part, then, not only in
the arts (in symphonic music, the balance maintained among the
various sections of the orchestra is partly responsible for the listener's
pleasure; in sculpture and painting, much of the aesthetic pleasure is
derived from the subtle balancing of part against part) but also in
many of the facets of everyday life—from a balanced diet to a balanced checkbook.

Balance is no less important in English prose—particularly in sentences. It is achieved essentially by constructing a sentence so that
two or more of its parts are grammatically equivalent or coordinate:
two independent clauses of approximately the same length and structure connected by a semicolon or a coordinating conjunction make a
balanced sentence:

The students protested vigorously, but the faculty seemed uncon-
cerned.

Similarly, balance can be achieved by playing one subordinate clause
off against another:

The man who takes seriously his responsibilities as a voter is the
citizen who helps most to make democracy work.

Words, phrases, and even sentences can be made parts of a balanced
structure. Parallelism is, of course, a major means of achieving balance.

Though balanced structure is being presented here as an asset to
the writer, it should not be used too frequently; overuse of balanced
structure results in stilted, pompous, artificial writing. When content
demands its use, it should be used, but not otherwise. The crispness
and fluidity of modern prose compared with the heaviness and for-

mality of earlier English prose stem in part from limiting the use of balanced sentence structure. Balanced structure is rather like food: enough of it, when needed, is good; too much of it is unpleasant.

1. What is the guiding purpose of the Goldsmith selection? Does your wording of the guiding purpose suggest that a number of balanced sentences and even balanced paragraphs would be appropriate? If not, reword your formulation so that it does.

2. How many balanced sentences do you find in the first paragraph? Analyze each to show the sentence elements that are in balance. Has Goldsmith overdone the use of balance in the paragraph? If you think so, rewrite one or more of the sentences—effectively—to reduce the amount of balance in the paragraph.

3. In the context of the essay, which sentence in each of the following pairs is more effective? Justify your answer.

a. (1) "The senses ever point out the way, and reflection comments upon the discovery" (paragraph 3).

   (2) After the senses have pointed out the way, reflection comments upon the discovery.

b. (1) "In short, we only desire to know what we desire to possess; and whatever we may talk against it, luxury adds the spur to curiosity, and gives us a desire of becoming more wise" (paragraph 3).

   (2) In short, we only desire to know what we desire to possess. Whatever we may talk against it, luxury adds the spur to curiosity, giving us a desire of becoming more wise.

c. (1) "On the other hand, the polite Chinese and civilized European seem even to love their enemies" (paragraph 4).

   (2) On the other hand, the polite Chinese seem even to love their enemies; the civilized Europeans love theirs too.

4. Taking into account not only the balanced sentence, but sentence rhythms and variety of structure as well, characterize Goldsmith's prose style in some detail.

Alternate selections for the study of Balance: Lloyd Morris, "A Coating of Cold Chocolate Sauce"; Jan Struther, "Feather Brooms."

Assignment: Find at least five examples of balanced sentences in your current reading in newspapers and periodicals. Copy out or bring to class the paragraph in which each sentence appears, and be prepared to comment on the effectiveness (or lack of it) achieved through the balance.

Subordination

General Winfield Scott

MARGARET LEECH

[1] THAT winter, the old General moved from the rooms he had rented from the free mulatto, Wormley, in I Street to Cruchet's at Sixth and D Streets. His new quarters, situated on the ground floor—a spacious bedroom, with a private dining-room adjoining—
5 were convenient for a man who walked slowly and with pain; and Cruchet, a French caterer, was one of the best cooks in Washington.

[2] In spite of his nearly seventy-five years and his increasing infirmities, the General was addicted to the pleasures of the table. Before his six o'clock dinner, his black body servant brought out
10 the wines and the liqueurs, setting the bottles of claret to warm before the fire. The old man had refined his palate in the best restaurants in Paris; and woodcock, English snipe, poulard, capon, and *tête de veau en tortue* were among the dishes he fancied. He liked, too, canvasback duck, and the hams of his native Virginia. Yet nothing,
15 to his taste, equaled the delicacy he called "tarrapin." He would hold forth on the correct method of preparing it: "No flour, sir—not a grain." His military secretary could saturninely foresee that moment, when, leaning his left elbow on the table and holding six inches above his plate a fork laden with the succulent tortoise, he would announce,
20 "The best food vouchsafed by Providence to man," before hurrying the fork to his lips.

[3] From his splendid prime, the General had retained, not only

a discriminating palate, but the defects suitable to a proud and ambitious nature. He had always been vain, pompous, exacting, jealous and high-tempered. Now that his sick old body could no 25 longer support the racking of its wounds, his irascibility had dwindled to irritation, and his imperiousness to petulance. His love of flattery had grown, and he often declared that at his age compliments had become a necessity. While taking a footbath, he would call on his military secretary to remark the fairness of his limbs. In company, 30 he spoke of the great commanders of history, and matched with theirs his own exploits at Chippewa and Lundy's Lane, at Cerro Gordo and Chapultepec. Near his desk stood his bust in marble, with shoulders bared; classical, serene and idealized. The walls were brilliant with his portraits at various ages, from the young General 35 Winfield Scott who had been victorious over the British in 1814 to the already aging General-in-Chief who had defeated the Mexicans in 1848. They were arresting figures, those generals on the walls; handsome, slender, heroic, with haughty eye and small, imperious mouth. Gold gleamed in spurs, in buttons and embroidery and huge 40 epaulettes, in the handle of the sword which had been the gift of Virginia; and one portrait showed the superb cocked hat, profusely plumed, that had earned for Scott the sobriquet of "Fuss and Feathers." He stood six feet, four and a quarter inches in height, and had been wont to insist on the fraction. But, swollen and dropsi- 45 cal, he spoke no longer of his size. He pointed instead to the bust, to the portraits, to show what he had been.

[4] Such was the commanding general of the Army of the United States in December of 1860, but not so did his compatriots see him. His eye had lost its fire and he could no longer sit a horse, but in 50 huge epaulettes and yellow sash he was still his country's hero. Europe might celebrate the genius of Napoleon; the New World had its Winfield Scott. For nearly half a century the republic had taken pride in his achievements as soldier and pacificator; and, if he now lived in a glorious military past, so did his fellow-countrymen. He 55 was the very figure to satisfy a peaceful people, fond of bragging of its bygone belligerence. The General was as magnificent as a monument, and no one was troubled by the circumstance that he was nearly as useless.

If parallelism applies to the structuring and positioning of equal sentence units, subordination applies to the structure and positioning of unequal units. Not all elements within the sentence are of equal importance. The backbone of the sentence consists of the subject and predicate; the noun—or noun substitute—and the verb: the person, place, or thing and the action it performs. The elements, then, which are subordinate must stand in some meaningful relation to the subject and predicate (or subjects and predicates). Most often this relation is descriptive or explanatory; the subordinate element may be adjectival, modifying a noun or noun substitute, or it may be adverbial, modifying a verb, adjective, or adverb. A "thing" may be modified in kind, color, size, identity, shape, quality. An action may be modified in cause, effect, time, place, purpose, or method. The elements in a sentence which stand in any of these relations to the main clause or to the major sentence elements are said to be subordinate. They may be single words, phrases, or clauses.

Why subordinate one idea to another? Part of the answer to this question might be put as another question: are not some ideas more important than others? Since they surely are, the writer gains in precision by being able to use the tool of subordination. He is able to emphasize (and de-emphasize), to vary the rhythms of his prose, to chisel the deep lines and etch the fine ones. The main point (or points) which the sentence is making should be put in the main clause, subsidiary points in subordinate units. The rule can most easily be understood by seeing what happens when this logical weighting is overturned and a minor point grammatically outweighs the major one:

a. When the plane crashed, killing twenty-two people, much valuable property was destroyed.

b. As the first rocket carrying a man to the moon took off, many people crowded around the entrance to the restricted area.

There is another method by which the writer can control and communicate relative weights within the sentence. It has been pointed out that words must be experienced in time (or, if you think of the printed page, in space). Any block of writing, then, has its strategic spots. This is true for the whole piece of writing; the beginning and ending have certain potentialities which the middle usually does not have. It is true for the paragraph; the topic sentence most often appears at either the beginning or the end. These same places (or times) are strategic points in the sentence. The midportion of the sentence is normally a position of de-emphasis or subordination; the beginning is stronger than the middle but not so strong as the end.

1. Give as many reasons as you can to justify which unit in each of the following groups you prefer:

a. (1) "In spite of his nearly seventy-five years and his increasing infirmities, the General was addicted to the pleasures of the table."

(2) The General was nearly seventy-five years old and had increasing infirmities. He was addicted to the pleasures of the table.

b. (1) His military secretary was saturnine. He could foresee what the General would do. He would lean his left elbow on the table. He would hold his fork six inches above his plate. The fork would be laden with succulent tortoise. "This is the best food vouchsafed by Providence to man," he would announce. Then he would hurry the fork to his lips.

(2) "His military secretary could saturninely foresee that moment, when, leaning his left elbow on the table and holding six inches above his plate a fork laden with succulent tortoise, he would announce, 'The best food vouchsafed by Providence to man,' before hurrying the fork to his lips."

c. (1) Because his love of flattery had grown, he often declared that at his age compliments had become a necessity.

(2) "His love of flattery had grown, and he often declared that at his age compliments had become a necessity."

d. (1) "While taking a footbath, he would call on his military secretary to remark the fairness of his limbs."

(2) He took a footbath and called upon his military secretary who remarked the fairness of his limbs.

(3) He would call on his military secretary to remark the fairness of his limbs while taking a footbath.

(4) He would call on his military secretary, while taking a footbath, to remark the fairness of his limbs.

e. (1) His bust stood near his desk. It was made of marble. His shoulders were bared. The statue was classical, serene, and idealized.

(2) "Near his desk stood his bust in marble, with shoulders bared; classical, serene and idealized."

2. Parallelism, balance, and subordination have been used in the following sentence: "The walls were brilliant with his portraits at various ages, from the young General Winfield Scott who had been victorious over the British in 1814 to the already aging General-in-Chief who had defeated the Mexicans in 1848." Rewrite the passage in at least three ways, using as many sentences as you need. Be prepared to point out the differences in meaning among the versions.

3. Point out as many other examples of parallelism and balance as you can find in paragraph 3, and explain for what purpose they are used in each example.

4. Why do you think there are so many compound sentences in paragraph 4? What would be gained or lost if some of the coordinate thoughts were subordinated to others? If you think the paragraph would benefit by some subordination, suggest which ideas you would subordinate and explain why you would do so.

5. Illustrate as many varieties of sentence structure as you can find in the selection. What is the construction of the majority of the sentences? What does this tell you about General Winfield Scott? about Margaret Leech?

6. Why is the simile, or comparison, at the end of paragraph 4 appropriate? Why is it placed where it is?

Alternate selection for the study of Subordination: René Fülöp-Miller, from *Triumph over Pain.*

Assignment: Following are two sets of lists of nouns and verbs which might be related to one another. Write up to a dozen sentences in one or more paragraphs using as many words (in their appropriate forms) from either set of paired lists as you can. Remember that some of these nouns and verbs, in whatever form or structure you use them, will and should be more important than others.

I

A	B
a lake	to find
a boat	to take
a dock	to sing
a man	to cry
a boy	to sail
a dog	to swim
a wind	to drown
a salmon	to walk
a birch tree	to laugh
a rock	to pray
a mountain	to flow
a church	to blow
water skis	to bark
rain	to call
a ripple	to catch
pine trees	to dance
moss	to smell
algae	to thank
driftwood	to try
a minnow	to be
a stream	to get
	to lose

II

A	B
a house	to go
a book	to guess
a fireplace	to call
a chimney	to cook
a stove	to wash
a sink	to climb
a woman	to hit
a frying pan	to fear
a bottle of milk	to catch
a rug	to sell
a door	to break
a window	to burn
a vase	to open
an egg	to smile
a chair	to hide
a fire	to take
a yawn	to think
a kiss	to surprise
a scream	to shake
a man	to hate
a clock	
a hammer	
a mouse	

Rhythm

August

CHARLES DICKENS

[1] THERE is no month in the whole year, in which nature wears a more beautiful appearance than in the month of August. Spring has many beauties, and May is a fresh and bloom-ing month, but the charms of this time of year are enhanced by
5 their contrast with the winter season. August has no such advantage. It comes when we remember nothing but clear skies, green fields and sweet-smelling flowers—when the recollection of snow, and ice, and bleak winds, has faded from our minds as completely as they have disappeared from the earth—and yet what a pleasant time it
10 is! Orchards and cornfields ring with the hum of labour; trees bend beneath the thick clusters of rich fruit which bow their branches to the ground; and the corn, piled in graceful sheaves, or waving in every light breath that sweeps above it, as if it wooed the sickle, tinges the landscape with a golden hue. A mellow softness appears
15 to hang over the whole earth; the influence of the season seems to extend itself to the very waggon, whose slow motion across the well-reaped field, is perceptible only to the eye, but strikes with no harsh sound upon the ear.

[2] As the coach rolls swiftly past the fields and orchards which
20 skirt the road, groups of women and children, piling the fruit in sieves, or gathering the scattered ears of corn, pause for an instant from their labour, and shading the sun-burnt face with a still browner

From *Pickwick Papers*, by Charles Dickens. Selection title by the Editors.

hand, gaze upon the passengers with curious eyes, while some stout
urchin, too small to work, but too mischievous to be left at home,
scrambles over the side of the basket in which he has been deposited 25
for security, and kicks and screams with delight. The reaper stops
in his work, and stands with folded arms, looking at the vehicle as
it whirls past; and the rough cart-horses bestow a sleepy glance upon
the smart coach team, which says, as plainly as a horse's glance can,
"It's all very fine to look at, but slow going, over a heavy field, is 30
better than warm work like that, upon a dusty road, after all." You
cast a look behind you, as you turn a corner of the road. The
women and children have resumed their labour: the reaper once
more stoops to his work: the cart-horses have moved on: and all
are again in motion. 35

[For treatment of this selection, see p. 212.]

Feather Brooms

JAN STRUTHER

[1] IT was obvious, from the moment when he shuffled round
the corner into the square, that he would leave it without having sold
a single broom; and I felt as I watched him from my window that
sinking of the heart, that small embarrassed misery, which you feel
when you see a grown-up about to play a practical joke on a child, 5
or when there is a little man at a party whose card tricks do not
quite come off.

[2] He evidently had not the faintest idea of how to sell feather
brooms, or anything else. Salesmanship, that widely studied art, was
a closed book to him, and he did not even seem to have common 10
sense to fall back upon. For one thing, he made no noise. The
people who come to sell things in the square are divided into three
classes: those who stand in the road and cry their wares, those who
knock timidly at the door and pitch hard-luck stories to the parlor-
maid, and those who ring the bell briskly and ask to see the lady 15

"Feather Brooms," from *Try Anything Twice*, by Jan Struther (London: Chatto
& Windus, 1938). Reprinted with the permission of Curtis Brown Ltd. on
behalf of the estate of Jan Struther.

of the house. The first class sell, roughly speaking, logs, muffins, and strawberries; the second, bootlaces, buttons, hairy writing-pads, and hand-made lace of distressing design; the third, water-softeners and labor-saving machines. Class I are legitimate and useful traders,
20 who make no demands on your time or your emotions; either you want logs, in which case you shout "Hi!," or else you have plenty, in which case you wait, partially deafened, until their uncouth but exciting roars have left the square. Class II are more difficult to deal with, because they hit you below the belt; somehow you never
25 seem to have run out of hand-made lace, and you generally salve your conscience by parting with your favorite pair of shoes, which you would have gone on wearing for years, for the benefit of their youngest daughter, who happens (they say, after a rapid and expert glance at your own feet) to take size three-and-a-half. Class III are
30 emissaries of the Tempter, wasters of time and wreckers of content. The only way to get rid of them is to keep a permanent case of scarlet fever in the house—and even then some of them have had it.

[3] But the old man with the feather brooms did not fit into any of these categories. He did not shout "Fine broom-O!" or any inar-
35 ticulate corruption of the old cry. He did not ring at a single bell, or even clamber down the steep area steps to tap at kitchen windows. He just pottered very slowly around the square, pausing uncertainly every few yards and gazing up at each house in turn, as though by the mere power of thought he could induce occupants to become
40 broom-conscious. But his will-power was evidently as weak and bleary as his eyes; too weak, at any rate, to pierce the well-knit brickwork, the prim, dry stucco of Sycamore Square: for nobody took any notice of him at all. Occasionally a lady of the house would shut her front door behind her, pause a moment on the step to
45 draw on her gloves and taste the fresh morning air, and then, with delicate leisured assurance, walk away up the square to do her morning's shopping in the King's Road. With unfailing regularity the old man missed his chance. All he did was to stand there as dumb as a lamp-post, making a small ineffective gesture with his
50 unwieldy handful of brooms. It was not surprising that the lady of the house either walked on without noticing him or else drew perceptibly aside. And when she had gone past he would blink resignedly and move on a few steps further to stare at the next house.

[4] My mind was exasperated and my heart wrung. Work became
55 impossible. I put down my pen and marched out into the square. There was, I felt, nothing in life I wanted less at that moment than

a new feather broom. Still, they could not cost more than a shilling, and that seemed a small price to pay for an eased conscience.

[5] "Here!" I called out. His face lit up hopefully as he shambled towards me. "How much?" 60

[6] "Five-and-six the long'ns. Free-and-six the short."

[7] "Good Lord," I said, aghast. "Surely that's rather a lot, isn't it?"

[8] "Ever tried to buy one in a shop, lidy?"

[9] "No," I admitted. 65

[10] "Ar," said the old man, and left it at that.

[11] "Well, I'm sorry," I said, "but I really can't afford to buy one." I expected pleading, protestation, possibly a drop in price. Instead, he gave an almost inaudible sigh, picked up his brooms and began to move away. Against such humility—or was it, after all, 70 such pride?—I was defenseless.

[12] "Look here," I said, "you can give me a three-and-sixpenny."

[13] He turned, handed me one of the shorter brooms and pushed the money with gnarled fingers into some unspeakable recess of his clothing. 75

[14] "You won't regret it, lidy," he said simply. "It's a nice straight bit o' cane, and the turkey fevvers is from Norwich, in Norfolk. I always makes 'em to last."

[15] "You *make* them?" I said, surprised at the contrast between his own unsavory person and the spruce beauty of his wares, all 80 shining bamboo and nodding plumes, with pieces of scarlet leather to hide the binding.

[16] "Yerss, lidy," he said. "Wiv my pore old rheumaticky fingers." He held out a dirty, shriveled claw. Somehow this, his only attempt at deliberate pathos, was the most heart-rending thing of all. 85 That he should be so pitiful an object was bad enough: that he should be conscious of it was unbearable. I said good-by rather curtly and went indoors. But he kept coming between me and my thoughts, and after a few minutes I had to go to the windows and look at him again. 90

[17] By this time he had reached the Barringtons' house, three doors away. The Barrington pram, as usual, was strapped to the area railings, and the Barrington baby was having its morning yell. Mrs. Barrington is one of those modern young mothers who hold that the time-honored practice of pram-jiggling is bad for a baby's nerves. 95 Grown-ups, it appears, have none. So Edward Barrington goes purple in the face from ten-thirty to ten-forty-five every morning, and if we

don't like it we can always shut our windows. The old man with the
brooms was standing by the pram looking down at the baby's con-
100 torted face and whirling fists.

[18] "Oy," I heard him say through the din. "Oy-oy-oy. Wassa
matter?" The Barrington baby went on yelling. The old man, who
had never heard of modern mother-craft, glanced inquiringly at the
front door, but nobody came. So he took out one of his brooms
105 and tickled the baby's face with it. The effect was magical. The
yelling stopped at once; it was followed by a few hysterical hiccups
and then by an unmistakable crow. Two starfish hands and two
woolen-booted feet shot simultaneously into the air towards the soft
waving feathers.

110 [19] "Thass better," said the old man. "Oy-oy-oy. Thass better."
He grinned toothlessly at the baby, and the baby grinned toothlessly
back at him. Again he tickled it; again it crowed with delight. But
at this moment the Barrington front door opened and the Barrington
Nannie appeared—puzzled, no doubt, by the untimely cessation of
115 the morning yell.

[20] "My precious lamb!" She flew down the steps like an aveng-
ing whirlwind and snatched up the baby in her arms.

[21] "You be off," she said sharply. "Pushing your dirty feathers
in the child's face. I've a good mind to send for the police." The
120 baby began howling again as she bore it off into the house.

[22] His one success over, the old man shouldered his brooms
again and trailed away up the square. His broken boots moved over
the flagstones like two misshapen toads.

Rhythm is so major an element of poetry that the student-writer
may not have realized that rhythm plays a role in good prose too.
Repetition is the essence of rhythm: in painting, the repetition of a
pattern or color or line produces visual rhythm; in music, the repetition of a pattern of beats produces rhythm; in poetry, the repetition
of a pattern of stressed and unstressed sounds produces rhythm. In
prose, rhythm is produced by the repetition—always with some variation possible—of patterns of stressed and unstressed words. Prose
rhythms are subtle and frequently so varied that a certain amount of
training and practice is needed before a reader can respond fully to
the best rhythmical prose.

In metered poetry, the rhythmical unit is the foot, consisting of
one stressed sound and one or more unstressed sounds arranged in
any one of several possible patterns; in prose, however, the rhythmical

unit ranges from the various parts of a sentence (words, phrases, clauses) to the whole sentence itself. For example, in the following sentences, the rhythmical units are indicated by slashes:

The boy,/ with a bedraggled looking dog behind him,/ ran to the corner,/ peered into the car,/ and then ran off again.

Higher education is considered a necessity today/ not only for the man who wants a professional career/ but also for the woman who wants to be a wife and mother.

The idea was loathsome./ The man who proposed it/ was even more loathsome.

Reading a sentence aloud to communicate its meaning will normally enable the reader to sense the rhythmical units of which it is composed.

An infinite variety of effects—of different movements—can be achieved through the varying lengths of rhythmical units and their relations within and between sentences. Several short units placed together in a sentence can result in choppy or staccato or clogged movement:

The gymnasium,/ completed only recently,/ towered embarrassingly,/ most faculty members thought,/ over the small, dilapidated buildings/ in which were taught/ the humanities,/ the social sciences,/ and the natural sciences.

Larger units strategically placed—and perhaps varied with one or two smaller units—can result in smooth, flowing movement:

For century after century after century,/ thinking man has exerted the best efforts of his mind and imagination/ to penetrate the mysteries of the natural world about him.

It must be pointed out here that no pat generalizations of any validity can be made about the best number of rhythmical units per sentence or the best relations among units or the best length of units. The only meaningful criteria to use in evaluating prose rhythms (or sentence movements) are the propriety of the movement to the content and the pleasure (or lack of it) felt by the reader as he reads. Sentences expressing smooth, flowing action or movement should move smoothly and flowingly; sentences expressing ideas rather than action or movement should move easily, without the clogging effect of several short units following one after another. Awareness of sentence movements and the ability to analyze them in the student's own writing as well as in the writing of prose masters will sharpen sensitivity and help in the achievement of rhythmically pleasing prose.

But there is more to sentence movement than the recognition of

214   The Sentence

rhythmical units. Any normal English sentence when read aloud (or even silently, for that matter) has certain words which the content demands giving more stress to than to others. Using the symbol ´ to indicate a stressed word (understanding that not all stressed words are equally stressed) and the symbol ˘ to indicate an unstressed word, we may show the normal reading of a sentence as follows:

   a. Lóoking aroŭnd tŏ seĕ whĕre thĕ bóat hăd beĕn tiéd,/ thĕ húnter wăs hórrified tŏ fĭnd/ thăt hĕ hăd beĕn léft alóne ŏn thĕ ísland.

This is a typical English sentence in its larger number of unstressed than stressed words and in the repetition—with variation—in the third unit of the basic rhythmical pattern of the first unit. The repetition is not so pronounced, however, that it makes the sentence singsong or "versified."

   b. Thĕ úp-grading/ ŏf stóck íssues/ bŭ thĕ Bóard mémbers/ fóoled búyers,/ séllers,/ ănd brókers tóo.

Sentence *b* has a movement quite different from that of sentence *a*: it has a larger percentage of stressed words (9 of 15 compared with 8 of 25 in *a*), and a stressed word follows a stressed word several times, whereas in sentence *a* every stressed word is separated from every other stressed word by at least one unstressed word. In addition, sentence *a*, with 25 words, has only 3 rhythmical units; *b*, with 15 words, has 6 rhythmical units. In over-all effect, sentence *a* moves with a certain rapidity which echoes its meaning; *b* has a clogged, somewhat staccato movement, a rather unpleasant movement.

In analyzing prose rhythms or sentence movement, it is always necessary to take into account not only the number, length, and interrelations of rhythmical units, but also the patterns of stressed and unstressed words for whatever effects they may create. Piling stressed word on stressed word may result in heavy, emphatic delivery or in slow, clogged movement; a large number of unstressed words separating stressed words usually results in light, rapid movement.

Closely related to prose rhythms are the sound patterns of sentences. Continuant consonants—consonants whose sounds can be drawn out when spoken aloud (*l, m, n, r*, for example)—aid in producing smoothness of movement; stop consonants (*b, d, k, p, t*, for example) help produce a staccato movement. The most skillful prose writer manages his sentences so that sound and movement are as appropriate as possible to his content.

Although readers will vary slightly one from another in the way in which they read almost any sentence, the content and context of most sentences will determine reading patterns essentially alike. For example, most readers would read the first sentence of the Dickens selection as follows:

There is no month in the whole year,/ in which nature wears a more beautiful appearance/ than in the month of August.

Though most readers will feel the pleasing rhythm of the sentence, analysis will show at least some of the means by which the rhythm has been achieved. First, each of the three units in the sentence has two stressed words—repetition of a pattern helping to produce rhythm. Second, each of the units repeats the pattern, ˘ ˘ ˘ ´ —repetition again. Third, the first unit with its stressed words, *month, year,* is balanced with subtle variation by the third unit with its stressed words, *month, August.* Finally, the large number of unstressed words—22 of 28—allows the sentence to move easily and lightly.

1. Analyze similarly sentences 2, 3, and 4 of the first paragraph. There are at least three kinds of repetition in sentence 2; what are they? Compare the number of stressed words with the number of unstressed words; what comment does this comparison enable you to make about the movement of the sentence? Is the movement appropriate to the content and context? Why or why not? What patterns in sentence 1 are repeated in sentence 2? What is the effect of the repetition? Sentence 4 has a much higher percentage of stressed words than have sentences 1 and 2; what does this suggest about the movement of sentence 4? Show why the movement of sentence 4 is appropriate to the content and context. What patterns in sentences 1 and 2 are repeated in sentence 4? To what effect?

2. Compare the length of the rhythmical units in sentences 5 and 6; in terms of content and context, what does your comparison reveal? In which of the two sentences are sound patterns more effectively used? Justify your answer.

3. Which of the sentences in the second paragraph moves most slowly, most haltingly? Which moves most rapidly? Why is the movement of these sentences appropriate to their content?

4. Analyze the rhythms in sentences 4, 5, and 6 of the second paragraph of "Feather Brooms." You will notice that in sentence 4 the *those who* construction appears three times, that in sentence 5 there are three clauses similarly constructed, and that in sentence 6 there is an *either . . . or* construction. What relations do you find between these various constructions and the rhythmical patterns?

5. Analyze the rhythms in the sentences which make up the dialogue between the broom peddler and the writer. What differences do you find between the patterns here and those in the sentences in paragraph 2? What do these differences suggest about the differences in rhythm

between spoken and fairly formally written English? What differences do you find between the rhythmical patterns of each of the speakers? How do you account for these differences?

Alternate selections for the study of Rhythms: John Milton, from *Areopagitica*; Hilaire Belloc, from "The Mowing of a Field."

Assignment: For each of the following, write a single sentence of some length in which the rhythm is as appropriate to the content as you can make it:

a. Describe an utterly placid mountain lake or river scene on a hot summer's day.

b. State, with as much emphasis as you can muster, an idea about which you have a strong conviction.

c. Convey something of the excitement during the closing minutes of a basketball or football game.

d. What is it like to travel at a high speed in a car or boat or train?

e. Describe a graceful couple dancing on ice skates.

f. Show how upset you were just after committing your worst social blunder.

g. Make your favorite food as appetizing to your reader as you can.

h. Defend your favorite newspaper against a violent attack.

i. Ask your parents for permission to do something they have hitherto forbidden.

j. What sensations do you have when you feel most sleepy?

Diction

Succinctness

Five *Haiku*

I

Since there is no rice . . .
  Let us arrange these
  Flowers
For a lovely bowl

II

I raised my knife to it
Then walked
Empty-handed on . . .
Proud rose of Sharon

III

Reciting scriptures . . .
I find a strange
Wondrous blue
In morning-glories

From *Japanese Haiku*. Reprinted with the permission of Peter Pauper Press, Mt. Vernon, N.Y.

IV

In the city park
  Contemplating
  Cherry-trees . . .
Strangers are like friends

V

Dead my old fine hopes
  And dry my dreaming
  But oh . . .
Iris, blue each spring!

[For treatment of these selections, see p. 226.]

Ready-Money Jack

WASHINGTON IRVING

[1] ON the skirts of the neighboring village there lives a kind of small potentate, who, for aught I know, is a representative of one of the most ancient legitimate lines of the present day; for the empire over which he reigns has belonged to his family time
5 out of mind. His territories comprise a considerable number of good fat acres; and his seat of power is in an old farm-house, where he enjoys, unmolested, the stout oaken chair of his ancestors. The personage to whom I allude is a sturdy old yeoman of the name of John Tibbets, or rather Ready-Money Jack Tibbets, as he is called
10 throughout the neighborhood.

[2] The first place where he attracted my attention was in the churchyard on Sunday; where he sat on a tombstone after the service, with his hat a little on one side, holding forth to a small circle of

From *Selected Prose*, by Washington Irving, ed. Stanley T. Williams (Rinehart Editions; New York: Rinehart & Company, Inc., 1950).

auditors; and, as I presumed, expounding the law and the prophets; until, on drawing a little nearer, I found he was only expatiating on 15 the merits of a brown horse. He presented so faithful a picture of a substantial English yeoman, such as he is often described in books, heightened, indeed, by some little finery peculiar to himself, that I could not but take note of his whole appearance.

[3] He was between fifty and sixty, of a strong, muscular frame, 20 and at least six feet high, with a physiognomy as grave as a lion's, and set off with short, curling, iron-gray locks. His shirt-collar was turned down, and displayed a neck covered with the same short, curling, gray hair; and he wore a colored silk neck-cloth, tied very loosely, and tucked in at the bosom, with a green paste brooch on 25 the knot. His coat was of dark-green cloth, with silver buttons, on each of which was engraved a stag, with his own name, John Tibbets, underneath. He had an inner waistcoat of figured chintz, between which and his coat was another of scarlet cloth, unbuttoned. His breeches were also left unbuttoned at the knees, not from any 30 slovenliness, but to show a broad pair of scarlet garters. His stockings were blue, with white clocks; he wore large silver shoe-buckles; a broad paste buckle in his hatband; his sleeve-buttons were gold seven-shilling pieces; and he had two or three guineas hanging as ornaments to his watch-chain. 35

[4] On making some inquiries about him, I gathered, that he was descended from a line of farmers that had always lived on the same spot, and owned the same property; and that half of the church-yard was taken up with the tombstones of his race. He has all his life been an important character in the place. When a youngster he was 40 one of the most roaring blades of the neighborhood. No one could match him at wrestling, pitching the bar, cudgel play, and other athletic exercises. Like the renowned Pinner of Wakefield, he was the village champion; carried off the prize at all the fairs, and threw his gauntlet at the country round. Even to this day the old people 45 talk of his prowess, and undervalue, in comparison, all heroes of the green that have succeeded him; nay, they say, that if Ready-Money Jack were to take the field even now, there is no one could stand before him.

[5] When Jack's father died, the neighbors shook their heads, and 50 predicted that young hopeful would soon make way with the old homestead; but Jack falsified all their predictions. The moment he succeeded to the paternal farm, he assumed a new character: took a wife; attended resolutely to his affairs, and became an industrious,

55 thrifty farmer. With the family property he inherited a set of old
family maxims, to which he steadily adhered. He saw to everything
himself; put his own hand to the plough; worked hard; ate heartily;
slept soundly; paid for everything in cash down; and never danced
except he could do it to the music of his own money in both pockets.
60 He has never been without a hundred or two pounds in gold by him,
and never allows a debt to stand unpaid. This has gained him his
current name, of which, by the by, he is a little proud; and has
caused him to be looked upon as a very wealthy man by all the
village.

65   [6] Notwithstanding his thrift, however, he has never denied himself the amusements of life, but has taken a share in every passing
pleasure. It is his maxim, that "he that works hard can afford to
play." He is, therefore, an attendant at all the country fairs and
wakes, and has signalized himself by feats of strength and prowess
70 on every village green in the shire. He often makes his appearance
at horse-races, and sports his half-guinea, and even his guinea at a
time; keeps a good horse for his own riding, and to this day is fond
of following the hounds, and is generally in at the death. He keeps
up the rustic revels, and hospitalities too, for which his paternal farm-
75 house has always been noted; has plenty of good cheer and dancing
at harvest-home, and, above all, keeps the "merry night," as it is
termed, at Christmas.

[7] With all his love of amusement, however, Jack is by no means
a boisterous jovial companion. He is seldom known to laugh even
80 in the midst of his gayety; but maintains the same grave, lion-like
demeanor. He is very slow at comprehending a joke; and is apt to
sit puzzling at it, with a perplexed look, while the rest of the company is in a roar. This gravity has, perhaps, grown on him with the
growing weight of his character; for he is gradually rising into patri-
85 archal dignity in his native place. Though he no longer takes an
active part in athletic sports, he always presides at them, and is
appealed to on all occasions as umpire. He maintains the peace on
the village green at holiday games, and quells all brawls and quarrels
by collaring the parties and shaking them heartily, if refractory. No
90 one ever pretends to raise a hand against him, or to contend against
his decisions; the young men have grown up in habitual awe of his
prowess, and in implicit deference to him as the champion and lord
of the green.

[8] He is a regular frequenter of the village inn, the landlady hav-
95 ing been a sweetheart of his in early life, and he having always con-

tinued on kind terms with her. He seldom, however, drinks anything but a draught of ale; smokes his pipe, and pays his reckoning before leaving the tap-room. Here he "gives his little senate laws"; decides bets, which are very generally referred to him; determines upon the characters and qualities of horses; and, indeed, plays now and then 100 the part of a judge, in settling petty disputes between neighbors, which otherwise might have been nursed by country attorneys into tolerable law-suits. Jack is very candid and impartial in his decisions, but he has not a head to carry a long argument, and is very apt to get perplexed and out of patience if there is much pleading. He gen- 105 erally breaks through the argument with a strong voice, and brings matters to a summary conclusion by pronouncing what he calls the "upshot of the business," or, in other words, "the long and the short of the matter."

[9] Jack made a journey to London a great many years since, 110 which has furnished him with topics of conversation ever since. He saw the old king on the terrace at Windsor, who stopped, and pointed him out to one of the princesses, being probably struck with Jack's truly yeomanlike appearance. This is a favorite anecdote with him, and has no doubt had a great effect in making him a most loyal 115 subject ever since, in spite of taxes and poors' rates. He was also at Bartholomew fair, where he had half the buttons cut off his coat; and a gang of pickpockets, attracted by his external show of gold and silver, made a regular attempt to hustle him as he was gazing at a show; but for once they caught a tartar, for Jack enacted as 120 great wonders among the gang as Samson did among the Philistines. One of his neighbors, who had accompanied him to town, and was with him at the fair, brought back an account of his exploits, which raised the pride of the whole village; who considered their champion as having subdued all London, and eclipsed the achievements of 125 Friar Tuck, or even the renowned Robin Hood himself.

[10] Of late years the old fellow has begun to take the world easily; he works less, and indulges in greater leisure, his son having grown up, and succeeded to him both in the labors of the farm and the exploits of the green. Like all sons of distinguished men, how- 130 ever, his father's renown is a disadvantage to him, for he can never come up to public expectation. Though a fine active fellow of three-and-twenty, and quite the "cock of the walk," yet the old people declare he is nothing like what Ready-Money Jack was at his time of life. The youngster himself acknowledges his inferiority, and has 135 a wonderful opinion of the old man, who indeed taught him all his

athletic accomplishments, and holds such a sway over him, that, I am told, even to this day, he would have no hesitation to take him in hands, if he rebelled against paternal government.

140   [11] The Squire holds Jack in very high esteem, and shows him to all his visitors, as a specimen of old English "heart of oak." He frequently calls at his house, and tastes some of his home-brewed, which is excellent. He made Jack a present of old Tusser's "Hundred Points of Good Husbandrie," which has furnished him with reading

145 ever since, and is his text-book and manual in all agricultural and domestic concerns. He has made dog's ears at the most favorite passages, and knows many of the poetical maxims by heart.

[12] Tibbets, though not a man to be daunted or fluttered by high acquaintances, and though he cherishes a sturdy independence

150 of mind and manner, yet is evidently gratified by the attentions of the Squire, whom he has known from boyhood, and pronounces "a true gentleman every inch of him." He is, also, on excellent terms with Master Simon, who is a kind of privy counsellor to the family; but his great favorite is the Oxonian, whom he taught to wrestle

155 and play at quarter-staff when a boy, and considers the most promising young gentleman in the whole county.

[For treatment of this selection, see p. 226.]

Paradox of
the American Woman

ERIC JOHN DINGWALL

[1] A STUDY of social trends shows that the gulf which separates the sexes in the United States with regard to their social and intellectual lives opened so early that it has become an American characteristic. The building of the vast new structure demanded so

5 much practical activity that men simply did not have the time to

From *The American Woman*, by Eric John Dingwall. Copyright 1957 by Eric John Dingwall. Reprinted by permission of Rinehart & Company, Inc., New York, Publishers. Selection title by the Editors.

attend to anything more than the work on hand. Thus, . . . woman stepped down from her pedestal to attend to social affairs when she was not dealing with the house and the education of the children. Since all women did not want to marry or did not have the opportunity to do so, other openings had to be found for them. But whatever course of action they chose to take, or had forced upon them, they were still, in a sense, the guardians of social intercourse, and thus the feminization of American culture was inevitable. Indeed, James Truslow Adams, in his interesting study of *The American*, has gone so far as to say that the feeling of guilt aroused in the man for his neglect of the woman has been partially assuaged by the fact that the woman, in turning away from the man, has managed to find fresh fields for her own life and interests apart from the home and domestic duties.

[2] What the American is capable of producing, when the obstructionist tactics of selfish groups are overcome, can be seen in such magnificent achievements as the T.V.A. (Tennessee Valley Authority) and other projects. Yet, with every fresh proposal the same wall of difficulties has to be surmounted, the same old arguments countered, and the same old fallacies exposed and refuted. But progress is being made; and in the United States progress is sometimes spectacular. Once informed opinion realises the inner meaning and origin of the tension and frustration that afflict society, then and then only will a beginning be made to end a state of affairs which make the United States an enigma to so many.

[3] At the very core of that puzzle stands the American woman, and it is only by understanding her relation to the industrial framework of American civilization that a true realisation of the basic factors operating in American society can be achieved. For with the freedom of the American woman from the mesh in which she is vainly struggling, will come the liberation of the American man from the invisible influences which retard his growth and stunt his mental development. We have not far to look to see what the American people are capable of achieving. In many of the more material and useful activities of the human race they stand supreme. It may have been merely an accident of history that their development has been along lines which have led them to their present condition. But, if I have interpreted that development at all correctly, it would seem that the general trend was inevitable. With Puritanism gone sour, and the age of private enterprise leading to unparalleled periods of prosperity and slumps in which Mammon stifled the things of the

mind and of the spirit, the position of woman became intolerable. "Equal rights" and the ideals of feminism contributed but little to the essentials for which she craved. With feminism triumphant she
50 lost her femininity, and with her femininity her peace of mind.

•   •   •   •   •

[4] The English-speaking world is linked by bonds which can hardly be broken by candid criticism of the varying cultures which make up this powerful combination of peoples. These links, intangible though many of them be, stem from fundamental ways of looking at
55 life and the belief in the freedom of the human spirit to climb upwards and onwards so long as its progress does not hinder and impede the same path in other people.

[5] The main difference between the two great blocs of English-speaking people is, I am convinced, the position of women in the
60 two societies. In the one case we have a culture through the development of which feminine influence has become dominant, and through this dominance a kind of infantilism and immaturity is spread among considerable portions of the population. In the other, as among the great Latin peoples, feminine influence is pronounced, but woman
65 has never attempted to usurp the position accepted by man, and thus bring him under her undisputed sway. Such an empire brings neither happiness nor peace of mind to her who rules it and nothing but neurotic restlessness to him who submits. This is one key to the American enigma, and through an understanding of the American
70 woman's place and sexual activities in the industrial society of the United States, the paradoxes and contradictions in American life may become resolved.

One of the major characteristics of poetry is compression—the saying of much in few words, each word carrying a maximum burden of meaning. The Japanese *Haiku* beautifully illustrates compression through economy of diction, or succinctness, as it is often called—an asset in prose as well as in poetry.

1. In *Haiku* I, there is communicated in the first line (including the three dots) one of the stark and tragic realities of life in seventeenth-century China—famine as a result of rice-crop failure; the remaining three lines show not only resignation to the famine, but the positive response to beauty—here, ironically, the beauty of nature which has failed to supply the foodstuff necessary to maintain life. This statement of the content, tone, and feelings shows how much is communicated through the fourteen words.

Taking into account not only the explicit words but also the turn in thought and feeling indicated by the sets of dots, summarize in your own words the essentials of all that is communicated through the *Haiku* II through V. Make a word count of each *Haiku* and of each of your summaries; what conclusions can you draw about professional writers of *Haiku*?

2. Study each *Haiku* to see whether it has any verbiage—any word or words that can be removed without destroying meaning. Be prepared to justify the deletion of any words you decide can be deleted. Can you substitute a single word for any combinations of words in any of the *Haiku* without destroying meaning or decreasing effectiveness? If so, where?

3. In the edition from which the *Haiku* were reprinted here, the second line has been split in two, a result of certain typographical considerations. In its purest form, the *Haiku* contains three lines, the first and third having five syllables each and the second, seven syllables. Write a *Haiku* on any one of the following or on a subject of your own choosing:

    a. a sudden change in weather

    b. a disappointed hope

    c. a disabled new car

    d. a tough steak

    e. a tattered coat

Apply the tests indicated in 2 above. If the tests show that your *Haiku* needs revision, revise it as many times as necessary to have it "pass" the tests; preserve the various versions for comparative analysis.

4. Washington Irving in "Ready-Money Jack" has written in straightforward, unadorned prose; it is not prose of great beauty, but it is efficient and economical in its diction. Here and there, however, Irving is guilty of a certain amount of wordiness; compare the two versions of the following sentence:

    a. "The first place where he attracted my attention was in the churchyard . . ." (paragraph 2).

    b. He first attracted my attention in the churchyard. . . .

Find five additional sentences in the essay which are needlessly wordy; revise each without changing the basic meaning; count the number of words you save in each of your revisions.

5. "Very" is one of the most overworked words in the language; as a result, most frequently it weakens rather than intensifies the word it modifies. Irving certainly overworks the word. Examine each use he makes of "very" to determine whether its use is legitimate or whether

its omission would improve the sentence or whether a more exact, more specific intensifier would improve the sentence; wherever you decide on the third of these possibilities, supply the better word. Be prepared to justify each of your decisions.

6. Find five sentences in which Irving uses parallelism to achieve succinctness; by reconstructing each of the sentences, show how much more wordy it would have been without the parallelism.

7. In no more than six sentences describe yourself and the clothing you are wearing today, achieving as far as you can the exactness, vividness, and succinctness that characterize Irving's third paragraph.

8. Compare the first paragraph of the Dingwall selection with the following version, rewritten to reduce the number of words in each of the sentences; determine whether each change is an improvement (in increasing succinctness), whether meaning has been seriously changed, or whether communication has been impaired.

> A study of social trends shows that the gulf separating the sexes socially and intellectually in the United States opened so early that it has become an American characteristic. Building the vast new structure demanded so much practical activity that men could do only the work on hand. Thus, woman stepped down from her pedestal to attend to social affairs when she was not educating the children and housekeeping. Since not all women wanted, or had the opportunity, to marry, other openings had to be found for them. But whatever action they chose to take, or had forced upon them, they were still the guardians of social intercourse; thus the feminization of American culture was inevitable. Indeed, James Truslow Adams, in his interesting study of *The American,* has said that the man's guilt feeling for his neglect of the woman has been partially assuaged because the woman, in turning away from the man, has found fresh fields for her own life and interests apart from home and domestic duties.

9. Classify the sentences in Dingwall's second and third paragraphs under the usual headings of simple, compound, complex, compound-complex. Do you find significantly greater succinctness in any one of the types of sentences compared with the others? What generalization, if any, can you make about the relation between types of sentences and succinctness?

Alternate selections for the study of Succinctness: John Ciardi, "An Ulcer, Gentlemen, Is an Unwritten Poem"; Ralph E. Lapp, from *Atoms and People.*

Theme Assignment: Toward the end of the selection, Dingwall says that in America ". . . we have a culture through the development of which feminine influence has become dominant, and through this dominance a kind of infantilism and immaturity is spread among considerable portions of the population." This is a double-barreled statement: you may agree with both "barrels" or disagree with both or with one or the other. Women in our country generally are dominant in all areas of homemaking, but they play only a minor role in holding political office. Women probably spend more consumer money than men do, but men still govern the New York Stock Exchange and the Chicago grain market. Women are largely responsible for family patterns of sociability, but commercial airlines, railroads, and steamship companies hire only men for the most responsible jobs. Evidences of immaturity and infantilism can be found in advertising and in many widely read periodicals; evidences of maturity, however, can be found in the creativity of American painters, musicians, and writers. Many conventions of businessmen and fraternal organizations supply evidences of infantilism, but American science gives abundant proof of intellectual maturity.

Write a theme in which you support your reactions to the Dingwall quotation; draw extensively on your own knowledge of American life for evidence to substantiate your views. Apply the tests indicated in 2 above to each of your sentences; succinctness is the particular virtue for which you are striving.

Cliché and Jargon

Hard Sell

"A TIME OF RECESSION IS THE MOST FAVORABLE TIME FOR A CHANGE IN COMPETITIVE POSITIONS"

[1] THIS statement, from a recent talk given by Marion Harper, President of McCann-Erickson Incorporated, contains both promise and warning.

[2] It raises a "stop-look-think" signal for all companies that sell to the public and rely on advertising as a major force in the distribution and sale of their merchandise. The reason is apparent, but worth stating:

[3] An individual consumer today may be relatively unaffected by business conditions and have discretionary money to spend. But he is no longer swept along on a free-flowing tide of buying. His need to "keep up with the Joneses" is no longer the motive force it represents in a climate of general prosperity. He stops, looks, considers and compares. You need to give him *new reasons* to buy what you have to sell.

When basic buying attitudes alter, when large sections of the public begin to make critical comparisons of competitive products, the standings in an industry become especially subject to change.

Advertisement in *The New York Times* for July 8, 1958. Reprinted by permission of the CBS Radio Network. Selection title by the Editors.

[4] In the past, new brands, new products have come to the fore in times like these. Companies have gotten ahead of competition during such periods by presenting a product keyed to new buying moods, or by presenting an established product in a new light.

[5] These conditions, and the opportunity they hold, point up the need for thorough revaluations. Preliminary to any revaluation of marketing strategy is an examination of the product itself. In addition to such obvious considerations as improvements that can readily be made in the product or its package—are there new uses for it? Are the things you are saying about it the things most likely to trigger the buying impulse of the consumer? What image do you want your prospects to have of your product? And what image do they actually have? Where is the best place to tell your story? How often do you tell it to the same prospect?

[6] All these questions tumble around in every executive's mind periodically. But at no time are they more valid and more deserving of answers than today.

AGREEMENT ON HARD SELL

[7] There's little argument about the *way* to sell most consumer products now. Reports C. James Proud, President of the Advertising Federation of America:

> There is a definite move under way in the industry toward the hard sell approach. Advertisers have been studiously neglecting the importance of price for many years, and have been talking in generalities rather than specific product features. All that is changing. The public today is more practical about its purchases.

But hard sell involves more than a change in approach and content. Hard sell also means applying more advertising influence on more prospects more often. And the target of all marketing men is to do this with no increase in budget.

[8] It can be done. But it can be done only through an unemotional appraisal of all media.

Today, the luxury of the big gesture—of being able to point with pride at advertising—is no longer affordable *for its own sake*.

If there are solid influence or institutional reasons which stand up under scrutiny, then color-spreads and broadcast spectaculars have a useful place in the advertising program. And their values, in addition to straight advertising performance, will always include their capacity to impress distributors, dealers, salesmen. *But advertising campaigns can no longer be rated on prestige factors alone.*

ABSOLUTE AND RELATIVE COSTS

[9] Before you open the door to consideration of such important factors as advertising impact, background for your message, the persuasiveness of what you have to say, one question needs a clear answer.

[10] The question concerns dollars and people. It is a two-part question.

[11] Part one is the absolute cost: "What can I get for my total budget, for $500,000, or $1,000,000 or $5,000,000?" And the second part is relative efficiency in different media: "How much does it cost to reach 1000 people?"

[12] For years advertising men have argued that you cannot *compare* the relative cost of reaching 1000 people by means of a magazine insertion with that of a newspaper page or that of a broadcast program. You can't do this, they say, because there are differences in *how* you reach people through different media. This is true. It is true that there are techniques special to each of the media which, when imaginatively used, result in an effective job. It's also true that there are differences in this effectiveness. But these observations by-pass the central fact that to get maximum value from his budget, an advertiser must necessarily compare the costs.

[13] The first step in any media consideration is to look at the *transportation* price-tag—the absolute cost, and the cost of getting the message to a number of prospects.

[14] This must be paid for in dollars. Dollars and dollars can be compared. The numbers of people to whom the advertising message is delivered can also be compared.

[15] Recognizing the need for cost comparisons, some time ago a leading advertising agency researched the subject, and its index has been reported in the trade press.

•　•　•　•　•

[16] The *absolute* costs on which these comparisons are based have tremendously wide variations. Currently, a black-and-white page in a leading magazine costs $26,275. The average network half-hour evening television program costs $87,200 for time and talent. These one-time costs become significant when you recognize:

Effectiveness is based on more than just a one-time advertising effort. Prospects remember and respond to your product story only if you tell it OFTEN ENOUGH.

WHAT CAN $46,000 BUY?

[17] The figure of $46,000 is more than the cost of a magazine page and it is less than the cost of a television program. Here is what it buys in network radio:

It buys 50 advertisements of hard-sell length with an estimated reach of almost 25 per cent of all U.S. families more than five times each within one week at a cost of under 80c for each thousand family impressions.

$46,000 delivers this on the CBS Radio Network. The campaign, designed for heavy promotion before holiday weekends, operates in this way. It gives the advertiser sponsorship of 40 five-minute segments and units within radio's most popular program schedule. Within these, he has 40 commercials, one minute in length. The programs include such daytime serials as *Ma Perkins, Second Mrs. Burton, Young Dr. Malone* and *Our Gal Sunday* . . . and such diverse weekend and evening programs as *Amos 'n' Andy, Robert Q. Lewis, Galen Drake, The World Tonight, Indictment, F.B.I. in Peace and War* and *Mitch Miller.* The $46,000 also includes sponsorship of ten smaller program units within the popular daytime dramatic serial lineup, and with these, ten 30-second commercial messages.

[18] In this plan, an advertiser sponsors almost FOUR HOURS of entertainment programs and news . . . with 45 SOLID MINUTES of time in which to sell . . . concentrated in one week.

[19] That's one kind of campaign—a saturation drive. What will $10,000 a week, for example, give you in a *continuing campaign?*

[20] Strong representation in daytime serials on CBS Radio is one possibility, if your product is bought primarily by housewives. There are no programs in all radio today which attract as many housewives in the home as these do. Or, in the same budget area, sponsorship of multiple news broadcasts a week delivers an audience of both men and women—and carries with it an identification with the most celebrated news staff in broadcasting, CBS News.

• • • • •

THE BEST CLIMATE FOR HARD SELLING

[21] The CBS Radio Network does more than compete favorably in terms of numbers and dollars and cost per thousand. (These, as stated, are *first* considerations for advertising efficiency.)

[22] Just as important is the fact that on CBS Radio, efficiency is *not* delivered at the expense of the good neighborhood every advertiser wants for his message. Your message has more force, more believability, when it is delivered in surroundings that people believe in and respect. *Where* you appear is frequently as important as what you say.

[23] CBS Radio, of all the networks, has consistently maintained the program framework from which such values can come.

[24] As a result, sponsors are associated with established personalities and programs. These are important associations for every advertiser who wants the extra values that programs *as* programs add to the total influence of the message. For example, each program in its own way requires *attentive listening*. The schedule is deliberately designed for "foreground" as distinct from "background" listening. (It is an interesting corollary that these programs also attract the greatest *numbers* of listeners.)

[25] As another example of extra values, the network itself is recognized nationally as the place in radio where exciting things happen. Its presentation of outstanding broadcasts in the public interest— such as *The Galindez-Murphy Case*; *Who Killed Michael Farmer?*— attracts the attention of leading newspapers and magazines, and of prominent people in government and public life.

PROTECTING YOUR SALES MESSAGE

[26] A basic condition of hard sell is that you have *time enough to tell your story*. And in broadcasting, an additional condition of *effective* hard sell is that your message be protected from the competition of other advertisers' commercials.

[27] TIME ENOUGH: You can't give reasons, point out features —so necessary today to make a sale—on match box covers or the broadcast equivalent: 6-second and 10-second spots. The *minimum* length of a commercial message on the CBS Radio Network is 30 seconds.

[28] PROTECTED LISTENING: Advertisers have shown concern lately over triple-spotting and other practices which lessen the effectiveness of the message. The CBS Radio Network—scheduling advertisements within *programs*—sets each sponsor's message apart from the next.

[29] A recently completed study, "Protected Listening," demonstrates in sound the advantage to the advertiser of the CBS Radio

Network's commercial placement policy as compared with other radio. The vice president and radio-television director of a major advertising agency, who heard this report, said:

> *CBS Radio has done a genuine service to the industry in pointing up this problem. It raises a very sound point which certainly is applicable to radio but which also extends through the whole communication business wherein advertisers want their message spotted where people will hear or see it.*

You may want to examine and listen to the "Protected Listening" study, yourself.

• • • • •

WHAT CAN NETWORK RADIO DO FOR YOU?

[30] No advertising message—even one as long as this—can give a detailed answer to that question. A useful answer has to be designed to fit your specific needs.

[31] How about the salesman just named "Champion Salesman of all Broadcasting"? And named by people who ought to know: the National Association of Direct Selling Companies. They said:

> *Those of us in the business of selling have long admired Arthur Godfrey as the champion salesman. The mark of a good salesman is the job he does in moving the products from the manufacturer's hands into the consumer's hands, and no one does this job better than Mr. Godfrey.*

His salary? Under $7500 a week (full network, time and talent) to make calls on over a million prospects a day.

[32] If there's a place in your thinking for a new way to organize your marketing approach—if what we've said touches on your problems—then there's a place in network radio for your advertising. We want your business. May we give you some specific answers to *your* questions?

WITH AN UPTURN FORECAST FOR LATER IN THE YEAR, NOW IS THE FAVORABLE TIME TO BUILD AN EXTRA SHARE OF MARKET FOR WHAT YOU HAVE TO SELL. CBS RADIO NETWORK

[For treatment of this selection, see p. 236.]

The Case of Alaska

ANOTHER good reason for prompt action in the case of Alaska is that it may help to clear the decks for the equally meritorious cause of statehood for Hawaii. For some curious reasons it has been decided that coupling the two was certain to spell the doom of each. This does not seem exactly rational, since the same action should be taken in respect to each claimant. But since this seems to be one of the political facts of life, at the moment, the best thing that can be done is to get action, first on one and then on the other.

The inexperienced speaker, called upon to "say a few words," notoriously becomes tongue-tied. Sometimes the inexperienced writer becomes "pen-tied"; more often, unfortunately, he does not. He not only writes too much but also thinks he has to "Write," with a capital W. Suppose he wants to say that it is raining hard. He will probably write one of two things: either "It is raining cats and dogs" or "The precipitation is profuse." Both are bad, for somewhat different reasons. "It is raining cats and dogs" is a cliché; "The precipitation is profuse" is jargon.

A cliché is an expression which was once fresh but has become exhausted from overuse. There is nothing intrinsically wrong with it; it is neither ungrammatical nor inexact. But it has been said so often that it no longer evokes any vivid image in the reader's mind; a writer uses it out of laziness or misunderstanding.

Students often ask how they can recognize clichés. Isn't *any* expression a cliché, they ask, because everything has been said before? Any expression can become a cliché if it is used too often, but expressions which already have been used too often are fairly easy to identify. If you hear half of an expression, and can supply the other half, it's a cliché. So, given these two lists:

as warm as _____

as free as _____

as comfortable as _____

as jumpy as _____

From an editorial, "Alaska's Statehood," *The New York Times*, June 16, 1958. Reprinted with the permission of The New York Times. Selection title by the Editors.

as sly as _____

as wise as _____

as pretty as _____

an old shoe
a picture
an owl
toast
a fox
a bird
a cat

you have no difficulty pairing them off. But not all clichés are comparisons. The following lists are equally easy to match:

sing for _____

pay _____

the straight _____

chip off _____

the sum _____

the old block
and substance
your supper
the piper
and narrow

All these expressions have their origin in human observation. They often derive from nature and were once concrete and imaginative. But now, when you read "as jumpy as a cat," for example, you don't picture a cat and think how apt the comparison is. Your mind simply clicks off the meaning "jumpy," and the writer might as well not have bothered with the rest. It is the writer's job to think up a new way of saying "jumpy" (jumpy as a jockey or a bingo player or a contestant in a spelling bee) or to say it straight. The word alone is stronger and clearer if it doesn't have to carry dead wood.

Jargon has two meanings. It may mean specialized shop- or trade-talk of a particular group. Thus, "audiovisual aids," "upward mobility," "ability to relate to his peers in a social situation," "hard sell," "Man, that's way out," "He hit the sack at twenty-three hundred," "The patient is spiking 104° in the afternoons" are all examples of the jargon of various groups. In general, this kind of writing should be avoided when the writer addresses any but the members of his own group. At best, it is the mark of the newcomer trying on his still-squeaky boots;

at worst, it is pretentious and ill-mannered. Again it should be emphasized that this type of jargon is perfectly acceptable when members of a particular group or profession are communicating with one another.

The other, more important meaning of the word "jargon" was explained by Sir Arthur Quiller-Couch in his *On the Art of Writing*. He calls jargon clumsy, roundabout, vague, "woolly," affected, "elegant" writing. The writer of jargon uses such meaningless, unnecessary phrases as "in connection with," "with regard to," "according as to whether." He never hits a point head-on, but prefers to walk all around it; instead of writing "no," Quiller-Couch says, he writes "The answer to the question is in the negative"; instead of writing "It is raining," he writes "The precipitation is profuse." He is in love with the sound of his own words, particularly if they are long. He dotes on "vague, woolly, abstract" nouns such as "case, instance, quality, thing, factor, character, condition, state." He is afraid to repeat himself and so uses what Quiller-Couch calls "the trick of Elegant Variation." So, he says, if the writer is talking of Byron, he cannot call him Byron twice on the same page, but uses instead affected variations: "that great but unequal poet," or "the meteoric darling of society." As an amusing example of honesty, of brevity, of concreteness, he cites " 'The hand that rocked the cradle has kicked the bucket.' "

1. Rewrite the following excerpts from the CBS Radio Network advertisement, identifying and then eliminating the stylistic disease from which each suffers:

   a. "a favorable time to build an extra share of market"

   b. "saturation drive"

   c. "stand up under scrutiny"

   d. "trigger the buying impulse"

   e. "CBS Radio has done a *genuine service* to the industry in *pointing up this problem. It raises a very sound point* which certainly is applicable to radio but which *extends through the whole communication business wherein advertisers want their message spotted* where people will hear or see it."

   f. "the motive force"

   g. "the hard sell approach"

   h. "efficiency is not delivered at the expense of the good neighborhood every advertiser wants for his message"

   i. "Before you open the door to such important factors as advertising impact"

   j. "these observations by-pass the central fact"

   k. "a black-and-white page"

l. "All these questions tumble around in every executive's mind periodically"

m. "It buys *50 advertisements of hard-sell length* with *an estimated reach* of almost 25 per cent of all U.S. families more than five times within one week at a cost of under 80c for *each thousand family impressions.*"

n. "a change in competitive positions"

2. What, if anything, does the ad gain by using so much jargon? What does it lose?

3. In your own words, summarize what the ad is saying. In doing so, keep these questions in mind: To whom is it addressed? What action, if any, is it recommending? When? Why?

4. Find at least two examples of clichés and two of jargon (Quiller-Couch style) in the paragraph from *The New York Times* editorial.

5. Rewrite one of the sentences in the paragraph, eliminating all the clichés and jargon you find.

Theme Assignment: Write a theme in which you try to convince a particular group that an action it is about to take is wrong. For example:

——a farmers' grange is planning to petition against a school tax.

——a hospital workers' union is planning to go out on strike.

——a group of refugees is planning a demonstration against a foreign diplomat visiting this country on official business.

——a group of teen-agers is planning to exclude a newcomer from its organization.

——a faculty committee is planning to abolish fraternities and sororities the following semester.

——a Congressional committee is considering a proposal to extend compulsory military training to women.

——a state highway commission is considering granting permission for billboards to be posted along the state turnpike.

Remember that—especially because you are addressing a specialized group—any insincerity on your part will be easily detected. Since you are trying to convince the opposition of your way of thinking, you must be direct and forceful. Your worst enemies will be clichés and jargon.

Concreteness

Musée des Beaux Arts

W. H. AUDEN

About suffering they were never wrong,
The Old Masters: how well they understood
Its human position; how it takes place
While someone else is eating or opening a window or just walking
    dully along;
5 How, when the aged are reverently, passionately waiting
For the miraculous birth, there always must be
Children who did not specially want it to happen, skating
On a pond at the edge of the wood:
They never forgot
10 That even the dreadful martyrdom must run its course
Anyhow in a corner, some untidy spot
Where the dogs go on with their doggy life and the torturer's horse
Scratches its innocent behind on a tree.

In Breughel's *Icarus*, for instance: how everything turns away
15 Quite leisurely from the disaster; the ploughman may
Have heard the splash, the forsaken cry,
But for him it was not an important failure; the sun shone
As it had to on the white legs disappearing into the green

Water; and the expensive delicate ship that must have seen
Something amazing, a boy falling out of the sky,
Had somewhere to get to and sailed calmly on.

[For treatment of this selection, see p. 243.]

A Memorable Hand

VIRGINIA WOOLF

[1] AFTER an hour or so—the sun was rapidly sinking, the
white clouds had turned red, the hills were violet, the woods purple,
the valleys black—a trumpet sounded. Orlando leapt to his feet.
The shrill sound came from the valley. It came from a dark spot
down there; a spot compact and mapped out; a maze; a town, yet girt 5
about with walls; it came from the heart of his own great house in the
valley, which, dark before, even as he looked and the single trumpet
duplicated and reduplicated itself with other shriller sounds, lost its
darkness and became pierced with lights. Some were small hurrying
lights, as if servants dashed along corridors to answer summonses; 10
others were high and lustrous lights, as if they burnt in empty ban-
queting halls made ready to receive guests who had not come; and
others dipped and waved and sank and rose, as if held in the hands
of troops of serving men, bending, kneeling, rising, receiving, guard-
ing, and escorting with all dignity indoors a great Princess alighting 15
from her chariot. Coaches turned and wheeled in the courtyard.
Horses tossed their plumes. The Queen had come.

[2] Orlando looked no more. He dashed downhill. He let himself
in at a wicket gate. He tore up the winding staircase. He reached his
room. He tossed his stockings to one side of the room, his jerkin 20
to the other. He dipped his head. He scoured his hands. He pared
his finger nails. With no more than six inches of looking-glass and
a pair of old candles to help him, he had thrust on crimson breeches,
lace collar, waistcoat of taffeta, and shoes with rosettes on them as

25 big as double dahlias in less than ten minutes by the stable clock.
He was ready. He was flushed. He was excited. But he was terribly
late.

[3] By short cuts known to him, he made his way now through
the vast congeries of rooms and staircases to the banqueting-hall,
30 five acres distant on the other side of the house. But half-way there,
in the back quarters where the servants lived, he stopped. The door
of Mrs. Stewkley's sitting-room stood open—she was gone, doubtless,
with all her keys to wait upon her mistress. But there, sitting at
the servant's dinner table with a tankard beside him and paper in
35 front of him, sat a rather fat, rather shabby man, whose ruff was a
thought dirty, and whose clothes were of hodden brown. He held a
pen in his hand, but he was not writing. He seemed in the act of
rolling some thought up and down, to and fro in his mind till it
gathered shape or momentum to his liking. His eyes, globed and
40 clouded like some green stone of curious texture, were fixed. He did
not see Orlando. For all his hurry, Orlando stopped dead. Was this
a poet? Was he writing poetry? "Tell me," he wanted to say, "everything in the whole world"—for he had the wildest, most absurd,
extravagant ideas about poets and poetry—but how speak to a man
45 who does not see you? who sees ogres, satyrs, perhaps the depths
of the sea instead? So Orlando stood gazing while the man turned
his pen in his fingers, this way and that way; and gazed and mused;
and then, very quickly, wrote half-a-dozen lines and looked up.
Whereupon Orlando, overcome with shyness, darted off and reached
50 the banqueting-hall only just in time to sink upon his knees and,
hanging his head in confusion, to offer a bowl of rosewater to the
great Queen herself.

[4] Such was his shyness that he saw no more of her than her
ringed hand in water; but it was enough. It was a memorable hand;
55 a thin hand with long fingers always curling as if round orb or
sceptre; a nervous, crabbed, sickly hand; a commanding hand too;
a hand that had only to raise itself for a head to fall; a hand, he
guessed, attached to an old body that smelt like a cupboard in which
furs are kept in camphor; which body was yet caparisoned in all
60 sorts of brocades and gems; and held itself very upright though perhaps in pain from sciatica; and never flinched though strung together
by a thousand fears; and the Queen's eyes were light yellow. All
this he felt as the great rings flashed in the water and then something
pressed his hair—which, perhaps, accounts for his seeing nothing
65 more likely to be of use to a historian. And in truth, his mind was

such a welter of opposites—of the night and the blazing candles, of the shabby poet and the great Queen, of silent fields and the clatter of serving men—that he could see nothing; or only a hand.

[5] By the same showing, the Queen herself can have seen only a head. But if it is possible from a hand to deduce a body, informed 70 with all the attributes of a great Queen, her crabbedness, courage, frailty, and terror, surely a head can be as fertile, looked down upon from a chair of state by a lady whose eyes were always, if the wax-works at the Abbey are to be trusted, wide open. The long, curled hair, the dark head bent so reverently, so innocently before her, 75 implied a pair of the finest legs that a young nobleman has ever stood upright upon; and violet eyes; and a heart of gold; and loyalty and manly charm—all qualities which the old woman loved the more the more they failed her. For she was growing old and worn and bent before her time. The sound of cannon was always in her 80 ears. She saw always the glistening poison drop and the long stiletto. As she sat at table she listened; she heard the guns in the Channel; she dreaded—was that a curse, was that a whisper? Innocence, simplicity, were all the more dear to her for the dark background she set them against. And it was that same night, so tradition has it, 85 when Orlando was sound asleep, that she made over formally, putting her hand and seal finally to the parchment, the gift of the great monastic house that had been the Archbishop's and then the King's to Orlando's father.

One of the most important ingredients which distinguish good writing from pedestrian writing, a work of art from a second-rate attempt, an A paper from a B, is concreteness. For it is not enough to be accurate; it is not even enough to have something to say—essential as both are to communication. The rule is easy enough to state: be specific. Never be satisfied with the abstract: *be specific.* Narrow down until you can narrow down no further. (Would you rather go on a blind date with "a girl" or with "a blue-eyed blond who won a beauty contest at Lake Champlain last summer"? with "a guy" or with "the six-foot-two life guard with the red Impala convertible"?) Never say "dress" when you mean "red wool jersey sheath"; "soldier" when you mean "top sergeant" or "rookie" or "company commander"; "animal" when you mean "tiger" or "deer" or "jaguar" or "puppy" or "skunk." Never say "go" when you mean "run," "drive at 60 miles an hour," "toddle," "skip," or "push your way through the crowd."

Auden could have written, "Suffering takes place while life is going on as usual" if he had wanted only to convey an idea. Virginia Woolf could have said, "You can see only a part of a person and know what that person is like."

The first step each of them took in the narrowing-down process was to give an example or examples. It would therefore be somewhat closer to Auden's meaning to write, "*The Old Masters knew that* suffering *always* takes place while life is going on as usual." He has gone to the masterpieces of painting to exemplify his abstraction. He has then gone on to use concrete noun after concrete noun, pinning down every thought or potential abstraction.

1. Point out how, in line 4, Auden has made concrete the abstraction "While life is going on as usual."

2. What other examples does he give in the first stanza? How has he pin-pointed or made concrete each of these examples?

3. What meanings of "the miraculous birth" occur to you? How many meanings do you think Auden intended? Find evidence within the poem to support your answer. If your answer is more than one, do you think this makes the poem less concrete? Why or why not?

4. Why did he not end the poem after the first stanza? Why would it have been more (or less, depending on your interpretation) effective if he had done so?

5. What does Auden do to make the abstract noun "everything" in line 14 concrete? Explain the use of the words "leisurely" (l. 15) and "calmly" (l. 21).

6. The "abstract" we made of the Virginia Woolf selection was "You can see only a part of a person and know what that person is like." Noting that she, too, employed an example to make this idea concrete, rewrite the sentence, substituting the appropriate concrete nouns for abstract ones; convey more specifically the meaning of the selection.

7. How does Virginia Woolf make you see the sunset?

8. Point out the ways in which Virginia Woolf made the following nouns in paragraph one concrete: "spot," "light," "men."

9. Account for the sentence structure in paragraph 2.

10. Point out the examples of concreteness in paragraph 3.

11. Show how, through the use of concrete detail, Virginia Woolf has Orlando "deduce . . . a body," and sense the Queen's "crabbedness," her "courage," her "frailty," and her "terror" from "a hand."

12. How is Orlando's "head" made vivid to the reader? What does the Queen deduce from it? What else in the selection bears out or gives further substance to her impression of Orlando?

13. What has the following sentence to do with organization of the whole: "And in truth, his mind was such a welter of opposites—of the night and the blazing candles, of the shabby poet and the great Queen,

of silent fields and the clatter of serving men—that he could see nothing; or only a hand"?

Alternate selections for the study of Concreteness: Washington Irving, "Ready-Money Jack"; Albert Camus, "A Thoroughly Negative Place."

Theme Assignment: The following words were spoken by Thomas Jefferson as part of his first inaugural address:

About to enter, fellow citizens, on the exercise of duties which comprehend everything dear and valuable to you, it is proper you should understand what I deem the essential principles of our government, and consequently those which ought to shape its administration. I shall compress them within the narrowest compass they will bear, stating the general principle, but not all its limitations. Equal and exact justice to all men, of whatever state or persuasion, religious or political; peace, commerce, and honest friendship with all nations, entangling alliances with none; the support of the State governments in all their rights, as the most competent administrations for our domestic concerns, and the surest bulwarks against antirepublican tendencies; the preservation of the general government in its whole constitutional vigor, as the sheet-anchor of our peace at home and safety abroad; a jealous care of the right of election by the people; a mild and safe correction of abuses which are lopped by the sword of revolution, where peaceable remedies are unprovided; absolute acquiescence in the decisions of the majority, the vital principle of republics, from which is no appeal but to force, the vital principle and immediate parent of despotism; a well-disciplined militia, our best reliance in peace and for the first moments of war, till regulars may relieve them; the supremacy of the civil over the military authority; economy in the public expense, that labor may be lightly burdened; the honest payment of our debts, and sacred preservation of the public faith; encouragement of agriculture, and of commerce as its handmaid; the diffusion of information and arraignment of all abuses at the bar of the public reason; freedom of religion, freedom of the press, and freedom of person, under the protection of the Habeas Corpus; and trial by juries impartially selected.

Jefferson said that he was simply stating "the general principle, but not all its limitations." Select one of these principles and write a theme defining, illustrating, or discussing it in as concrete terms as possible.

Active Verbs

The Storm

THOR HEYERDAHL

[1] TWO days later we had our first storm. It started by the trade wind dying away completely, and the feathery, white tradewind clouds, which were drifting over our heads up in the topmost blue, being suddenly invaded by a thick black cloud bank which rolled
5 up over the horizon from southward. Then there came gusts of wind from the most unexpected directions, so that it was impossible for the steering watch to keep control. As quickly as we got our stern turned to the new direction of the wind, so that the sail bellied out stiff and safe, just as quickly the gusts came at us from another
10 quarter, squeezed the proud bulge out of the sail, and made it swing round and thrash about to the peril of both crew and cargo. But then the wind suddenly set in to blow straight from the quarter whence the bad weather came, and, as the black clouds rolled over us, the breeze increased to a fresh wind which worked itself up into
15 a real storm.

[2] In the course of an incredibly short time the seas round about us were flung up to a height of fifteen feet, while single crests were hissing twenty and twenty-five feet above the trough of the sea, so that we had them on a level with our masthead when we ourselves
20 were down in the trough. All hands had to scramble about on deck

246

bent double, while the wind shook the bamboo wall and whistled
and howled in all the rigging.

[3] To protect the radio corner we stretched canvas over the rear
wall and port side of the cabin. All loose cargo was lashed securely,
and the sail was hauled down and made fast around the bamboo yard. 25
When the sky clouded over, the sea grew dark and threatening, and
in every direction it was white-crested with breaking waves. Long
tracks of dead foam lay like stripes to windward down the backs of
the long seas; and everywhere, where the wave ridges had broken
and plunged down, green patches like wounds lay frothing for a long 30
time in the blue-black sea. The crests blew away as they broke, and
the spray stood like salt rain over the sea. When the tropical rain
poured over us in horizontal squalls and whipped the surface of the
sea, invisible all round us, the water that ran from our hair and
beards tasted brackish, while we crawled about the deck naked and 35
frozen, seeing that all the gear was in order to weather the storm.

[4] When the storm rushed up over the horizon and gathered
about us for the first time, strained anticipation and anxiety were
discernible in our looks. But when it was upon us in earnest, and
the *Kon-Tiki* took everything that came her way with ease and buoy- 40
ancy, the storm became an exciting form of sport, and we all delighted
in the fury round about us which the balsa raft mastered so adroitly,
always seeing that she herself lay on the wave tops like a cork, while
all the main weight of the raging water was always a few inches
beneath. The sea had much in common with the mountains in such 45
weather. It was like being out in the wilds in a storm, up on the
highest mountain plateaus, naked and gray. Even though we were
right in the heart of the tropics, when the raft glided up and down
over the smoking waste of sea we always thought of racing downhill
among snowdrifts and rock faces. 50

[5] The steering watch had to keep its eyes open in such weather.
When the steepest seas passed under the forward half of the raft,
the logs aft rose right out of the water, but the next second they
plunged down again to climb up over the next crest. Each time the
seas came so close upon one another that the hindmost reached us 55
while the first was still holding the bow in the air. Then the solid
sheets of water thundered in over the steering watch in a terrifying
welter, but next second the stern went up and the flood disappeared
as through the prongs of a fork.

[6] We calculated that in an ordinary calm sea, where there were 60
usually seven seconds between the highest waves, we took in about

two hundred tons of water astern in twenty-four hours. But we hardly
noticed it because it just flowed in quietly round the bare legs of
the steering watch and as quietly disappeared again between the logs.
65 But in a heavy storm more than ten thousand tons of water poured
on board astern in the course of twenty-four hours, seeing that loads
varying from a few gallons to two or three cubic yards, and occasionally much more, flowed on board every five seconds. It sometimes broke on board with a deafening thunderclap, so that the
70 helmsman stood in water up to his waist and felt as if he were
forcing his way against the current in a swift river. The raft seemed
to stand trembling for a moment, but then the cruel load that weighed
her down astern disappeared overboard again in great cascades.

•   •   •   •   •

[7] When the weather moderated, it was as though the big fish
75 around us had become completely infuriated. The water round the
raft was full of sharks, tunnies, dolphins, and a few dazed bonitos,
all wriggling about close under the timber of the raft and in the
waves nearest to it. It was a ceaseless life-and-death struggle; the
backs of big fishes arched themselves over the water and shot
80 off like rockets, one chasing another in pairs, while the water round
the raft was repeatedly tinged with thick blood. The combatants
were mainly tunnies and dolphins, and the dolphins came in big
shoals which moved much more quickly and alertly than usual. The
tunnies were the assailants; often a fish of 150 to 200 pounds would
85 leap high into the air holding a dolphin's bloody head in its mouth.
But, even if individual dolphins dashed off with tunnies hard on their
heels, the actual shoal of dolphins did not give ground, although
there were often several wriggling round with big gaping wounds in
their necks. Now and again the sharks, too, seemed to become blind
90 with rage, and we saw them catch and fight with big tunnies, which
met in the shark a superior enemy.

[8] Not one single peaceful little pilot fish was to be seen. They
had been devoured by the furious tunnies, or they had hidden in
the chinks under the raft or fled far away from the battlefield. We
95 dared not put our heads down into the water to see.

Standard grammars point out that the function of verbs is to make
an assertion or to communicate action or state of being. The verb is
the very heart of most English sentences; except in dialogue where the
verb may be clearly implied in context, a "sentence" without a verb

fails to communicate. So important a part of speech deserves the attention of every writer.

Beyond one or two generalizations, however, little of value can be said in the abstract about the most effective use of verbs. The generalizations are, first, to use verbs in the active voice rather than the passive whenever possible and, second, to use the most vivid and appropriate verb to communicate action rather than vaguely suggesting action.

"He kicked the ball" (active voice) is a crisp sentence.

"The ball was kicked by him" (passive voice) emphasizes the ball rather than the man and reverses the normal forward movement of English sentences.

"He went over the fence" is far less effective than "He clambered over the fence" because the action is left vague and general.

English as a language is rich in verbs, and care in the selection of just the right verb will do much to improve writing.

1. List five particularly effective verbs (or verbals) in the first paragraph of the selection from *Kon-Tiki*. Why are they as effective as you think they are? List at least two synonyms for each of the five; are any of your synonyms more effective than Heyerdahl's verbs? Why or why not?

2. Heyerdahl did not take advantage of every opportunity in the first paragraph to use vivid verbs. Would changing any of his verbs improve the paragraph? Why or why not?

3. Why is the passive voice ("were flung") in the first sentence of paragraph 2 justifiable? What quality do "hissing," "whistled," and "howled" (paragraph 2) have in common? Why is their use here effective?

4. Change the passive verbs in the second sentence of paragraph 3 to active verbs. Have you improved the original? Explain.

5. In paragraphs 4 and 5, are verbs or nouns and adjectives more important in achieving vividness? Rewrite parts of both paragraphs, changing as many verbs and nouns and adjectives as necessary to increase vividness.

6. Analyze the verbs in the rest of the selection, accounting for the effectiveness of those you think are effective and substituting more effective verbs for those you think are ineffective. Remember that the value of any technique will be reduced through overuse.

Alternate selection for the study of Active Verbs: Virginia Woolf, "A Memorable Hand."

Assignment: Substitute five alternatives for each of the verbs in the sentences on the following page; arrange each set of your alternatives in ascending order of effectiveness:

1. The professor walked into the lecture hall.
2. The boys ate the food greedily and audibly.
3. The boat was brought into its pier by an experienced, licensed pilot.
4. The minister spoke with great feeling about his deepest convictions.
5. The group went up the steep mountain side, constantly aware of the danger of a misstep.
6. Democracy forces equality even upon those who least want it.
7. Most advertising today insults the intelligence of the mature reader.
8. An ignorant critic retards the growth of the creative artist.
9. Frequent consultation of a dictionary helps the writer to increase his vocabulary.
10. The tasteful use of cosmetics can add to a woman's beauty.

Levels of

Diction

"Say, Bud!"..."Hiya, Baby!"

JACQUES BARZUN

[1] THE thing about the U.S. "which nobody can deny" is not that we are jolly good fellows. Half the world hates us, at sight or on principle. But nobody can deny that we have the best table manners of any people. The abolition of the toothpick, the injunction against using the napkin as buckler or towel, the rediscovery of the 5 right side of the fork (while the English continue to pile up the curved side of theirs with mouthfuls of balanced diet) are worthy of all praise.

[2] We go too far, quite often, we fall into the genteel and curl the little finger, or subdue chewing to lip motions that make a woman 10 look as if she were expecting a kiss. With care and a fork, surely, one should be able to imitate the French mopping-up operations and not let good sauce or gravy go to waste. But the American principle is sound: not to make others disgusted at the sight of their fellow man. It is all the more important in a democracy where one has to 15 endure close and continual contact with everybody else. The marvel of our collective training may be seen in any restaurant or dining car. Regardless of differences of income, speech, and occupation,

those one looks at are eating in a civilized manner. The exception
20 is so rare as to be memorable.

[3] But the table is only one of the places of public resort, and
talk forms a larger part of our impact on one another than eating
in common. Of our spoken manners, the European would say that
we have none. By his standards, we are rude or uncouth when we
25 are not downright impudent. Americans who have lived even a short
time abroad notice this on their return—as did the young lady who
wrote to the papers of her experience at the airport. She somehow
got separated from her husband and, looking bewildered, was asked
by an attendant what the matter was. She said "I've lost my hus-
30 band." To which his rejoinder was: "Don't worry, baby, we'll get
you another." And he probably took her by the elbow to show her
the right way.

[4] Lord Chesterfield would have gone about it differently, no
doubt, but it is a mistake to consider the American rude or uncouth.
35 He is casual, free-and-easy, intimate. He is using to the limit his
new-found privilege—tremendous when you come to think about
it—of addressing anybody at will, without bowing and scraping or
having to fear the consequences of forwardness. The worst that can
happen to him is what we call the brushoff, some equally intimate
40 formula for saying "Run along, I'm busy."

[5] None of this has elegance; casualness can get tiresome, but
the observer has no right to compare it with drawing-room *politesse*.
It must be compared with the average of underling behavior abroad,
which may be very high indeed and then again very low—as in the
45 brutal snarl of the European petty official or the obsequious shop-
keeper cringe. Whatever we may think, the one thing sure is that
casual American manners, in spite of their seeming rudely personal,
are quite *im*personal. "They're nothing to do with you"—as the guy
himself would say. And the headlines of his paper prove him right.
50 When Governor Stevenson's chances for the nomination began to
improve, the tabloid scarehead bore the simple words: "Stevie's
Rolling."

[6] If the situation were no more complicated than this, we could
lean back and let time take care to rub down the edges and do the
55 burnishing. The forces working toward a general raising of our common behavior are enormous. The airport attendant's son will go to
college and have some of the surface crudity removed. The daughter
meanwhile reads magazines and newspapers in which the propaganda
for etiquette is as incessant as it is solemn. Her wedding, we may be

sure, will be true to Emily Post or not take place at all. Through 60
the women's social ambition for their offspring, the men acquire
somewhat gentler manners and by the next generation a new crop
of well-reared youth has to be credited to our institutions—to the
very freedom which in its first outbursts we may deplore.

[7] But a complication does enter in and qualifies this natural 65
evolution. I have in mind the relations of the better-mannered to
the rest and to one another. We have to recognize that there still is
in the United States some difference of upbringing as between the
workingman and the "genteel," even though that gap has been
leaped by many an executive who started in the ranks. The desire 70
to ignore the gap expresses itself in the refusal to talk about manners
at all. It is considered undemocratic, snobbish, lacking in manliness,
to notice their existence. We deny or disbelieve that manners are
"little morals." And yet the most genuinely American in this respect
will choose a college for their sons or a club for themselves on 75
grounds of congeniality and tone that are, in the last analysis, taste
in manners. In their own actions, moreover, these Americans instinc-
tively apply the double standard, though it does not *feel* double in
the daily routine. As he goes up to his office, the businessman will
talk to any of the men who run his tier of elevators without any 80
sense of constraint on either side. But he calls them Joe or Pete
whereas they say Mr. Jones. Where then is the equality? In this,
that Mr. Jones wouldn't dream of speaking to them as I heard an
elderly Senator do down South: "Boy, I'm in a hurry, take me up!"
A kind of familiarity, joking and kidding, are mutually accepted, and 85
special favors are asked for as man to man, not as master to servant.

[8] Out in the street, though, the social contract breaks down. The
cabdriver and his fare don't know each other, and as often as not
the driver feels that he must reaffirm Liberty, Equality, and Fraternity
the moment a stranger enters his territory. He calls me Big Boy, 90
asks personal questions, turns the radio on for the track results,
and blows cigar smoke into my compartment, all with the best
humor and fullest indifference to my comfort. If I have a headache
and want silence or if I want to tell him the quickest route at that
particular time of day, I have to use diplomacy so as not to offend 95
and alienate him. To get my money's worth I must wheedle my own
employee. The cash nexus has something to do with this: I mustn't
think that because I pay him I can order him about. He's a free
man, doing me a favor, really, and the tip I am supposed to give
him, whether or not I feel satisfied, is but a meaningless ritual. Hence 100

it will happen (not strangely but logically) that the taxi man I meet repeatedly will become less aggressive, more deferent, as we get to know each other better.

[9] Cabdrivers here serve as a mere example. They are not a 105 marked species and I was careful to say that "as often as not" their behavior is such. In the same way shopgirls will assert their independence by going on with private conversation while you wait patiently. You had better be patient. Throughout the day you will run into a dozen similar types who seem to resent your inquiry, your 110 grammar, your manners. If, as with the cabbie, the strangeness wears off because the same doorman, the same waiter, the same boy from the dry cleaners has managed to identify you, then, ninety-nine times out of a hundred, a beautiful friendship begins. You're pals. They'll do anything for you; they pull the word "Sir" out of their uncon- 115 scious where it has been repressed for so long, and you've regained your lost equality.

[10] This characteristic phenomenon (don't say it's human—anything people do is human) is a clue to what goes on in the higher echelons. It's quite simple: all the echelons want love—why not 120 make it the chorus of a popular song? It rings sad and true. We may think of ourselves as higher-ups, but we make one another as nervous as cats and want to be reassured: "I won't bite or scratch, please don't you either." What the old aristocrats believed about the discomforts of democracy was a shrewd guess. The competition of 125 each with all, they said, will make people touchy, envious, ill at ease. There will be no protection to one's self-love such as comes from a fixed rank or status. In a hierarchy your rank may not be high but it is yours for keeps; it gives you that clear look and firm tread, for no one can belittle you or step on your toes with impunity. 130   [11] This is doubtless an embellished view of rank, and it leaves out of account our American kindliness born of prosperity and much moving about. But the lack of some protection for self-love does leave us open to brushing, or we wouldn't put so much cotton-wool in our manners. Is it a coincidence that the compulsory lovey-dovey 135 style began about twenty years ago, shortly after the Great Crash? Certainly the first Washington joke under Roosevelt was about his greeting a visitor: "Sorry, John, but I didn't catch your last name." The new brotherhood of man born of calamity and teamwork in reconstruction is with us yet. One of the knottiest questions in any 140 business relation is just when to begin calling your correspondent

Charlie. Too soon, you're rushing the deal; too late he thinks you don't really like him. Why should he care? That is easy to guess. If you were already on familiar terms, he would attach no significance to any little thing that was said or done between you. That great word "informal," which we work to death, means the sigh of relief that 145 comes when the bars are down and the vests unbuttoned. But until then the conventions are as real as in the court of Louis XIV.

[12] Consider the conference manners in a group where not everybody is Charlie yet. You can't hear the facts for the purring. Nobody dares say: "This is my view." They all say: "I'm only thinking out 150 loud of course—" a form of indecent exposure that nobody minds because it proves defenselessness. To contradict the previous speaker argues premeditation, so you begin: "I agree in general with everything you say, but don't you think that—" It shows mutual respect, it is log-rolling on the intellectual plane. I have actually heard: "Give 155 me your thinking, and then I'll give you mine"—another lilt for a popular song. And I am wrong, on reflection, in ascribing this cakewalk to the New Deal. Part of it is an old American tradition that Benjamin Franklin describes as his own technique for getting things done: put your idea in such a way that others will think it originated 160 with them. That's the way to subdue the ego and redistribute the wealth of ideas in one operation.

[13] To be sure, the law of diminishing returns will ruin the game in time. I once attended as a guest an informal session of a very popular course in How to Get Ahead (for women it's the Charm 165 School), and heard some recent graduates tell the wonders of the system. One pimply youth declared that whereas before he had suffered from an "inferior complex," now he thought nothing of addressing this large and distinguished audience—why? Because he was a success. He had made himself into a good mixer to whom everybody 170 was "really wonderful." He could now develop a liking not only for people he liked but for people he didn't like. The whole world liked him in return and that was success. His family believed in him from the start, which helped him to maintain an "I'll show you" attitude. Toward the rest of the world he was invariably lighthearted, 175 cheerful, and free. Add to this a good memory for names and faces— so that you can say right off: "You're Frank Sims in cosmetics," or "How's that growling appendix of yours?"—and life holds no terrors.

[14] Most of us shudder at the thought of those hearty handshakes and are speechless at the naïveté that cannot see the worthlessness 180

of cordiality by formula. But the march of psychology is like everything else among us, varied in pace, though not unpredictable. The
Hackle-Riser school of thought has by now caught up with the folly
and indignity of Excessive Lubrication. One more effort, one more
185 scraping down and coat of varnish on the next generation, and our
revolting young sycophant will be like the suave salesman who
entered my office, whipped out a card, extended a hand, and said:
"I want you to meet me."

[15] Taking the broad view, what is going on in American man-
190 ners is our characteristic process of education. We start with raw
materials and the first licks must be adapted to the simple thoughts
of large numbers. We begin "democratic" then turn "scientific,"
which means becoming shamelessly self-conscious and mechanical.
Gradually the grossness purges itself. We must not forget that what
195 we have undertaken, no other society has tried: we do not suppress
half of mankind to refine part of the other half. We let it spread
out in the daylight to do the best it can. So one may question
whether it is fair to complain at once of popular crudity and of
popular efforts to correct it.

200   [16] And after all, who are we higher-ups to sneer at the pimply
youth turned good mixer, when all around us we see leaders of industry, finance, and the professions turning into patterns of public
relations? Not all succumb but all are vulnerable because our world
is composed entirely of the likes of us, equals. By consent, our lives
205 are more and more in one another's hands, we do not feel strong or
independent even when we have the means or power, and we must
compensate besides for the anonymity of statistical living. On top of
these emotional reasons come the practical ones based on our political
and economic structure. We have to sell and we have to get votes. If
210 the presidential candidates must kiss babies, the salesmen must try to
like their customers, and the big shots must endear themselves to one
another by diminutives. To cry out with delight, "Why, Morgan!" is
still too formal: Morg's the word.

[17] But what should be the goal, the ideal, by which to try and
215 shape improved American manners? The principle that we must not
give others cause for disgust or contempt is important but negative.
What can we aim at beyond avoiding offense? The answer, I think,
lies in one word: conversation. I once told a friend who, I know,
loves good conversation how surprised I was that he could stand the
220 company of a man I met at his house and found totally uninteresting.

Ted explained that they had been to the same Western college, though
several years apart, and were active alumni. "And so," said Ted,
"when we're alone, we talk Wabash." The phrase has stayed with us
as a means of describing conversation that is null and void, a reckless
squandering of words. Among the uneducated it is truly wonderful 225
how many times an idea is repeated before it is let go. It is as if each
party were not quite sure the language would carry across—a sad
thought for democrats. In more fluent circles, the bane is not repetition
but interruption. The eyes wander while the lips go on—interruption
from within.   230

[18] I like to watch her. She is handsome and intelligent like so
many ladies of Dallas, and evidently proud of her careful suburbanity.
Excellent drinks have been served. The talk has come to life in one
corner, and naturally those engaged in it have momentarily stopped
reaching for things, so she looks around for a dish of peanuts, a box 235
of cigarettes, and, having heard that it is rude to break in, she signals
in pantomime to the person whose eye she has at last caught. People
turn and stop one by one; the damage is done. You cannot reweave a
fabric that has frayed to bits. She does this again and again—to her
family, her children, to the guests she has herself adroitly launched 240
into debate. "See here," one wants to say, "hospitality is not all food
and drink. On the contrary, we want to forget our appetites a little
and refresh ourselves with new faces by an exchange of what dwells
behind the face. Let us be and let us talk." O. Henry did warn us
that "in Texas discourse is seldom continuous," but I am disappointed 245
just the same, and to that extent my hostess has failed.

[19] Is it because our manners are inept that many people prefer
an evening of bridge or playing chamber music? Either takes as much
practice as conversation, if not more, but at the end they feel less
jarred, the time seems better spent, no words have passed except 250
functional ones. It would be sad to think that ordinary democratic
society was being reduced to communion without words. The trouble
is not all on the surface. Those who are bored by triviality are too
easily put off by other subjects, and especially by the clash of tastes
and opinions. The old habits need a shaking out. From mutual toler- 255
ance here in America, we began by excluding the expression of religious views, then of political opinions, finally of all controversial
utterance whatever. In many a circle that has intellectual pretensions
you hardly dare talk freely about an actress or a movie for fear that
your remarks will hit the favorite of someone present. Possessiveness 260

and self-love can hardly go farther. The net effect is to make everybody talk Wabash, which is like the abdominal complaint known as
Variable Dullness. The livelier minds conclude that anything is better
than conversation. An unhappy friend of mine used to anesthetize
265 himself with drink. His well-wishers pleaded, "But you're so much
more agreeable when you're sober!" To which he would reply,
"Maybe, but other people are so much more boring."

[20] Work itself suffers from our systematic blandness. It was a
recent Secretary of Defense who said that what this country needed
270 was Tertiary Flap. This he defined as the hammering out of differences sharply expressed. It is normal and healthy, he adds, and helps
to get things done. It obviously does not speak well for our poise and
confidence in one another if the assumption is that the slightest breath
of criticism must destroy the thing criticized. That assumption is so
275 revoltingly stupid that I make a point of never using a certain phrase
in common use, just because it implies that criticism is necessarily
hostile and mean. I found it hard at first to break the habit because
it is so widely shared. But now I don't preface a personal remark by
saying: "I'm very fond of Tom, *but* . . ."

280   [21] Thinking in this vein opens a wide field of observation. One
begins to notice how often others say: *"Frankly,* I prefer Lucky
Strikes." Frankly! Good God! It also turns out that what they have
been telling you is their *personal* opinion. When they apply to you on
some point, they excuse themselves with the formula, "I'm asking just
285 for information." So! He won't make use of it, won't use it against me.
To ask for use would be impertinent, cavalier, but if it's just for
information, I can afford to tell him. It makes one pine for Lydia, the
Lady of the Aroostook in William Dean Howells, who isn't any less
delightful because we're told: "Lydia wants to know."

290   [22] In this reproving mood, I confess I also begin to look
askance at all the laughing and grinning that is *de rigueur.* I am all
for finding comedy wherever life will let us. I think Shakespeare was
right to scatter humorous scenes in tragedies—the same idea would
improve most of our Broadway comedies. But I don't see why every
295 committee meeting has to open with strenuous ha-ha's about nothing
at all. Everybody brings his cackle under pressure and has to let it
out before work can start. Is it meant to show that he's not taken in
by what he's doing, that he's above it? Or alternatively is it a confes-
sion that he's an ass and knows it, but—saving grace!—he has a sense
300 of humor?

[23] Modern man's humor is a secretion he thinks would be dangerous to hold in. This is why, no doubt, it has become impossible, at the end of a quiet evening party, to say "Thank you" like a rational creature—just as it was impossible to say just "Good evening" on arrival. What takes place instead is a whinnying of mares and friendly 305 snarling of stallions. When alone at home you see the image of it in the magazines. This led an inspired critic of our manners, Mr. Charles Morton, to summon advertisers who use pictures to "wipe off that grin." After a definitive study of the facts, he reports: "Three people fondling cigarette lighters: something is convulsing them. Woman 310 about to put an enormous dessert in a refrigerator already chockfull: the very idea has brought her to the point of hysterics." With such training in deterging folly, Mr. Morton should go on to tackle public figures and newspaper photographers. In any situation except kissing their wives, our leaders invariably show their full set of teeth. Two of 315 them shaking hands have of course more to laugh at, but even so . . . Meanwhile the voice of the people has embodied the affectation in a decisive phrase—a sentence, rather, from which there is no appeal:

[24] "He hasnasensayoomer." 320

[25] Manners as anxious and also as yielding as ours are a disadvantage not only to those who like to keep their activities separate and either really work, or play, or talk. They also put everyone at the mercy of the uninhibited. In public places, it becomes less and less possible to recover one's privileges when infringed. The sign may 325 plainly say No Smoking and one may be suffering from a cold or an allergy, but the boorish will light up. One stands the discomfort rather than make a fuss. If two couples meet unexpectedly on the train, their loud joy at the surprise, and all the news since they last met, have to be heard by many who would prefer to read. The captive audience is 330 shackled by its own excessive gentility—as was shown in the case of the radio commercials in the Washington buses. We are law-abiding to a point just this side of martyrdom.

[26] But if life is to remain tolerable in the promiscuous modern world, a sharper line will have to be drawn between positive and 335 negative rights to comfort in public utilities. It may be a comfort to the sailor across the aisle to be strumming on his banjo. But the negative comfort of the rest of the car should make him desist. Coming back to your hotel at 2 A.M. with colleagues you've met at the convention, you may find it natural to pursue the discussion down the 340

deserted halls; but the sleep of your neighbors—so negative it seems quite useless—should make you shut up. We are so numerous, so tightly packed, our devices are so powerful and so inspiring to childish imaginations, that we must vigilantly protect ourselves and the unrep-
345 resented public too. It was only a few months ago that a railroad proposed to floodlight from the trains the thickly peopled regions through which they passed.

[27] And speaking of the childish, it is important not to let misplaced kindness to the young encourage them to forget themselves and
350 go berserk in public. I have seen a whole subway car of adults terrorized by eight or ten schoolboys who wanted a roughhouse on the way home—satchels flying in people's faces, feet trampled on, and never a sign that the little barbarians were not alone in the place or that their behavior was not to be expected. Who can wonder then at
355 the vandalism which the keepers of our national shrines and parks report annually? Six million dollars' worth of damage to public property, some of it irreparable, most of it the result of indulging whims at others' expense.

[28] The proof that a democracy is not by nature irresponsible but
360 knows how to raise itself to civilized behavior can be found every summer at Jones Beach near New York. The city's thousands are there in close proximity and utopian perfection. There are no messes, no flying papers or cigarette butts, nothing but reasons to admire the collective self-discipline. When one thinks of the manners of the
365 populace a hundred years ago, this seems like the wholesale conversion of sinners. To go to a theater then was to risk having clothes torn or spat upon, to see the show interrupted by yells and missiles, and to court insult and violence at the slightest mishap.

[29] On the strength of our progress I do not even despair of seeing
370 some of my friends as civilized at home as they are at the theater. I do not mean that they are domestic rowdies, but that their carelessness often comes to the same thing. They will, for instance, allow their dog to do nearly everything except eat the guests. Yet if one arrived at the party in blue jeans, with a cake of soap and a towel, they would
375 feel hurt. Offenses through the dog would make a long chapter, beginning with the inhospitable yapping that greets the sound of the doorbell. Small children, too, are positive comforts to the owner that should yield within reason to the negative pleasure of the guests. And finally, the word might go around that a large cocktail party is
380 not just an opportunity for abandoned acts—holes burned in rugs and

table tops, cigarettes crushed out in *canapés* or floating in drinks, sticky hands wiped on upholstery, half-eaten olives cached atop your books. But perhaps all this is just a weak modern expression of the need for saturnalia—another subject altogether.

[30] The more one thinks about manners the more one recognizes 385 that the very idea is full of contradictions. One wants people to be tactful, but knows that to exercise tact is fatiguing and destroys sociability. No tact, then, formal manners which are like signals telling everybody how matters stand. But how rigid and silly and pompous! Let's be natural. Yes, but in the best of us nature is self-centered and 390 easily detestable by all. One hates to hear even oneself going on, how much more that unquenchable bore Bumpus. And Mrs. O'Grundy who calls herself Organdy now her husband's dead, what an insufferable social climber! . . . .

[31] Here let me pause and digress, to make the dear lady amends 395 and lay a votive offering at the feet of snobbery. Thou maligned virtue! Or if that is too strong, let me say Worthy Effort Misunderstood—and sometimes misapplied. How wrong of Longfellow to call *Excelsior* a "strange device." Climbing is the basic device—look at Evolution, one laborious social climb over the bodies of unfashionable 400 dodos and dinosaurs. The ape in us is primordial and we should cheer when he apes something better. To emigrate and become an American is to climb. To follow etiquette and eat peas only off your own knife is sheer affectation—at first. To value education and buy books one does not quite understand—what is this but another climb upward? 405

[32] Our favorite reading in modern times, the novel, is a school of snobbery. All the characters we are not meant to imitate are ticked off by the author's snobbish instincts: "His hair was parted in the middle and thickly plastered with oil." "Elsie bobbed her head and said 'Pleased to meetcha.' " Shame on you, novelists! Your character 410 traits are nothing but hasty generalizations, like race prejudice. But glory to you also for leading us on toward that perfect delicacy of manners which you alone possess. It is thanks to you perhaps that our Western world is now outwardly one class in clothes, manners, and common thoughts—one world, if we do not dig too deep. It is to your 415 fussing about trivial detail, perhaps, that we enjoy another unique American spectacle: the workman respectful of his hands and wearing gloves at his work—gloves, which were once the appanage of the princes of the Church, then of the noble lords, whom next the bourgeois aped, until now they have found their true place with their 420

utility. Gentlemen of labor, let nothing you dismay. And you who are not to the manner born, snob on, snob on—good always comes of it.

[33] If the objector points to Hollywood as the revolting apotheosis of snobbery, he can be told that Hollywood is only the court of Louis XIV over again. The bootlicking, the brief authority and the plunges from the heights, the desire to be seen and seen with, the refusal of grade A to talk to grade B, the prostitution of every kind, interspersed unquestionably with talent, integrity, and lofty contempt—those are the people and the manners of Versailles. We can esteem ourselves lucky if California drains off from our midst the unrepresentative snobs *à outrance*.

[34] Who then is representative? Since I have involved the novelists, I give you Mr. Rex Stout's Archie Goodwin. In his thirties, a drinker of milk who packs a gun and takes shorthand, full of brains but not willing to let them show in public, he is the idealization of American manners. Compare his relation to his employer Nero Wolfe with Dr. Watson's to Sherlock Holmes. Archie is impudent and will be annoying if it relieves his feelings. At the end of thirty years, Watson was on less familiar terms with his friend and equal Holmes than Archie can be with a new client after ten minutes. Archie's vocabulary is also more extensive gutterwards, which makes him and not Nero Wolfe the memorable speaker. Holmes would not have stood it. Wolfe has to stand it. And he reaps ample benefits. Archie is loyal, infinitely more helpful because more emancipated than Watson, and just as devoted when circumstances require.

[35] The one thing Archie does not tolerate and uses every ingenuity to puncture is affectation. No bad thing to tilt at, though to suspect affectation can itself become a pose. But such is the mood of Archie's generation, the median American style in manners. They are manners for universal, that is, democratic use. Why change when going from the family circle to the world of strangers? There are no strangers any more. True, the freight of feeling carried by these manners is slight. Feeling is nobody's business but your own—which includes your feeling about yourself. And this, favorable or not, it is your duty to suppress. You can make up for impersonality by giving casualness a twist others may recognize. Thus do we sort one another out for friendship, or more, or less, from among our common kind.

[For treatment of this selection, see p. 270.]

FROM *My Zip Gun Army*

IRA H. FREEMAN

[1] IT was the end of the road for me when the bus turned off King's Highway four miles beyond Warwick, N. Y. I never felt so alone, helpless, trapped and scared in my life.

[2] The sign at the entrance read: "New York State Training School for Boys." I had made it all right—president of the mighty Deacons, the club with the meanest rep and heaviest artillery in Brooklyn. Now from the top of the ladder I had hit bottom. As we drove in, I got a sinking sensation that my days as a big sahib of the Little People were over. I was in the cooler now, all the way in.

[3] "Cheer up, Frenchie." The supervisor slapped me on the back. "You ain't going to the electric chair."

[4] For two hours on the ride up from New York he had been trying to persuade me that I would like the training school. I stared silently at all the damn red and gold trees. I did not believe one word he said.

[5] The school grounds were as neat and depressing as Prospect Park. Red brick buildings stood around a large mall. Beyond lay athletic fields, a sparkling lake and, in the distance, the blue Ramapos and foothills of the Catskills.

[6] "You don't see any fences or walls or armed guards, do you?" the supervisor asked me proudly.

[7] "What a dump!" I said. I had been to the stupid country once on a summer vacation. To squares it might look prettier and smell sweeter than the Bedford-Stuyvesant section of Brooklyn where I came from. But what was there to do in these boondocks? I guessed there wasn't a candy store for miles, much less a bar.

[8] We were herded through two locked doors into the reception area and searched to the skin. They actually looked inside our mouths. Even the headbeaters [police] of the 79th Precinct were not that thorough.

[9] It griped me to have to put on "state-o" or official clothes. They

didn't look very sharp: gray corduroy trousers, blue denim shirt, sneakers, workshoes, a Navy pea jacket and a knitted watchcap.

[10] I managed to swallow some of the supper slop—macaroni, 35 bread, milk and salad. I wished I were back in Lenny's candy store at Fulton Street and Carlton Avenue having some chips and coke.

[11] Then we were locked up for the night in tiny, single rooms with a grate at the bottom of the door and a window that opened only four inches. The walls pressed in even closer than they had in my cell 40 at Youth House in New York, where I could at least look out through the heavy wire screening.

[12] I lay back on my lumpy mattress, so shook up I could not sleep. It bugged me to be cooped up alone in this narrow cage. I had no idea what was going to happen to me or how long they would keep 45 me here.

[13] I tried to imagine my Deacons pacing the turf [gang territory] or talking about me in Lenny's candy store. "We gotta keep the club together till Frenchie gets back," they would be saying—I hoped.

[14] Although I had been busted [arrested] less than two weeks 50 ago, I was homesick already. I was only 14-and-a-half and had never really been away from home before. I thought about my family as I never had when I lived at home.

[15] "You little hood," my older brother Larry had said when I was saying goodby to my folks in Brooklyn Children's Court. "You 55 ought to be shot for what you doin' to Ma."

[16] "Hush," my mother reproved Larry. "Don't say that to your brother." She begged me to pray to God to make me a better boy. She didn't cry, but she looked so sad that the tears came to my eyes.

[17] "Thirteen arrests." The judge shook his head over my file. 60 "Gang fighting, shootings, burglary, stealing a car. . . . I don't know what to make of you. Your parents are hardworking, religious people in pretty good circumstances. Your I. Q. is extraordinarily high. Why do you do these things?"

[18] I shrugged. What a dumb question. Every boy I knew did 65 these things. Maybe I just did more of them and better.

[19] "Well, son," the judge said, "I'm going to send you up to the country for a few months to straighten yourself out."

[20] "The country" meant the training school. Warwick was the place for hard guys like me, the cop fighters, gang leaders, kids who 70 had committed murder, rape, arson, robbery, every crime in the book. As long as you were between 12 and 16, had an I. Q. over 70 and were bad enough, you were in.

[21] I made up my mind that I would stand it until Christmas. If I didn't get out legally by then, I would breeze [run away].

[22] I was kept in the reception area for two weeks of inoculations and silly interviews by psychologists and social workers. Then, my orientation finished, I moved into a cottage. Almost 500 boys were grouped according to age or toughness in 15 cottages. About half were Negroes from New York. I found many boys I knew from West-inghouse Vocational or John Marshall Junior High School, and from clubs in Bedford-Stuyvesant and nearby turfs.

[23] We boys lived on the main floor of the cottage. Our "cottage parents" occupied the second floor. Either the cottage father or a relief man was on duty day and night, and all doors were kept locked. At 5:30 a.m. Mr. Schultz, the cottage father, walked through the "dorm-o," rapping on the metal cots with his keys. "Rise and shine." After morning slop, as we called breakfast, I had to join the others in cleaning the cottage. We swept and scrubbed the whole place like mad for 40 minutes.

[24] "Shine the floor like this, man," Chigger told me. With a rub-rag under each foot he began dancing over the highly waxed linoleum like Fred Astaire. Each boy had his own style of doing this, humming a bop tune and snapping his fingers. I found it was fun and invented a real crazy step. Rocking on the wax was repeated after every meal throughout my stay in the school.

[25] While we were trucking over the linoleum, a mild little man smoking a pipe wandered in. I was surprised to learn that this casual visitor was Superintendent A. Alfred Cohen.

[26] "Welcome to training school, Carl," he greeted me. I was amazed that the head man in the place should know my name so soon. Afterward I discovered that he knew everyone. He always used boys' real names, not their gang nicknames.

[27] "If you have a problem," he told me, "take it up first with your supervisors. If they can't help, come to me. You'll see me around."

[28] I did see him often, roving the grounds, bareheaded, hands in pockets, puffing his pipe. Boys would stop him any time to pour out their troubles. He was never too busy to listen.

●　●　●　●　●

[29] I was stretched on my bed one afternoon staring at the ceiling. I could hear kids yelling from the softball field, but I preferred to lie alone in my hole. Mr. Wall came in.

[30] "What's the matter with you, Frenchie?"

[31] "Mr. Wall, nothing personal, but I want out, out, out. From now on I'm going to be the worst state-o bum that ever went to this
115 training school. I'm going to force you people to send me home or ship me to a real prison, I don't care which."

[32] "You out of your mind?" he said.

[33] In his usual miraculous way Mr. Cohen appeared. "What's this powwow about?"

120 [34] "Same old thing, Mr. Cohen." Mr. Wall sighed hopelessly.

[35] Mr. Cohen nodded and sat down next to me on the bed. Nobody said a thing while he stuffed his pipe. I remembered what he had once said to me: "If you ever have a problem, come to me."

125 [36] "I got a problem, Mr. Cohen," I said wryly.

[37] "I know," he answered. "Your committee is of the opinion that it would be dangerous to send you home. If I should overrule the committee, do you think you could stay out of trouble at home?"

130 [38] "Mr. Cohen," I gasped, choked by new hope, "please, please!"

[39] "You didn't encourage us during your Easter leave," he said. "Why do you believe you could stay out of trouble now?"

[40] "I can do whatever I put my mind to," I argued. "Did I ever let you down?"

135 [41] "I have great hopes for you," Mr. Cohen said. "I'd like to see you finish school, go through college. What about that?"

[42] "Try me, just try me." I could hardly draw breath while I waited for his answer. He took his pipe out of his mouth and blew smoke.

140 [43] I studied his face to see if one of his famous hunches was coming.

[44] All of a sudden Mr. Cohen slapped my thigh. "Mr. Wall, process this boy to leave in four days."

[45] I leaped straight for the ceiling, howling like a fire siren. I
145 hugged Mr. Cohen and wished I could tell him of the love I had for him. I put a bear hug on my cottage father. I kissed Mrs. Wall and took a poke at every boy in the cottage.

[46] On my last night, while the boys were giving me the traditional good-luck beating, I cried a bit, though not from pain.

150 [47] I kept my promise to Little Al and never got busted again. The Deacons nearly flipped when I came home and told them I had

jumped smooth. But they gradually came around to my idea of converting the bopping club into a baseball and social club. We called it the Imperial Deacons. Of course we had to defend the turf a few times against invasions, but we never went down on a real raid again.   155

[48] Eight of the members could not stand it this way and joined the Army to see some action in Korea. Three of them never came back.

[49] Remembering what my supervisors had urged, I continued my education. It wasn't easy. Fourteen New York City high schools 160 rejected me because of my bad record, but I finally shoehorned into one. My brother Larry, who was an honor graduate of the last school, had to appeal personally to the principal to get me in.

[50] After high school it took me five years of plugging to get a college diploma. All the way through high school and college I kept 165 working to support myself and bring money home. I worked for years as a room clerk in a YMCA residence from 4 p.m. to midnight, and later as a hospital orderly from midnight to 8 a.m. Drinking coffee, I would try to stay awake to study between tours of the wards. Some days I felt I would never make it, but I kept plodding along. Mr. 170 Cohen wrote often to give me a lift.

[51] The grind paid off at last. Today I am a research technician in a university biological laboratory and I hope to enter medical school.

[52] Occasionally I run into a few of the old gang. No less than 175 twenty have served time for some adult crime. Half a dozen are junkies. Some are dead—of junk, disease or injuries in a brawl. Only one or two—like Chukker who became a commercial artist—are doing all right.

[53] I have returned to the training school often. Sixty percent of 180 Mr. Cohen's "alumni" now have no further trouble with the law, compared with 20% when he took over eleven years ago.

[54] Mr. Cohen keeps my graduation picture by his desk and I make speeches to the boys. Out of 10,283 training school boys since 1932, only six are college graduates. Most of the other college men 185 don't let on they ever went there. But I am not ashamed. I am forever grateful to Little Al, to his dedicated staff, to my parents, and even to the judge, who did me more of a favor than he thought. Thanks to all of them, I know I'm going to make it.

[For treatment of this selection, see p. 270.]

FROM *Down on the Tennessee*

RICHARD PIKE BISSELL

[1] IT was October and the trees were turning and there was a blue haze in the hills and ravines. Once we passed an old-time saddlebag cabin right beside the river and it looked like a scene from the opening of the old West, with about six hounds sprawled around, 5 two or three rangy-looking men leaning against a buckboard wagon, and a woman in a sunbonnet emptying a pail. And we passed Pittsburg Landing, and Shiloh Battlefield, and Mousetail Eddy, Petticoat Riffle, and Widow Reynolds Bar, and Gin Landing, and Fowlkes Tribble, and a lot of other places with names like that.

10 [2] I was up sitting on the leather bench listening to the endless talk about steamboats and steamboating one afternoon and finally there was a lull in the torrent of river talk.

[3] Captain Warren turned to me. "Dude, something has got to be done about that cook's legs. You're such a flash with the girls, now I 15 want you to speak to her."

[4] "Aw listen, Cap. . . ."

[5] "I mean it. You're the very man for the job. I'm mighty pleased to have such a versatile Mate aboard."

[6] "All right, I'll go in and say, 'The Captain says your legs is 20 dirty. Wash em!' "

[7] "That's fine. Go and do it."

[8] "Aw listen, Cap. . . ."

[9] "Go and do it. Now," he said. "By the way, Dude, what in hell does that pair of ground-hogs use their wonderful private bathtub 25 for?"

[10] "They keep their clothes in it," I said.

[11] I got up and went down to the deck room. Birdie's husband, Vergil, was asleep on a pile of junk line.

[12] I went up to the galley. Birdie was sitting on a chair eating 30 peanut butter out of the jar, with a spoon.

[13] "Listen, Birdie," I said. "You ain't supposed to eat that right out of the jar."

[14] "Ah lahks it," she said.

[15] The sink was all piled up with dishes, and two full garbage pails were spilling onto the floor. Vergil was so dang lazy, instead of emptying a full pail he would go and get another empty one. 35

[16] "This place looks like hell," I said. "Why don't Vergil empty that garbage?"

[17] "Vergil he's around someplace. He says his hand hurts where he sawed it on them plums." 40

[18] "Birdie," I said. "Come here with me."

[19] She got up and slopped after me and I went down the main cabin to her room and went in. You never saw such a mess but I'm not going to describe it.

[20] I went in the bathroom and took a couple of cracker boxes 45 and some wadded-up clothes out of the tub and turned on the water.

[21] "What you fixin to do, Mate?" she said, taking out her Bruton's snuff and helping herself.

[22] The tub got pretty full and I tested the water and turned it off. I couldn't find any soap, so I went out to the galley after some. 50

[23] "You stay right there," I said.

[24] "Mighty strange goins-on," she said.

[25] I came back with a big bar of Ivory. "Birdie, if you like your job on here, get in that tub and take a bath. It's a rule. Maybe you don't understand on account of never workin on a boat before, but 55 the cook gotta take a bath every day. That's the state law."

[26] "What state?" she says.

[27] "Tennessee," I said.

[28] "Ain't no law like that in Alabama."

[29] "You want me to give you that bath?" 60

[30] "Huh uh," she says. "Go way, boy," and she began to haul her dress off.

[31] I went out.

[32] "Especially the legs, Birdie," I said. "Especially the legs."

[33] "Especially the laigs," she said. "Mah God, what a state." 65

[34] I went back up to the pilothouse. "Your cook's in the bathtub, Cap. She looks just like Claudette Colbert," I said.

[35] Captain Warren reached in his breast pocket and handed me an Antonio and Cleopatra. "Have a good cigar, Dude," he said. "You know, on deck you leave something to be desired at times. But, boy, 70

I wouldn't trade you for all the mates on the Mississippi River and Tributaries and the Red River of the North."

[36] "Thank you, Captain," I said. "Perhaps my deck work will improve as I grow older. When do we get to Sheffield?"

75   [37] "In a couple of hours," he said, and commenced to roar. "In the bathtub! You better go down and see that our little Alabama rose don't drown."

You gotta work real hard to get the hang of this writing stuff. It's a lot tougher than it looks. English may be the mother tongue, all right, but Mother never worried none about unity, coherence, and all that junk.

If, on reading the preceding paragraph, you became immediately aware—and perhaps disapprovingly aware—of the inappropriateness of our addressing college students in such "English," then you are also aware that there are various levels of diction in English and that appropriateness is a major criterion in the choice of a level of diction for a given kind of communication. Without attempting to make a highly formal and rigid classification of the levels of diction, it is nevertheless useful to draw a few distinguishing lines among the various levels.

The most formal English is used in such writings as learned articles on scholarly subjects addressed to scholars, philosophical treatises, documents of historical import (*The Constitution of the United States,* for example), reports and minutes of parliamentary bodies. Somewhat less formal English—though still formal—is used in such writings as good newspaper editorials, articles in periodicals addressed to an educated and cultivated audience (*Harper's, Atlantic Monthly, Saturday Review,* for example), formal correspondence between educated people, college students' term papers and most expository themes. Informal English is appropriate for social correspondence, the casual conversation of educated people, certain kinds of personal (or informal) essays.

The lines distinguishing these levels, one from another, are not hard and fast. Many words are quite correct and appropriate on all levels; the place of some words has changed with time, and the place of other words will change with time. What was once a slang or objectionable word may now be a standard word, and what is now a highly formal word or expression may become appropriate for informal usage.

Appropriateness of diction depends on whether the communication is written or spoken, on the speaker or writer, on the reader or listener, and on the circumstances under which the communication takes place. Spoken English is usually less formal than the most formal English, but sometimes it may be just as formal—a sermon, for example, or even

at times a university commencement address or the citations read aloud
to recipients of honorary degrees. For a college professor to order
groceries over a telephone as though he were lecturing on archaeology
would obviously be inappropriate; for the grocery clerk to address the
professor as he would his bowling club intimates would be just as inappropriate. The college student who writes, "The collation served after
the jam session was super" or "The iniquities of the Nazis were pretty
hard to take" is guilty of mixing levels of diction, one or another of
which is inappropriate.

Provincialisms and dialects, technical or trade vocabularies, and slang
form additional levels of diction. Except in fiction in which characters
are made to speak as they would in a particular part of the country
or with a particular foreign-language background, there is normally no
place for provincialisms and dialects in written communication of any
formality. Technical or trade vocabularies (the golfer's "birdie,"
"eagle," and "divot"; the horse racer's "win," "place," and "show"; the
college student's "flunk," "crib," and "cut"; the newspaper man's "lead,"
"head," and "cut") have a place only in the communication—usually
informal—among members of the group or trade for which the vocabulary came into being. For a golfer to avoid golf terms or for a reporter
to avoid newspaper terms would be just as inappropriate as for a
student to write in tennis or baseball terms about agrarian reforms in
nineteenth-century England.

Slang is defined in part by the *American College Dictionary* as
"language . . . regarded as below the standard of cultivated speech."
Slang is never admitted into the most formal writing and only rarely
into less formal writing. There are two chief objections to slang: it is
usually ineffective, vague, unimaginative (the dance was swell; the food
was lousy), and it frequently is in vogue for only a short time; when
the vogue dies, communication is impaired. Occasionally a slang expression is effective, however, and it may have a long enough life to
become quite respectable. The use of a particularly effective slang
expression in informal or semiformal writing just because it is effective
and lends variety is not objectionable; but it must be remembered that
a little slang goes a long way.

Slang should not be confused with colloquialisms—the style, diction,
and usage of informal communication. And the diction most characteristic of colloquial speech should not be mixed with the diction
peculiar to more formal written communication. The *American College
Dictionary*, in pointing out that there is nothing "bad" about colloquial
English, says that "it is merely a familiar style used in speaking rather
than in writing."

It is obviously impossible to draw up exhaustive lists of words
appropriate to various types of written communication that will guide

you into using appropriate diction. Reading various types of writing; analyzing the diction of occasional pieces of writing; listening to and conversing with people of various occupations, professions, and levels of society; remaining constantly aware of the necessity for propriety of diction in your own writing; and consulting a dictionary to find out whether a given word is slang or a colloquialism or a provincialism, say, will do much to help you avoid serious errors in diction.

1. Formulate the guiding purpose of Barzun's essay and character-ize as exactly as you can the audience for which you think Barzun was writing. Precisely how do you characterize the tone of the essay?

2. Which sentence in each of the following pairs is more formal; which is more appropriate to the content and tone? Justify your answer.

a. (1) "She somehow got separated from her husband . . ." (para-graph 3).

   (2) She somehow was separated from her husband.

b. (1) "If the situation were no more complicated than this, we could lean back and let time take care to rub down the edges and do the burnishing" (paragraph 6).

   (2) If the situation were no more complicated than this, we could permit time to ameliorate it.

c. (1) "Is it a coincidence that the compulsory lovey-dovey style began about twenty years ago, shortly after the Great Crash?" (paragraph 11).

   (2) Is it a coincidence that compulsory informality began about twenty years ago, shortly after the Wall Street debacle?

d. (1) "He had made himself into a good mixer to whom every-body was 'really wonderful' " (paragraph 13).

   (2) He had made himself into a socially acceptable person to whom everyone was consistently polite.

e. (1) "The principle that we must not give others cause for dis-gust or contempt is important but negative" (paragraph 17).

   (2) The principle that we must not gripe others is important but negative.

3. Classify each of the following words or expressions—as used in context—under one or more of the following levels: formal, informal, colloquial, slang; evaluate the propriety of each:

a. bane (paragraph 17)
b. suburbanity (paragraph 18)
c. well-wishers (paragraph 19)

    d. cackle (paragraph 22)
    e. secretion (paragraph 23)
    f. light up (paragraph 25)
    g. irreparable (paragraph 27)
    h. saturnalia (paragraph 29)
    i. ticked off (paragraph 32)
    j. apotheosis (paragraph 33)
    k. No bad thing to tilt at (paragraph 35)
    l. mopping-up operations (paragraph 2)
  m. brushoff (paragraph 4)
    n. scarehead (paragraph 5)
    o. phenomenon (paragraph 10)

4. It is obvious from the preceding questions that Barzun has mixed several levels of diction throughout his essay—seemingly a violation of the consistency considered above as a virtue in writing. Is this mixing of levels a flaw or a justifiable technique in this essay? Make clear the criteria on which you base your answer.

5. Jacques Barzun is a graduate school professor and dean at Columbia University. Select five sentences from the essay that seem completely appropriate in the writing of a highly trained academician; then select five more sentences that you might not have expected from such an author. Comment, in terms of context and tone, on the propriety of each of the sentences, and be prepared to justify your selection.

6. The Freeman selection appeared originally as an article in *Life* magazine; what is the guiding purpose of the piece and to what audience is it addressed?

7. List all the words and expressions in the Freeman article that fall under the heading of "technical or trade vocabulary" and all those under the heading of slang. After consulting relevant dictionaries, explain the origin of at least five of the words in each of your lists.

8. At what point in the Freeman article did you suspect that the narrator had had at least some higher education? What specific words gave you a clue?

9. At what level of diction is the Freeman article as a whole written? What inconsistencies in levels of diction do you find? Are they functional or a blemish in the writing?

10. Choose two paragraphs—not necessarily in succession—that do not contain dialogue but do contain slang or "technical or trade vocabulary" or both; rewrite each paragraph in formal English. In terms of content and context, what is gained or lost by your revisions?

11. In the selection from Bissell's "Down on the Tennessee," there is a considerable difference between the level of diction used in the dialogue and that used in the rest of the selection. How do you

classify the levels used? Is the difference disturbing or functional? Why?

12. What is the tone of the Bissell excerpt? How does the sentence structure of the first paragraph contribute to establishing the tone?

13. List several provincialisms Bissell uses; do they add to or detract from the effectiveness of the whole? Justify your answer.

Alternate selections for the study of Levels of Diction: Carl Sandburg, "Getting Education"; Robert Benchley, "The Children's Hour"; Thomas B. Macaulay, "The Country Squire."

Theme Assignment: Everyday situations demand different kinds of manners and different levels of diction—including, often enough, "technical or trade vocabularies" and even slang. A conversation with a garage mechanic about fixing your car will sound quite different from the instructions you may give to a barber or beauty shop operator about cutting your hair. Though you may at all times be polite, your manner of ordering in a diner will (and should) be quite different from your manner of ordering in an exclusive and expensive restaurant. Your behavior and levels of diction will be quite different when you are in a funeral home and a sports arena, a college classroom and a student lounge, a bank and a butcher shop.

Write a richly illustrated theme on differences in manners and levels of diction in various everyday situations; you need not, of course, limit yourself to the situations in the preceding paragraph. This is your opportunity to use some of the techniques of narration—particularly dialogue—to develop an expository idea.

Connotation and Denotation

A Thoroughly Negative Place

ALBERT CAMUS

[1] THE unusual events described in this chronicle occurred in 194— at Oran. Everyone agreed that, considering their somewhat extraordinary character, they were out of place there. For its ordinariness is what strikes one first about the town of Oran, which is merely a large French port on the Algerian coast, headquarters of the Prefect 5 of a French Department.

[2] The town itself, let us admit, is ugly. It has a smug, placid air and you need time to discover what it is that makes it different from so many business centers in other parts of the world. How to conjure up a picture, for instance, of a town without pigeons, with- 10 out any trees or gardens, where you never hear the beat of wings or the rustle of leaves—a thoroughly negative place, in short? The seasons are discriminated only in the sky. All that tells you of spring's coming is the feel of the air, or the baskets of flowers brought in from the suburbs by peddlers; it's a spring cried in the marketplaces. 15 During the summer the sun bakes the houses bone-dry, sprinkles our walls with grayish dust, and you have no option but to survive those days of fire indoors, behind closed shutters. In autumn, on the other

hand, we have deluges of mud. Only winter brings really pleasant
20 weather.

[3] Perhaps the easiest way of making a town's acquaintance is
to ascertain how the people in it work, how they love, and how they
die. In our little town (is this, one wonders, an effect of the climate?)
all three are done on much the same lines, with the same feverish
25 yet casual air. The truth is that everyone is bored, and devotes himself to cultivating habits. Our citizens work hard, but solely with the
object of getting rich. Their chief interest is in commerce, and their
chief aim in life is, as they call it, "doing business." Naturally they
don't eschew such simpler pleasures as love-making, sea-bathing,
30 going to the pictures. But, very sensibly, they reserve these pastimes
for Saturday afternoons and Sundays and employ the rest of the week
in making money, as much as possible. In the evening, on leaving
the office, they forgather, at an hour that never varies, in the cafés,
stroll the same boulevard, or take the air on their balconies. The
35 passions of the young are violent and short-lived; the vices of older
men seldom range beyond an addiction to bowling, to banquets and
"socials," or clubs where large sums change hands on the fall of
a card.

[4] It will be said, no doubt, that these habits are not peculiar to
40 our town; really all our contemporaries are much the same. Certainly
nothing is commoner nowadays than to see people working from
morn till night and then proceeding to fritter away at card-tables, in
cafés and in small-talk what time is left for living. Nevertheless there
still exist towns and countries where people have now and then an
45 inkling of something different. In general it doesn't change their lives.
Still, they have had an intimation, and that's so much to the good.
Oran, however, seems to be a town without intimations; in other
words, completely modern. Hence I see no need to dwell on the
manner of loving in our town. The men and women consume one
50 another rapidly in what is called "the act of love," or else settle
down to a mild habit of conjugality. We seldom find a mean between
these extremes. That, too, is not exceptional. At Oran, as elsewhere,
for lack of time and thinking, people have to love one another without knowing much about it.

55 [5] What is more exceptional in our town is the difficulty one may
experience there in dying. "Difficulty," perhaps, is not the right word;
"discomfort" would come nearer. Being ill is never agreeable, but
there are towns that stand by you, so to speak, when you are sick;
in which you can, after a fashion, let yourself go. An invalid needs

Write a theme describing a place, much as Camus describes Oran, giving it a special significance. This place may be the town or city in which you grew up, the resort where you spent your childhood vacations, the home of a friend or relative, a town in which you were once stranded (or lost), the place you always dream of seeing, or a place made famous by your favorite author. Make generous use of connotative meanings and connotative words to convey your impression to the reader.

small attentions, he likes to have something to rely on, and that's 60 natural enough. But at Oran the violent extremes of temperature, the exigencies of business, the uninspiring surroundings, the sudden nightfalls, and the very nature of its pleasures call for good health. An invalid feels out of it there. Think what it must be for a dying man, trapped behind hundreds of walls all sizzling with heat, while 65 the whole population, sitting in cafés or hanging on the telephone, is discussing shipments, bills of lading, discounts! It will then be obvious what discomfort attends death, even modern death, when it waylays you under such conditions in a dry place.

[6] These somewhat haphazard observations may give a fair idea 70 of what our town is like. However, we must not exaggerate. Really, all that was to be conveyed was the banality of the town's appearance and of life in it. But you can get through the days there without trouble, once you have formed habits. And since habits are precisely what our town encourages, all is for the best. Viewed from this angle, 75 its life is not particularly exciting; that must be admitted. But, at least, social unrest is quite unknown among us. And our frank-spoken, amiable, and industrious citizens have always inspired a reasonable esteem in visitors. Treeless, glamourless, soulless, the town of Oran ends by seeming restful and, after a while, you go complacently to 80 sleep there.

[7] It is only fair to add that Oran is grafted on to a unique landscape, in the center of a bare plateau, ringed with luminous hills and above a perfectly shaped bay. All we may regret is the town's being so disposed that it turns its back on the bay, with the result 85 that it's impossible to see the sea, you always have to go to look for it.

[8] Such being the normal life of Oran, it will be easily understood that our fellow citizens had not the faintest reason to apprehend the incidents that took place in the spring of the year in question and were (as we subsequently realized) premonitory signs of the grave 90 events we are to chronicle. To some, these events will seem quite natural; to others, all but incredible. But, obviously, a narrator cannot take account of these differences of outlook. His business is only to say: "This is what happened," when he knows that it actually did happen, that it closely affected the life of a whole populace, and that 95 there are thousands of eyewitnesses who can appraise in their hearts the truth of what he writes.

[9] In any case the narrator (whose identity will be made known in due course) would have little claim to competence for a task like this, had not chance put him in the way of gathering much information, 100

and had he not been, by the force of things, closely involved in all that he proposes to narrate. This is his justification for playing the part of a historian. Naturally, a historian, even an amateur, always has data, personal or at second hand, to guide him. The present
105 narrator has three kinds of data: first, what he saw himself; secondly, the accounts of other eyewitnesses (thanks to the part he played, he was enabled to learn their personal impressions from all those figuring in this chronicle); and, lastly, documents that subsequently came into his hands. He proposes to draw on these records whenever this
110 seems desirable, and to employ them as he thinks best. He also proposes . . .

[10] But perhaps the time has come to drop preliminaries and cautionary remarks and to launch into the narrative proper. The account of the first days needs giving in some detail.

Dictionary definitions often list synonyms, other words which have the same meaning as the word being defined. Yet it is never possible to use these words interchangeably. For example, under the word "habitation," one dictionary lists "dwelling, residence, domicile, home" as synonyms. But you will never see a sampler embroidered "Domicile, sweet domicile." And you will never read "The young heiress took up habitation at the mansion." You expect a lease to say that the "premises are to be occupied as a private dwelling"; you do not expect it to say that "the place is to be lived in as a home."

Words do not mean only what they "mean" literally (denotative meaning); they carry with them an aura of surrounding meaning—suggestive, emotional overtones of meaning which come to mind when you hear or see them (connotative meaning).

These connotative meanings vary to some extent from person to person: "bread" can never mean the same thing to someone who has been a war prisoner that it means to a baker or a farmer. Time and history may alter the connotative meanings of a word—"bomb," for example. Some words have more connotative meanings than others. Think of the differences between a marketing list and a menu: in making up a marketing list, you might include "rolls" and "crabmeat"; these might appear on a menu as the mouth-watering item: "King Crab on Toasted Bun." Although "jasmine" is defined as "any of a genus of shrubs of the olive family," you would never open a book by your favorite mystery writer and read "The air was heavy with the smell of a shrub of the olive family." And, finally, the context of a word may give it connotative meaning. "Hat" may seem a bland

enough word, yet its connotative meaning varies considerably (while its denotative meaning remains the same) in these sentences:

His *hat* was in the ring.
She put on her *hat* and marched out the door.
All that was visible on the surface of the lake was a *hat*.
She must have that *hat* and no other one.

1. What words rich in connotative meaning are there in the first paragraph of the Camus selection? How do you account for or explain your answer?

2. What is the topic sentence of the second paragraph? Which words or groups of words throughout the paragraph contribute to the meaning of the topic sentence by their connotations?

3. What do the following connote (a) in the context of the Camus selection and (b) to you, out of this context:

pigeons	sea bathing
the beat of wings	stroll
the rustle of leaves	fritter
bakes	cafés
sprinkles	boulevard
baskets of flowers	balconies
peddlers	card tables
deluges	banquets
closed shutters	"socials"

4. Use each of the words or phrases in question 3 in a sentence which gives it connotations different from those it has in context. If some of these words and phrases carry the same connotations for you both in and out of context, then use them in a sentence which again illustrates these connotations.

5. List as many sentences as you can find in the selection which confine themselves exclusively to conveying straightforward denotative meaning.

6. What sort of event do you expect is about to take place in Oran? What gives you that impression?

Alternate selections for the study of Connotation and Denotation: Nicholas Monsarrat, "Around-the-World Grouch"; William Faulkner, "The Spirit of Man."

Theme Assignment: Places have particular meanings for people a a result of things that have happened to them there, or perhaps merel as a result of reading about them.

small attentions, he likes to have something to rely on, and the natural enough. But at Oran the violent extremes of temperature the exigencies of business, the uninspiring surroundings, the sudden nightfalls, and the very nature of its pleasures call for good health. An invalid feels out of it there. Think what it must be for a dying man, trapped behind hundreds of walls all sizzling with heat, while the whole population, sitting in cafés or hanging on the telephone, is discussing shipments, bills of lading, discounts! It will then be obvious what discomfort attends death, even modern death, when it waylays you under such conditions in a dry place. [65]

[6] These somewhat haphazard observations may give a fair idea of what our town is like. However, we must not exaggerate. Really, all that was to be conveyed was the banality of the town's appearance and of life in it. But you can get through the days there without trouble, once you have formed habits. And since habits are precisely what our town encourages, all is for the best. Viewed from this angle, its life is not particularly exciting; that must be admitted. But, at least, social unrest is quite unknown among us. And our frank-spoken, amiable, and industrious citizens have always inspired a reasonable esteem in visitors. Treeless, glamourless, soulless, the town of Oran ends by seeming restful and, after a while, you go complacently to sleep there. [70][75][80]

[7] It is only fair to add that Oran is grafted on to a unique landscape, in the center of a bare plateau, ringed with luminous hills and above a perfectly shaped bay. All we may regret is the town's being so disposed that it turns its back on the bay, with the result that it's impossible to see the sea, you always have to go to look for it. [85]

[8] Such being the normal life of Oran, it will be easily understood that our fellow citizens had not the faintest reason to apprehend the incidents that took place in the spring of the year in question and were (as we subsequently realized) premonitory signs of the grav events we are to chronicle. To some, these events will seem qu natural; to others, all but incredible. But, obviously, a narrator c not take account of these differences of outlook. His business to say: "This is what happened," when he knows that it ac happen, that it closely affected the life of a whole pop there are thousands of eyewitnesses who can appr the truth of what he writes. [90][95]

[9] In any case the narrator (whose iden in due course) would have little claim t this, had not chance put him in the wa

had he not been, by the force of things, closely involved in all
that he proposes to narrate. This is his justification for playing the
part of a historian. Naturally, a historian, even an amateur, always
has data, personal or at second hand, to guide him. The present
105 narrator has three kinds of data: first, what he saw himself; secondly,
the accounts of other eyewitnesses (thanks to the part he played, he
was enabled to learn their personal impressions from all those figuring in this chronicle); and, lastly, documents that subsequently came
into his hands. He proposes to draw on these records whenever this
110 seems desirable, and to employ them as he thinks best. He also
proposes . . .

[10] But perhaps the time has come to drop preliminaries and
cautionary remarks and to launch into the narrative proper. The
account of the first days needs giving in some detail.

Dictionary definitions often list synonyms, other words which have
the same meaning as the word being defined. Yet it is never possible
to use these words interchangeably. For example, under the word
"habitation," one dictionary lists "dwelling, residence, domicile, home"
as synonyms. But you will never see a sampler embroidered "Domicile, sweet domicile." And you will never read "The young heiress
took up habitation at the mansion." You expect a lease to say that
the "premises are to be occupied as a private dwelling"; you do not
expect it to say that "the place is to be lived in as a home."

Words do not mean only what they "mean" literally (denotative
meaning); they carry with them an aura of surrounding meaning—
suggestive, emotional overtones of meaning which come to mind when
you hear or see them (connotative meaning).

These connotative meanings vary to some extent from person to
person: "bread" can never mean the same thing to someone who has
been a war prisoner that it means to a baker or a farmer. Time and
history may alter the connotative meanings of a word—"bomb," for
example. Some words have more connotative meanings than others.
Think of the differences between a marketing list and a menu: in
making up a marketing list, you might include "rolls" and "crabmeat";
might appear on a menu as the mouth-watering item: "King
n Toasted Bun." Although "jasmine" is defined as "any of a
shrubs of the olive family," you would never open a book
vorite mystery writer and read "The air was heavy with
a shrub of the olive family." And, finally, the context of
give it connotative meaning. "Hat" may seem a bland

small attentions, he likes to have something to rely on, and that's 60
natural enough. But at Oran the violent extremes of temperature,
the exigencies of business, the uninspiring surroundings, the sudden
nightfalls, and the very nature of its pleasures call for good health.
An invalid feels out of it there. Think what it must be for a dying
man, trapped behind hundreds of walls all sizzling with heat, while 65
the whole population, sitting in cafés or hanging on the telephone,
is discussing shipments, bills of lading, discounts! It will then be
obvious what discomfort attends death, even modern death, when it
waylays you under such conditions in a dry place.

[6] These somewhat haphazard observations may give a fair idea 70
of what our town is like. However, we must not exaggerate. Really,
all that was to be conveyed was the banality of the town's appearance
and of life in it. But you can get through the days there without
trouble, once you have formed habits. And since habits are precisely
what our town encourages, all is for the best. Viewed from this angle, 75
its life is not particularly exciting; that must be admitted. But, at
least, social unrest is quite unknown among us. And our frank-spoken,
amiable, and industrious citizens have always inspired a reasonable
esteem in visitors. Treeless, glamourless, soulless, the town of Oran
ends by seeming restful and, after a while, you go complacently to 80
sleep there.

[7] It is only fair to add that Oran is grafted on to a unique landscape, in the center of a bare plateau, ringed with luminous hills
and above a perfectly shaped bay. All we may regret is the town's
being so disposed that it turns its back on the bay, with the result 85
that it's impossible to see the sea, you always have to go to look for it.

[8] Such being the normal life of Oran, it will be easily understood
that our fellow citizens had not the faintest reason to apprehend the
incidents that took place in the spring of the year in question and
were (as we subsequently realized) premonitory signs of the grave 90
events we are to chronicle. To some, these events will seem quite
natural; to others, all but incredible. But, obviously, a narrator cannot take account of these differences of outlook. His business is only
to say: "This is what happened," when he knows that it actually did
happen, that it closely affected the life of a whole populace, and that 95
there are thousands of eyewitnesses who can appraise in their hearts
the truth of what he writes.

[9] In any case the narrator (whose identity will be made known
in due course) would have little claim to competence for a task like
this, had not chance put him in the way of gathering much information, 100

and had he not been, by the force of things, closely involved in all
that he proposes to narrate. This is his justification for playing the
part of a historian. Naturally, a historian, even an amateur, always
has data, personal or at second hand, to guide him. The present
105 narrator has three kinds of data: first, what he saw himself; secondly,
the accounts of other eyewitnesses (thanks to the part he played, he
was enabled to learn their personal impressions from all those figuring in this chronicle); and, lastly, documents that subsequently came
into his hands. He proposes to draw on these records whenever this
110 seems desirable, and to employ them as he thinks best. He also
proposes . . .

[10] But perhaps the time has come to drop preliminaries and
cautionary remarks and to launch into the narrative proper. The
account of the first days needs giving in some detail.

Dictionary definitions often list synonyms, other words which have
the same meaning as the word being defined. Yet it is never possible
to use these words interchangeably. For example, under the word
"habitation," one dictionary lists "dwelling, residence, domicile, home"
as synonyms. But you will never see a sampler embroidered "Domicile, sweet domicile." And you will never read "The young heiress
took up habitation at the mansion." You expect a lease to say that
the "premises are to be occupied as a private dwelling"; you do not
expect it to say that "the place is to be lived in as a home."

Words do not mean only what they "mean" literally (denotative
meaning); they carry with them an aura of surrounding meaning—
suggestive, emotional overtones of meaning which come to mind when
you hear or see them (connotative meaning).

These connotative meanings vary to some extent from person to
person: "bread" can never mean the same thing to someone who has
been a war prisoner that it means to a baker or a farmer. Time and
history may alter the connotative meanings of a word—"bomb," for
example. Some words have more connotative meanings than others.
Think of the differences between a marketing list and a menu: in
making up a marketing list, you might include "rolls" and "crabmeat";
these might appear on a menu as the mouth-watering item: "King
Crab on Toasted Bun." Although "jasmine" is defined as "any of a
genus of shrubs of the olive family," you would never open a book
by your favorite mystery writer and read "The air was heavy with
the smell of a shrub of the olive family." And, finally, the context of
a word may give it connotative meaning. "Hat" may seem a bland

enough word, yet its connotative meaning varies considerably (while its denotative meaning remains the same) in these sentences:

His *hat* was in the ring.
She put on her *hat* and marched out the door.
All that was visible on the surface of the lake was a *hat*.
She must have that *hat* and no other one.

1. What words rich in connotative meaning are there in the first paragraph of the Camus selection? How do you account for or explain your answer?

2. What is the topic sentence of the second paragraph? Which words or groups of words throughout the paragraph contribute to the meaning of the topic sentence by their connotations?

3. What do the following connote (a) in the context of the Camus selection and (b) to you, out of this context:

pigeons	sea bathing
the beat of wings	stroll
the rustle of leaves	fritter
bakes	cafés
sprinkles	boulevard
baskets of flowers	balconies
peddlers	card tables
deluges	banquets
closed shutters	"socials"

4. Use each of the words or phrases in question 3 in a sentence which gives it connotations different from those it has in context. If some of these words and phrases carry the same connotations for you both in and out of context, then use them in a sentence which again illustrates these connotations.

5. List as many sentences as you can find in the selection which confine themselves exclusively to conveying straightforward denotative meaning.

6. What sort of event do you expect is about to take place in Oran? What gives you that impression?

Alternate selections for the study of Connotation and Denotation: Nicholas Monsarrat, "Around-the-World Grouch"; William Faulkner, "The Spirit of Man."

Theme Assignment: Places have particular meanings for people as a result of things that have happened to them there, or perhaps merely as a result of reading about them.

Write a theme describing a place, much as Camus describes Oran, giving it a special significance. This place may be the town or city in which you grew up, the resort where you spent your childhood vacations, the home of a friend or relative, a town in which you were once stranded (or lost), the place you always dream of seeing, or a place made famous by your favorite author. Make generous use of connotative meanings and connotative words to convey your impression to the reader.

Imagery

The Lapham Drawing-Room

WILLIAM DEAN HOWELLS

THE Lapham drawing-room in Nankeen Square was in
the parti-coloured paint which the Colonel had hoped to repeat in
his new house: the trim of the doors and windows was in light green
and the panels in salmon; the walls were a plain tint of French grey
paper, divided by gilt mouldings into broad panels with a wide 5
stripe of red velvet paper running up the corners; the chandelier
was of massive imitation bronze; the mirror over the mantel rested
on a fringed mantel-cover of green reps, and heavy curtains of
that stuff hung from gilt lambrequin frames at the window; the
carpet was of a small pattern in crude green, which, at the time 10
Mrs. Lapham bought it, covered half the new floors in Boston. In
the panelled spaces on the walls were some stone-coloured landscapes,
representing the mountains and cañons of the West, which the
Colonel and his wife had visited on one of the early official railroad
excursions. In front of the long windows looking into the Square 15
were statues, kneeling figures which turned their backs upon the
company within-doors, and represented allegories of Faith and Prayer
to people without. A white marble group of several figures, expressing an Italian conception of Lincoln Freeing the Slaves,—a Latin
negro and his wife,—with our Eagle flapping his wings in approval, 20
at Lincoln's feet, occupied one corner, and balanced the what-not of

From *The Rise of Silas Lapham*, by William Dean Howells, ed. George Arms
(Rinehart Editions; New York: Rinehart & Company, Inc., 1949). Selection
title by the Editors.

281

an earlier period in another. These phantasms added their chill to
that imparted by the tone of the walls, the landscapes, and the
carpets, and contributed to the violence of the contrast when the
25 chandelier was lighted up full glare, and the heat of the whole
furnace welled up from the registers into the quivering atmosphere
on one of the rare occasions when the Laphams invited company.

[For treatment of this selection, see p. 289.]

Subtle Voices

HAL BORLAND

[1] IT hasn't really warmed up yet, but when we went for a
walk this evening we heard the first few peepers and we knew the
silence had ended. The silence which began with the last scratchy
note of the last katydid, progressed through the brittle-dry rustle of
5 leaves on the road, deepened into the echo of the owl hoot and the
fox bark. At its greatest depth it was a silence so profound that I
could hear the whisper of snowflakes nudging each other as they
fell. Now it has ended in the rush of flowing water, the quack of
beach ducks and American mergansers on the river, and the tentative
10 trill of the hylas.

[2] These, of course, are only the obvious voices. So, too, are most
of the bird songs which precede the great chorus. The robins already
sing a little at dawn, and so do the song sparrows, but their songs
seem a little hoarse and hesitant. But at the marsh down the road
15 the blackbirds, both the red-shouldered ones and the rusties, newly
arrived from the South, are in full voice at midday.

[3] The subtler voices call for other listening, however. I feel them
with all my senses, listening with my skin, as insects listen. Then I
am aware of the outriders of the great insect hordes—the ants, the
20 first hungry bees, the first wasps, the earliest beetles, the minute flies,
which tap the opening buds. They are barely humming, but I know

that back of them is the whole season's insect life and loudness. The silence will not return until frost bites deep in another Autumn.

• • • • •

[4] One of the most difficult of all sounds to put down on paper is the song of a bird. The reason is that vocal music is primarily a matter of vowel sounds with their consonants giving a familiar form rather than a sound of their own. Try to translate bird songs into words and you run into all kinds of stumbling blocks. For instance, even the familiar song of the chickadee is nearly always transcribed as chick-a-dee-dee-dee-, but it might as accurately be set down as sip-o'-tea-tea-tea-.

[5] The whippoorwills are calling every night now. It is generally conceded that although individual whippoorwills have a sharp variation in voice quality they all make sounds that translate as "whip poor will." An allowable variant is "whup-poo-ree." But I can with equal plausibility say that those on our mountainside are serenading my wife, saying over and over, "Bar-bar-ree, Bar-bar-ree!"

[6] It was Thoreau, I believe, who translated the call of the Baltimore oriole as, "Eat it, Potter, eat it!" A change of consonants makes that, "Beat it, rotter, beat it!" Another of the local orioles' songs is quite obviously, "I'm an oriole, suh!" uttered with a fine Eastern Shore of Maryland accent.

[7] When I was a boy I was quite sure that the meadow larks of the Colorado plains said, most melodically, in mid-June, "This is the time of the equinox." In April they said, "Now is the time to build a nest." And in September it was, "Summer is gone and now it's Fall."

• • • • •

[8] We speak of the wind and its voices, but most of the voices are in the trees. And even those voices vary from season to season, almost from month to month. They are speaking today, as the Fall winds rise—the winds, not the gales which have, beyond denial, voices all their own.

[9] The oaks speak today with a heavy voice, crisp with the crispness of their leaves. The big maples have a strong voice, with their big leaves rustling and thousands of them. At first listening one might think there was little difference between the voice of the oaks and that of the maples, but stand in an oak grove and listen, then move to a clump of maples. The difference is clear, a softer voice in the maples with their softer leaves and looser stems.

60   [10] The whisperers, of course, are the members of the willow
family, the poplars in particular. Aspens and cottonwoods whisper
in anything but an absolute calm; give them a breeze and you can
hear them afar, fairly chattering, their heart-shaped leaves on long,
limber stems, each leaf dancing against a dozen others. The birches
65 come a close second in their whispering, the small gray birches in
particular; as their leaves crisp with September they, too, almost
chatter.

     [11] The evergreens, the pines and spruces and hemlocks, hum
rather than speak, and theirs is closest of all to music. The music
70 of the pines is heard best at night, and best of all on a Winter night
when their deciduous brothers of the woodland stand stark in the
starlight. But the big Norway spruce outside my study is singing a
September song today.

[For treatment of this selection, see p. 289.]

The Smell of London

SINCLAIR LEWIS

     [1] THE smell of London is a foggy smell, a sooty smell, a
coal-fire smell, yet to certain wanderers it is more exhilarating, more
suggestive of greatness and of stirring life, than spring-time hillsides
or the chill sweetness of autumnal nights; and that unmistakable
5 smell, which men long for in rotting perfumes along the Orinoco, in
the greasy reek of South Chicago, in the hot odor of dusty earth
among locust-buzzing Alberta wheatfields, that luring breath of the
dark giant among cities, reaches halfway to Southampton to greet
the traveler. Sam sniffed at it, uneasily, restlessly, while he considered
10 how strange was the British fashion of having railway compartments
instead of an undivided car with a nice long aisle along which you
could observe ankles, magazines, Rotary buttons, clerical collars, and
all the details that made travel interesting.

     [2] And the strangeness of having framed pictures of scenery

behind the seats; of having hand straps—the embroidered silk cover- 15
ing so rough to the finger tips, the leather inside so smooth and cool—
beside the doors. And the greater strangeness of admitting that these
seats were more comfortable than the flinty Pullman chairs of America. And of seeing outside, in the watery February sunshine, not
snow-curdled fields but springtime greenness; pollarded willows and 20
thatched roofs and half-timbered façades—

[3] Just like in the pictures! England!

[For treatment of this selection, see p. 289.]

Knoxville: Summer 1915

JAMES AGEE

[1] WE are talking now of summer evenings in Knoxville,
Tennessee in the time that I lived there so successfully disguised to
myself as a child. It was a little bit mixed sort of block, fairly solidly
lower middle class, with one or two juts apiece on either side of
that. The houses corresponded: middle-sized gracefully fretted wood 5
houses built in the late nineties and early nineteen hundreds, with
small front and side and more spacious back yards, and trees in the
yards, and porches. These were softwooded trees, poplars, tulip trees,
cottonwoods. There were fences around one or two of the houses,
but mainly the yards ran into each other with only now and then a 10
low hedge that wasn't doing very well. There were few good friends
among the grown people, and they were not poor enough for the
other sort of intimate acquaintance, but everyone nodded and spoke,
and even might talk short times, trivially, and at the two extremes of
the general or the particular, and ordinarily nextdoor neighbors talked 15
quite a bit when they happened to run into each other, and never
paid calls. The men were mostly small businessmen, one or two very
modestly executives, one or two worked with their hands, most of
them clerical, and most of them between thirty and forty-five.

²⁰   [2] But it is of these evenings, I speak.

[3] Supper was at six and was over by half past. There was still
daylight, shining softly and with a tarnish, like the lining of a shell;
and the carbon lamps lifted at the corners were on in the light, and
the locusts were started, and the fire flies were out, and a few frogs
²⁵ were flopping in the dewy grass, by the time the fathers and the children came out. The children ran out first hell bent and yelling those
names by which they were known; then the fathers sank out leisurely
in crossed suspenders, their collars removed and their necks looking
tall and shy. The mothers stayed back in the kitchen washing and dry-
³⁰ ing, putting things away, recrossing their traceless footsteps like the
lifetime journeys of bees, measuring out the dry cocoa for breakfast.
When they came out they had taken off their aprons and their skirts
were dampened and they sat in rockers on their porches quietly.

[4] It is not of the games children play in the evening that I want
³⁵ to speak now, it is of a contemporaneous atmosphere that has little
to do with them: that of the fathers of families, each in his space of
lawn, his shirt fishlike pale in the unnatural light and his face nearly
anonymous, hosing their lawns. The hoses were attached at spiggots
that stood out of the brick foundations of the houses. The nozzles
⁴⁰ were variously set but usually so there was a long sweet stream of
spray, the nozzle wet in the hand, the water trickling the right fore-
arm and the peeled-back cuff, and the water whishing out a long
loose and low-curved cone, and so gentle a sound. First an insane
noise of violence in the nozzle, then the still irregular sound of
⁴⁵ adjustment, then the smoothing into steadiness and a pitch as accurately tuned to the size and style of stream as any violin. So many
qualities of sound out of one hose: so many choral differences out
of those several hoses that were in earshot. Out of any one hose,
the almost dead silence of the release, and the short still arch of
⁵⁰ the separate big drops, silent as a held breath, and the only noise the
flattering noise on leaves and the slapped grass at the fall of each
big drop. That, and the intense hiss with the intense stream; that,
and that same intensity not growing less but growing more quiet
and delicate with the turn of the nozzle, up to that extreme tender
⁵⁵ whisper when the water was just a wide bell of film. Chiefly, though,
the hoses were set much alike, in a compromise between distance
and tenderness of spray (and quite surely a sense of art behind this
compromise, and a quiet deep joy, too real to recognize itself), and
the sounds therefore were pitched much alike; pointed by the snorting
⁶⁰ start of a new hose; decorated by some man playful with the nozzle;
left empty, like God by the sparrow's fall, when any single one of

them desists: and all, though near alike, of various pitch; and in
this unison. These sweet pale streamings in the light lift out their
pallors and their voices all together, mothers hushing their children,
the hushing unnaturally prolonged, the men gentle and silent and 65
each snail-like withdrawn into the quietude of what he singly is
doing, the urination of huge children stood loosely military against
an invisible wall, and gentle happy and peaceful, tasting the mean
goodness of their living like the last of their suppers in their mouths;
while the locusts carry on this noise of hoses on their much higher 70
and sharper key. The noise of the locust is dry, and it seems not to
be rasped or vibrated but urged from him as if through a small
orifice by a breath that can never give out. Also there is never one
locust but an illusion of at least a thousand. The noise of each locust
is pitched in some classic locust range out of which none of them 75
varies more than two full tones: and yet you seem to hear each
locust discrete from all the rest, and there is a long, slow pulse in
their noise, like the scarcely defined arch of a long and high set
bridge. They are all around in every tree, so that the noise seems
to come from nowhere and everywhere at once, from the whole shell 80
heaven, shivering in your flesh and teasing your eardrums, the boldest
of all the sounds of night. And yet it is habitual to summer nights,
and is of the great order of noises, like the noises of the sea and of
the blood her precocious grandchild, which you realize you are hearing only when you catch yourself listening. Meantime from low in 85
the dark, just outside the swaying horizons of the hoses, conveying
always grass in the damp of dew and its strong green-black smear of
smell, the regular yet spaced noises of the crickets, each a sweet cold
silver noise threenoted, like the slipping each time of three matched
links of a small chain.   90

[5] But the men by now, one by one, have silenced their hoses
and drained and coiled them. Now only two, and now only one, is
left, and you see only ghostlike shirt with the sleeve garters, and
sober mystery of his mild face like the lifted face of large cattle
enquiring of your presence in a pitchdark pool of meadow; and now 95
he too is gone; and it has become that time of evening when people
sit on their porches, rocking gently and talking gently and watching
the street and the standing up into their sphere of possession of the
trees, of birds hung havens, hangars. People go by; things go by. A
horse, drawing a buggy, breaking his hollow iron music on the 100
asphalt; a loud auto; a quiet auto; people in pairs, not in a hurry,
scuffling, switching their weight of aestival body, talking casually,
the taste hovering over them of vanilla, strawberry, pasteboard and

starched milk, the image upon them of lovers and horsemen, squared
105 with clowns in hueless amber. A street car raising its iron moan;
stopping, belling and starting; stertorous; rousing and raising again
its iron increasing moan and swimming its gold windows and straw
seats on past and past and past, the bleak spark crackling and curs-
ing above it like a small malignant spirit set to dog its tracks; the
110 iron whine rises on rising speed; still risen, faints; halts; the faint
stinging bell; rises again, still fainter; fainting, lifting, lifts, faints
forgone: forgotten. Now is the night one blue dew.

Now is the night one blue dew, my father has drained, he has coiled
the hose.
Low on the length of lawns, a frailing of fire who breathes.
Content, silver, like peeps of light, each cricket makes his comment
over and over in the drowned grass.
A cold toad thumpily flounders.
Within the edges of damp shadows of side yards are hovering children nearly sick with joy of fear, who watch the unguarding of a
telephone pole.
Around white carbon corner lamps bugs of all sizes are lifted elliptic,
solar systems. Big hardshells bruise themselves, assailant: he is
fallen on his back, legs squiggling.
Parents on porches: rock and rock: From damp strings morning
glories: hang their ancient faces.
The dry and exalted noise of the locusts from all the air at once
enchants my eardrums.

[6] On the rough wet grass of the back yard my father and mother
have spread quilts. We all lie there, my mother, my father, my uncle,
115 my aunt, and I too am lying there. First we were sitting up, then
one of us lay down, and then we all lay down, on our stomachs, or
on our sides, or on our backs, and they have kept on talking. They
are not talking much, and the talk is quiet, of nothing in particular,
of nothing at all in particular, of nothing at all. The stars are wide
120 and alive, they seem each like a smile of great sweetness, and they
seem very near. All my people are larger bodies than mine, quiet,
with voices gentle and meaningless like the voices of sleeping birds.
One is an artist, he is living at home. One is a musician, she is living
at home. One is my mother who is good to me. One is my father
125 who is good to me. By some chance, here they are, all on this earth;
and who shall ever tell the sorrow of being on this earth, lying, on
quilts, on the grass, in a summer evening, among the sounds of the

night. May God bless my people, my uncle, my aunt, my mother, my good father, oh, remember them kindly in their time of trouble; and in the hour of their taking away.   **130**

[7] After a little I am taken in and put to bed. Sleep, soft smiling, draws me unto her: and those receive me, who quietly treat me, as one familiar and well-beloved in that home: but will not, oh, will not, not now, not ever; but will not ever tell me who I am.

Communication is essentially sharing, mutual participation or exchange. Before it can take place at all, there must be some community of experience between the sender and the recipient. All people, no matter how much they differ in surroundings, in history, in personality, in beliefs, discovered and continue to experience the world around them through their senses. They all see, hear, touch, taste, and smell the world. Therefore one extremely effective means of verbal communication is to evoke or create imagined sense impressions. These sense impressions are *images*; images in general are referred to as imagery.

Imagery may result from a simple reference to an impression of one or another of the senses: "the trim of the doors and windows was in light green and the panels in salmon" (Howells); it may use one sense to call forth another: "strong green-black smear of smell" (Agee); it may employ onomatopoeia—sound which echoes meaning: "last scratchy note of the last katydid" (Borland); it most often is created by or combined with a figure of speech—with a simile, for example: "There was still daylight, shining softly and with a tarnish, like the lining of a shell" (Agee) or with personification: "I could hear the whisper of snowflakes nudging each other as they fell" (Borland). But *any* sense impression is an image.

1. In "The Lapham Drawing-Room," Howells says, "These phantasms added their chill to that imparted by the tone of the walls, the landscapes, and the carpets . . . ." What are the "phantasms"? How does he convey their "chill"? What images, if any, does he employ to convey the "chill" of the walls? the landscapes? the carpets?

2. Point out an example of contrasting imagery in the Howells selection. What does this contrast, basic to the structure of the paragraph, tell us about the Laphams?

3. Enumerate all the elements which contribute to the effectiveness of the following phrases from the first of the selections by Hal Borland:

"the brittle-dry rustle of leaves on the road"
"deepened into the echo of the owl hoot and the fox bark"

"the rush of the flowing water"
"the quack of beach ducks and American mergansers on the
river"
"the tentative trill of the hylas"

4. Explain what Borland means by "listening with my skin" in
the same selection.

5. What fact of human experience forms the basis of the humor
in the second of the Borland selections?

6. List every example you can of imagery in the third Borland
selection. Which of these images combines onomatopoeia with auditory imagery (imagery of sound)? Explain your answer, accounting for the specific relevance of each sound to the meaning of the
image.

7. To which of the senses is the dominant appeal in "The Smell
of London" by Sinclair Lewis? What differences are there among "a
foggy smell, a sooty smell, a coal-fire smell"? Do they all belong to
"the luring breath of a dark giant among cities"? Explain your answer.

8. Where is contrast of olfactory images (images of smell) used
in the Lewis selection? Why do you think Lewis uses it?

9. What other types of images—visual, auditory, tactile, gusta-
tory—are there in this selection?

10. Lewis says that "to certain wanderers" the smell of London is
"more exhilarating, more suggestive of greatness and of stirring
life, than spring-time hillsides or the chill sweetness of autumnal
nights . . . ." How does his description bear out the statement that
the smell of London is suggestive of greatness and of stirring life?
How do Borland's descriptions of "spring-time hillsides" and "the
chill sweetness of autumnal nights" suggest greatness and stirring life?
Which do you find more effective? Why?

11. Select examples of all types of images in the James Agee
excerpt. Account for the effectiveness of at least three.

12. What is the tone or mood of the Agee selection? What sentence
or sentences explicitly state the thoughts that create that mood? How
does the imagery so richly used throughout contribute to the tone?
Which images do so, for example?

13. Justify the statement that Agee had many of the qualities of
the poet.

14. Which of the four writers whose works are illustrated in this
section do you think most skilled in the use of imagery? Justify your
answer on the basis of the selections here.

Alternate selections for the study of Imagery: Hans Zinsser,
"Mamie"; John H. Randall, "Eternally Old, Eternally New"; Margaret
Leech, "General Winfield Scott"; Charles Dickens, "August."

Theme Assignment: You are the first human being to complete a round trip to another planet. You have been asked to write for the newspapers a detailed description of the planet. This must, of course, be understandable not only to scientists (for whom you would make a separate technical report) but to laymen. So, although it is an experience no one else has had, you must translate it into terms everyone will understand—sense impressions. Write the account, making liberal use of more than one type of imagery.

or

Take as your laboratory whatever place you happen to be in when you read this assignment. Write a description of it as you experience it with your senses.

Figurative Language

Advice to the Writer

BEN JONSON

FOR a man to write well, there are required three neces-
saries—to read the best authors, observe the best speakers, and much
exercise of his own style. In style, to consider what ought to be written, and after what manner, he must first think and excogitate his
5 matter, then choose his words, and examine the weight of either.
Then take care, in placing and ranking both matter and words, that
the composition be comely; and to do this with diligence and often.
No matter how slow the style be at first, so it be labored and accurate;
seek the best, and be not glad of the forward conceits or first words
10 that offer themselves to us: but judge of what we invent, and order
what we approve. Repeat often what we have formerly written; which
beside that it helps the consequence, and makes the juncture better,
it quickens the heat of imagination, that often cools in the time of
setting down, and gives it new strength, as if it grew lustier by the
15 going back. As we see in the contention of leaping, they jump farthest
that fetch their race largest; or as in throwing a dart or javelin, we
force back our arms to make our loose the stronger. Yet, if we have
a fair gale of wind, I forbid not the steering out of our sail, so the
favor of the gale deceive us not. For all that we invent doth please
20 us in the conception of birth, else we would never set it down. But
the safest is to return to our judgment, and handle over again those

From *Timber, or Discoveries Made upon Man and Matter*, by Ben Jonson.
Selection title by the Editors.

things the easiness of which might make them justly suspected. So did the best writers in their beginnings: they imposed upon themselves care and industry; they did nothing rashly; they obtained first to write well, and then custom made it easy and a habit. By little and little 25 their matter showed itself to them more plentifully; their words answered, their composition followed; and all, as in a well-ordered family, presented itself in the place. So that the sum of all is, ready writing makes not good writing, but good writing brings on ready writing. Yet when we think we have got the faculty, it is even then 30 good to resist it, as to give a horse a check sometimes with a bit, which doth not so much stop his course as stir his mettle. Again, whither a man's genius is best able to reach, thither it should more and more contend, lift, and dilate itself; as men of low stature raise themselves on their toes, and so ofttimes get even, if not eminent. 35 Besides, as it is fit for grown and able writers to stand of themselves, and work with their own strength, to trust and endeavor by their own faculties; so it is fit for the beginner and learner to study others and the best. For the mind and memory are more sharply exercised in comprehending another man's things than our own; and such as 40 accustom themselves and are familiar with the best authors shall ever and anon find somewhat of them in themselves: and in the expression of their minds, even when they feel it not, be able to utter something like theirs, which hath an authority above their own. Nay, sometimes it is the reward of a man's study, the praise of quoting 45 another man fitly; and though a man be more prone and able for one kind of writing than another, yet he must exercise all. For as in an instrument, so in style, there must be a harmony and consent of parts.

[For treatment of this selection, see p. 294.]

Conqueror and Lover

HELEN WADDELL

[1] IT was long after sunset, but the crescent moon above Notre Dame was still no more than a glimmering sickle in the harvest glow of the sky. The inner radiance that is the mystery of the light

of the Ile de France slept on its towers. Abelard, rounding the last
bend above the Clos des Vignerons, halted in the stride that had
carried him through twenty miles of the Seine valley. Often as he
had seen it, this beauty never failed to catch him by the throat.
Before him rode the island with its towers, glimmering like some
great white-sailed ship that he had seen, bearing into Nantes from
the vast spaces of the open Loire, or a wild swan, resting a moment
in mid flood. It had the air of a winged victory, stayed of its own
volition in its imperious way. "Queen among cities, moon among
stars," his brain was beating out the lovely rhythms, "island of royal
palaces: and in that island hath Philosophy her royal and ancient
seat, who alone, with Study her sole comrade, holding the eternal
citadel of light and immortality, hath set her victorious foot on the
withering flower of the fast-aging world."

[2] *The withering flower.* The light on the banks had dimmed, the
river darkened, but still the island glowed with that unearthly light,
as though its fountains were within. Abelard swung down the river
road, his blood pulsing in a strange exaltation that was the climax
of his mood. Never had he so felt the richness of living as in these
last days, never been so joyously aware of the urge of creation. The
name of his new book had flashed on him, *Sic et Non,* and he had
stood astonished and charmed at its simplicity and its absoluteness.
His scholars were out of Paris, but he had hardly been aware of the
emptiness of his days, for he had plunged headlong into a rereading
of the Fathers, and the surge of St. Augustine's prose rose and fell
in his brain. He was drinking little and eating less, but something
was wine in his blood, and all the day and half the night reading
could not daunt the restlessness that fevered him. Today it had driven
him out, but the miles of the Seine valley had only set his pulse
beating to a headier rhythm. Paris rode there to greet him, unearthly
and proud: but the man who swung down the river-path to enter it
came as both conqueror and lover.

Like rhythm and imagery, figurative language might be thought to
be the province of poetry rather than prose. But it does have its place
in prose: it can make the difference between dull, lifeless prose and
sparkling, imaginative prose; between prose that only partially communicates and prose that communicates exactly, efficiently, and effectively.

Figurative language uses words in senses other than the literal; yet
the words convey precise meaning. In the sentence, "The car shot up
the road," "shot" cannot be understood literally, but any reader knows

what the sentence means. Similarly, "He walks like an elephant" cannot be understood literally; a man cannot actually walk like an elephant, but his lumbering gait can suggest an elephant's walk.

Simile and metaphor are the two most frequently used figures of speech. A simile expresses a comparison between two unlike things which have one or more points in common: "He ate like a pig"; "The house was like a barn"; "The party was as noisy as a circus on opening night." A metaphor, by speaking of one thing in terms of another or by identifying one thing with another, implies a comparison between two unlike things which have one or more points in common: "The little boy clawed at his food"; "The store had mountains of fruit on one counter"; "He planted the knockout blow in the midsection."

Other frequently used figures in everyday speech as well as in more formal writing are metonymy, "the use of the name of one thing for that of another to which it has some logical relation, as 'scepter' for 'sovereignty,' or 'the bottle' for 'strong drink' " (*American College Dictionary*); synechdoche—a special form of metonymy—"by which a part is put for the whole or the whole for a part, the special for the general or the general for the special, as in 'a fleet of ten *sail*' (for *ships*), or 'a *Croesus*' (for a *rich man*)" (*American College Dictionary*); personification, in which human qualities and characteristics are attributed to inanimate objects, as "This old car eats up gas by the gallon"; hyperbole, in which gross or fanciful exaggeration is used, as "I'd fly to the moon just to see him laugh"; and litotes, which achieves understatement through the negation of the opposite of what is meant, as "The president of the United States is a man of no little importance."

Writing in which figures of speech are appropriately used can be effective for a number of reasons. When comparison is the basis of the figure (simile and metaphor particularly), the writer has the opportunity of achieving compression, since he speaks of one thing in terms of another—"two for the price of one." In addition, figurative language—by its very definition—uses words in new and sometimes startling ways; the reader can be surprised or even shocked into heightened awareness of rich meaning. Finally, good figurative language is the product of the creative imagination: the reader can get something of the same pleasure from figurative language that he does from a painting or a piece of sculpture.

1. In Jonson's sentence beginning, "As we see in the contention of leaping . . ." precisely what is being compared with what? Would you label the comparison a simile or a metaphor? Why? Is the comparison appropriate and effective in context? Why or why not?

2. What figure does Jonson use in the next sentence? Is it appropriate? effective? Justify your answer.

3. Identify and classify the remaining figures in the Jonson passage, commenting briefly on the appropriateness and effectiveness of each.

4. Precisely what effect is lost by changing "glimmering sickle" to "glimmer" in the first sentence of the Waddell excerpt?

5. In Waddell's fourth sentence, is "this beauty never failed to catch him by the throat" a literal or a figurative statement? Explain.

6. In the next sentence, identify a metaphor and two similes; what contributions do the similes make to the description of Paris?

7. Find at least three examples of personification in Waddell's first paragraph and comment on the effectiveness of each.

8. What figure of speech is in "his brain was beating out the lovely rhythms"? What does it contribute to the over-all effect of the paragraph?

9. Analyze the second paragraph of the Waddell selection: comment in detail on figurative language, imagery, sentence rhythms, and connotative diction.

Alternate selections for the study of Figurative Language: Rutherford Platt, from *The River of Life*; René Fülöp-Miller, from *Triumph over Pain*.

Assignment: Metaphors which have been in long and frequent use can lose their power to evoke comparison; such metaphors are called dead metaphors (a special kind of cliché). Following are some examples:

> the table leg
> the neck of a bottle
> the heart of the matter
> the leaves of a book
> to hammer a point home

a. Add five dead metaphors from everyday speech to the list above.

b. Create a fresh metaphor to describe each of the following:

> the landing of a plane
> the atmosphere in a college examination room
> the sensation of hunger
> a building on fire
> a thunderstorm

c. Find in your daily reading, or create, an effective example of metonymy, synechdoche, litotes, and hyperbole; be prepared to account for the effectiveness of each.

Tone

This Telegram Smells

ERIC SEVAREID

[1] SUNDAY is the day set aside to make mothers happier, with the by-product of increased happiness among florist, telegraph, and telephone companies; and if the President can issue a statement about Mother's Day, I see no reason why a fellow who makes a living out of statement-issuing shouldn't tag along.   5

[2] I've been looking over the new Western Union form telegrams for the occasion; I know the company means well, but—well, it's like the political movement to make the rose the national flower. What I mean is, filial sentiment, like the rose petal, is a pretty delicate thing, which flourishes better in quiet and private passages. I   10 can't help thinking officialdom is a pretty heavy burden for so tender a thing as the rose; men and women who become national institutions get gray and solemn, I've noticed; and I should think the institutionalized rose might wither pretty fast.

[3] I hope Western Union won't feel hurt or anything if I suggest   15 that one's feeling toward his mother is also a special, private sort of thing that doesn't do too well under conditions of mass or public manufacture, though, goodness knows, every politician, editorial writer, and popular preacher is in the business along with W.U.

20   [4] What I mean is, don't you think you've gone a little too far
this year, Western Union? I mean this Mother's Day telegram form
bearing the picture of a carnation and giving off the *perfume* of the
carnation when you sniff it closely. Your publicity release says:
"Western Union people are excited about the idea of adding scent
25 to sentiment on Mother's Day telegrams." Well, I'm not. I won't
argue with you about the carnation being the Mother's Day flower;
I don't know who passed such a law, though if you say so, I suppose that's official, too; but mothers are differing individuals and you
take my mother for example. As I recall, she doesn't *like* carnations;
30 allergic to them, or something. Furthermore, she's the old-fashioned-
type mother, and telegrams still frighten her. You go and hand her
a telegram that smells like a flower and I know just what's going to
happen—she'll think somebody *is* dead, this time, and faint away.
On the whole, I think you did better with those singing telegrams;
35 I imagine your success with that just carried you away, and if W.U.
people are allowed to *telephone* maybe you better get the board of
directors together for another look at this thing—for Operation Re-
think, as my advertising pals would call it.

       [5] I notice you're covering a lot more territory this year, includ-
40 ing Mother's Day messages for grandmothers, aunts, and even girl
friends' mothers. It might be better if they had their *own* days—I'm
sure you wouldn't object—but lumping them all together this way
sort of blurs the lines of authority, and if I know anything about
women I think you're going to mess up some relationships that were
45 doing all right up to now.

       [6] And take those thirty-one suggested messages—some, as you
point out, in rhyme—where the sender just makes an X. Don't you
think that makes it a little too much like an election or a public-
opinion poll? I noticed your footnote saying: "for only a few cents
50 additional the word 'love' can be added to any of the above texts,"
but even so . . . .

       [7] Another thing. That first message is pretty neat, the one that
goes: "You don't need satin to be pretty; or perfume to be sweet;
you're a very dear mother; who simply can't be beat." That one.
55 *My* mother used to teach English and she was a bear on punctuation.
She's going to notice right away that you've cluttered it up with semi-
colons where commas ought to be and I'm afraid it might spoil her
whole day.

[For treatment of this selection, see p. 303.]

Not a Game She Likes to Play

INEZ ROBB

[1] SURE, I like to play games: Spin-the-Pan, Croquet, Post Office, Hearts, Footsie—you name it.

[2] But Russian Roulette is not my dish. Nor am I in any mood to play games, no matter how elaborate, with Civil Defense in which the stakes are life and death for millions of Americans. 5

[3] I don't know how Civil Defense operated in your home town last week when the Federal Civil Defense Administration decreed a mock hydrogen bomb attack across the nation. But in my home town, which is New York, it was a farce.

[4] Oh, yes, it was pronounced a great success by the authorities 10 because eight million New Yorkers disappeared from the sidewalks for from eight to ten minutes, the length of this "serious" test. In that interim, you could have shot a cannon (how quaint in this atom age!) up or down Broadway or Fifth Avenue or Riverside Drive and never plugged a soul except police and Civil Defense wardens. 15

[5] And where were all the obedient millions who so promptly "took cover" once the warning sirens blew? Well, an appalling percentage of them were standing placidly behind plate-glass windows in the store fronts of Fifth, Park, and Madison Avenues and Broadway, Maiden Lane, Lexington Avenue, Forty-second Street and the 20 Bowery. Or in equally flimsy "cover" all over the city.

[6] What this "mock" drill—and what an apt word!—proved is that the sidewalks of New York can be cleared in nothing flat. What that fact itself proves is beyond my grasp.

[7] Why Civil Defense authorities had to prove once more that 25 New Yorkers—and, presumably, all town dwellers—will quickly clear their streets by stepping through the nearest door, as ordered, is also beyond me. They proved this fact conclusively on November 28, 1951, when the first city-wide atom air raid test emptied the streets in two or three minutes. 30

[8] As a survivor of a little wartime bombing, I thought the 1951

drill a fiasco completely divorced from reality. It was obvious that
time that somehow the safety of the individual had been confused
with cleared streets and empty sidewalks!

₃₅   [9] In the intervening three and one-half years, I had every confidence that Civil Defense had devised some really adequate, horse-
sense safety measures.

[10] But the most recent drill was a dreary and frightening repetition of the initial atom drill in 1951. As far as this participant in
₄₀ both drills could see, nothing new had been added.

[11] Why, ten years after the explosion of the first atom bomb,
are there no adequate, intelligent drills or plans to protect as many
persons as possible? Why, after a decade, is Civil Defense still playing games?

₄₅   [12] It is ridiculous for Civil Defense to pat itself on the back
because it can clear streets. A hydrogen bomb is not needed for that.
Anyone can do the same thing, given enough stench bombs.

[For treatment of this selection, see p. 303.]

FROM *Directions to Servants*

JONATHAN SWIFT

[1] WHEN your master or lady calls a servant by name, if
that servant be not in the way, none of you are to answer, for then
there will be no end of your drudgery: and masters themselves allow,
that if a servant comes when he is called, it is sufficient.

₅   [2] When you have done a fault, be always pert and insolent, and
behave yourself as if you were the injured person; this will immediately put your master or lady off their mettle.

[3] If you see your master wronged by any of your fellow servants,
be sure to conceal it, for fear of being called a tell-tale: however,
₁₀ there is one exception in case of a favourite servant, who is justly
hated by the whole family; who therefore are bound, in prudence,
to lay all the faults they can upon the favourite.

[4] The cook, the butler, the groom, the marketman, and every

other servant who is concerned in the expenses of the family, should act as if his master's whole estate ought to be applied to that servant's particular business. For instance, if the cook computes his master's estate to be £1000 a year, he reasonably concluded that £1000 a year will afford meat enough, and therefore he need not be sparing; the butler makes the same judgment; so may the groom and the coachman; and thus every branch of expense will be filled to your master's honour.

[5] When you are chid before company (which, with submission to your masters and ladies, is an unmannerly practice), it often happens that some stranger will have the good nature to drop a word in your excuse; in such a case you will have a good title to justify yourself, and may rightly conclude, that whenever he chides you afterwards, on other occasions, he may be in the wrong; in which opinion you will be the better confirmed, by stating the case to your fellow servants in your own way, who will certainly decide in your favour: therefore, as I have said before, whenever you are chidden, complain as if you were injured.

[6] It often happens, that servants sent on messages are apt to stay out somewhat longer than the message requires; perhaps two, four, six, or eight hours, or some such trifle; for the temptation, to be sure, was great, and flesh and blood cannot always resist. When you return, the master storms, the lady scolds; stripping, cudgelling, and turning off is the word. But here you ought to be provided with a set of excuses, enough to serve on all occasions: for instance, your uncle came fourscore miles to town this morning on purpose to see you, and goes back by break of day to-morrow: a brother servant, that borrowed money of you when he was out of place, was running away to Ireland: you were taking leave of an old fellow servant, who was shipping for Barbadoes: your father sent a cow to you to sell, and you could not get a chapman till nine at night: you were taking leave of a dear cousin who is to be hanged next Saturday: you wrenched your foot against a stone, and were forced to stay three hours in a shop before you could stir a step: some nastiness was thrown on you out of a garret window, and you were ashamed to come home before you were cleaned, and the smell went off: you were pressed for the sea service, and carried before a justice of peace, who kept you three hours before he examined you, and you got off with much ado: a bailiff, by mistake, seized you for a debtor, and kept you the whole evening in a spunging house: you were told

your master had gone to a tavern, and came to some mischance, and
55 your grief was so great, that you inquired for his honour in a hundred taverns between Pall Mall and Temple Bar.

[7] Take all tradesmen's parts against your master, and when you are sent to buy anything, never offer to cheapen it, but generously pay the full demand. This is highly to your master's honour, and may
60 be some shillings in your pocket; and you are to consider, if your master has paid too much, he can better afford the loss than a poor tradesman.

[8] Never submit to stir a finger in any business but that for which you are particularly hired. For example, if the groom be drunk or
65 absent, and the butler be ordered to shut the stable door, the answer is ready,—"An please your honour, I don't understand horses": if a corner of the hanging wants a single nail to fasten it, and the footman be directed to tack it up, he may say he does not understand that sort of work, but his honour may send for the upholsterer.

70 [9] Masters and ladies are usually quarrelling with the servants for not shutting the doors after them: but neither masters nor ladies consider that those doors must be open before they can be shut, and that the labour is double to open and shut the doors; therefore the best, and shortest, and easiest way is to do neither. But if you are
75 so often teazed to shut the door, that you cannot easily forget it, then give the door such a clap as you go out, as will shake the whole room, and make everything rattle in it, to put your master and lady in mind that you observe their directions.

[10] If you find yourself to grow into favour with your master
80 or lady, take some opportunity in a very mild way to give them warning; and when they ask the reason, and seem loth to part with you, answer, that you would rather live with them than any body else, but a poor servant is not to be blamed if he strives to better himself; that service is no inheritance; that your work is great, and your
85 wages very small. Upon which, if your master has any generosity, he will add 5s. or 10s. a quarter rather than let you go: but if you are baulked, and have no mind to go off, get some fellow servant to tell your master that he has prevailed upon you to stay.

[11] Whatever good bits you can pilfer in the day, save them to
90 junket with your fellow servants at night; and take in the butler, provided he will give you drink.

[12] Write your own name and your sweetheart's, with the smoke of a candle, on the roof of the kitchen or the servants' hall, to show your learning.

[13] If you are a young, sightly fellow, whenever you whisper your 9 5 mistress at the table, run your nose full in her cheek; or if your breath be good, breathe full in her face; this I have known to have had very good consequences in some families.

[14] Never come till you have been called three or four times; for none but dogs will come at the first whistle; and when the master 1 0 0 calls "Who's there?" no servant is bound to come; for "Who's there" is nobody's name.

[15] When you have broken all your earthen drinking vessels below stairs (which is usually done in a week), the copper pot will do as well; it can boil milk, heat porridge, hold small beer, or, in 1 0 5 case of necessity, serve for a jordan: therefore apply it indifferently to all these uses; but never wash or scour it, for fear of taking off the tin.

[16] Although you are allowed knives for the servants' hall at meals, yet you ought to spare them, and make use of your master's. 1 1 0

[17] Let it be a constant rule, that no chair, stool, or table, in the servants' hall or the kitchen, shall have above three legs; which has been the ancient and constant practice in all the families I ever knew, and it is said to be founded upon two reasons: first, to show that servants are ever in a tottering condition; secondly, it was 1 1 5 thought a point of humility, that the servants' chairs and tables should have at least one leg fewer than those of their masters. I grant there has been an exception to this rule with regard to the cook, who, by old custom, was allowed an easy chair to sleep in after dinner; and yet I have seldom seen them with above three legs. 1 2 0 Now this epidemical lameness of servants' chairs is, by philosophers, imputed to two causes, which are observed to make the greatest revolutions in states and empires; I mean love and war. A stool, a chair, or a table is the first weapon taken up in a general romping or skirmish; and after a peace, the chairs, if they be not very strong, 1 2 5 are apt to suffer in the conduct of an amour, the cook being usually fat and heavy, and the butler a little in drink.

"Tone" is one of those words whose meaning is perfectly clear until you try to explain it. We speak of one violin as having a better "tone" than another, and we know what we mean without thinking in technical or even semi-technical terms. We speak of "tones" of color—the "tones" of Van Gogh's yellows, for example—without consciously referring to pigment. We say that an animal responds to the "tone" of his trainer's voice; we are all familiar with the parental admonition, "Don't take that tone with me!"

The animal trainer can express, and the animal respond to, praise, anger, a specific command, even fear in the presence of danger—a feeling, a mood, a spirit. So, too, the child whose parent has warned him about his "tone" has been expressing, perhaps, defiance or resentment or fretful unwillingness to assume responsibility—also a feeling, a mood, a spirit.

The written word communicates tone just as surely as does a musical instrument or a color on canvas or an animal trainer's or disobedient child's voice. The feeling, mood, or spirit of the writer is conveyed through every device he employs: organization; beginning and ending; paragraphing; sentence length and structure; sentence rhythms; word order; levels of diction; and choice of images, figures of speech, nouns, and verbs. And yet it is something more than the sum of all these parts; it is an elusive but not illusory flavor cooked in as if by magic.

Sometimes an author will write in fury, and the straightforward presentation of facts will imply his mood; sometimes he will say the opposite of what he means (irony) to point up the ridiculousness of a given attitude or state of affairs. His tone may be gentler, though his intention may still be to point up one or another human foible. His tone may be grim, gay, resigned, distraught, despairing, elated, triumphant, defiant, exalted, nostalgic, admiring, respectful, cold, affectionate, or as many other possible variations as there are emotions or situations to produce emotions.

Unless there is reason for a change, the writer should strive for unity of tone, rooting out of his writing all violations of unity. For example, he should not say, "Every man, woman, and child must be prepared to make great sacrifices in this hour of our country's need, by golly." You would not expect final examination instructions to read: "Students are herewith informed that any written matter will be taken as *prima facie* evidence that they are bad little boys and girls who aren't going to behave themselves." Similarly, in your own writing, you should avoid hopping from tone to tone, as for example: "It is my intention to show that juvenile delinquency almost always occurs in areas where people are squashed together like sardines."

1. Eric Sevareid and Inez Robb are each writing of some social ill. What are the ills? Do both writers employ the same tone? How would you describe the tone each employs? Why do (or don't) they use the same tone?

2. Explain why use of the first person is appropriate to the tone of each of the two essays. Are the reasons the same for both? What other person of the verb does Sevareid employ? Why does he use it?

3. What level of diction does Sevareid use? Give ten words or

expressions to verify your answer. Is the term "filial sentiment" an example of the level you have said he employs? If not, why does he use it?

4. Are the expressions "What I mean is," "or something," "or anything," "Operation Re-think" examples of jargon? Why does Sevareid use them?

5. Account for the number of questions in the essay and for the number of words italicized.

6. Comment on the contribution of the ending to the tone of the Sevareid essay.

7. Comment on the connotations (in context) of the following words or groups of words from the Robb essay. What contribution does each make to the tone?

"Spin-the-Pan, Croquet, Post Office, Hearts, Footsie"
"it was a *farce*"
"never *plugged* a soul"
"an *appalling* percentage"
"standing placidly behind plate-glass windows"
"equally flimsy 'cover' "
"a fiasco completely divorced from reality"
"horse-sense safety measures"
"dreary and frightening repetition"
"ridiculous"
"stench bombs"

8. What tone is reflected in the following: "Sure, I like to play games," "you name it," "beyond my grasp," "also beyond me," "pat myself on the back"?

9. What is the predominant type and length of sentence in the Robb essay? Analyze the rhythm of a sentence you consider typical in length and structure. What contribution to the tone of the piece is made by sentence lengths, sentence structure, and sentence rhythms?

10. Are paragraph length and methods of development relevant to Robb's tone? Explain.

11. The tone of the Swift selection derives from the cumulative use of one particular device. What is this device and what tone does it convey? Illustrate your answer from the essay. Do you think the repeated use of this device becomes monotonous here? Why or why not?

12. What is Swift really saying about servants? about masters?

13. What method of development is used in paragraph 6 of the Swift essay? Why is it appropriate to the central idea of the paragraph? Justify the comparative length of this paragraph.

Alternate selections for the study of Tone: Alistair Cooke, "It's a Democracy, Isn't It?"; Morris R. Cohen, "Philosophy in Wartime— An Apologia"; Demosthenes, from "On the Crown"; Richard P. Bissell, from "Down on the Tennessee."

Theme Assignment: Employing the same tone as Swift uses, write a set of instructions to one of the following:

entering freshmen
professors
younger sisters and brothers
upper seniors
sales personnel in department stores
pet owners

or

Write a theme commenting on a particular advertising campaign or "gimmick" which has struck you as forcibly as Eric Sevareid was struck. This campaign should, as his example did, reflect a broader attitude or institution about which you are also commenting. You may either approve or disapprove of the campaign and the institution, adopting whatever tone is appropriate. For example, a soap campaign and cleanliness in this country; a bread ad and the emphasis on nutrition; an advertising campaign for a "weight and figure control salon" and the emphasis on youth; toothpaste ads and attitudes toward doctors.

or

Write a theme on A-bomb drills. You may take any of a great number of attitudes toward them: for example, they should be conducted more frequently and more rigorously; they should be discontinued altogether; they are fine the way they are. Be sure to give justifying evidence for your position and to display a tone appropriate to it.

Index of Authors
and Titles

307